THE LAST WORD
my life as a gangland boss

THE LAST WORD
my life as a gangland boss

EDDIE
RICHARDSON

headline

First published in 2005
by HEADLINE BOOK PUBLISHING

1

A CIP catalogue record for this title
is available from the British Library

ISBN 0 7553 1400 X (hardback)
ISBN 0 7553 1500 6 (trade paperback)

Text design by Viv Mullett
Typeset in Aldine 721BT by Avon DataSet Ltd, Bidford on Avon
Printed and bound in Great Britain by
Clays Ltd St Ives plc

HEADLINE BOOK PUBLISHING
A division of Hodder Headline
338 Euston Road
London NW1 3BH

www.headline.co.uk
www.hodderheadline.com

This book is dedicated to my family and all the
friends who have been loyal to me

And to my very good friend Harry Rawlings,
who sadly died in September 2005
as this book was going to press

The paintings featured on the chapter
opening pages are by Eddie Richardson.
www.eddierichardson.com
PO Box 381, Beckenham, BR3 4US

CONTENTS

ACKNOWLEDGEMENTS

I would like to thank Martina Cole for her support and enthusiasm, and for introducing me to Val Hudson, who made this book happen. Thanks also to Lorraine Jerram and everyone at Headline. Special thanks are due to Jean Ritchie, who has made the book flow.

FOREWORD

BY MARTINA COLE

When Eddie told me he was writing a book, I was thrilled. I had often said that he should set the record straight. Tell his side of the story in his own words. He is a natural raconteur, and tells wonderful stories, often against himself, but always with a great deal of humour.

When I read his manuscript, I could almost hear him talking. I was not only enjoying the tale of his life, but I was also intrigued to learn, at first hand, the truth of the stories written about him.

This is the final word on an era which, although passed, is still in the forefront of everyone's minds, especially those, like me, who have a deep interest in the days when real criminality was a way of life, a means to an end.

Eddie's life is interesting, that will become apparent to anyone who reads his story, but it is also a true and honest account of someone who has lived through the worst that life can throw at them, and survived. Not only survived, but who has also made a good and decent life for himself, despite, or maybe because of the experiences he talks about in this book. His art, his love of painting, and his abiding loyalty to family and friends come across with stunning clarity. His memories are full of colour and detail, no matter how shocking the content.

We went on a trip down the Thames once and as we sailed along he told me stories about every place we passed. It was fascinating, but more than anything what struck me most was the total honesty of the man. That is the Eddie I know.

But for me, the main thing that I took away from reading his story was his determination to live life to the full. We have many mutual friends and, like me, they wish him the best that life can offer. Read this, and so will you. Because this is a roller-coaster ride, and an insight into his world that will keep you gripped from the first page.

PROLOGUE

WE DECIDED TO HAVE A
TEAR-UP

I was thirty-one years old, fit and full of energy. I should have been getting on with all the things I wanted to do with my life: instead, I was in the secure unit at Durham prison, facing a fifteen-year sentence. This was the Bastille of the British prison system, a prison within a prison where the most dangerous offenders were caged.

Why was I there? I was Eddie Richardson, one of the notorious Richardson brothers, leaders of the so-called 'torture gang' whose exploits had been splashed across the newspapers for weeks. The very mention of our name was enough to inspire terror from the public and respect from the hardest of criminals. We were the most feared London gangsters, with a reputation that went before us, and long prison stretches ahead of us.

The regime at Durham was unremittingly harsh, the atmosphere tense. As young men facing long sentences we were held in close confinement, rubbing against each other and the punitive system. We were bound together in one thing only: the screws – the toughest in the prison system – hated us, and we hated them, which helped unite us into a formidable force.

E Wing, which housed the secure unit, was covered by infrared cameras, and the screws had personal radios to call for help: state of the art stuff in the sixties. Around the walls of the jail were surveillance nests where, during a previous time of unrest, soldiers with machine guns had been posted.

Our block was on four floors, with iron staircases between the landings. On each of the landings was an open sluice where buckets were emptied in the mornings. The stench was awful, but you got used to it. The food was appalling slop brought over from the main prison, always cold by the time it arrived. The screws' offices at the end of each landing were fronted with gates of steel bars, behind which they locked themselves away.

A few months after my brother Charlie and I arrived at Durham, fresh from seeing our names and photographs plastered across every newspaper in the country, a new governor took over. He was determined to toughen things up for his celebrity charges. As well as me and Charlie, E Wing contained some dangerous and determined men: there was Dennis Stafford, serving life for murdering a rival in the fruit-machine business; Johnnie Hilton, who killed a milkman during an armed robbery on a dairy; John Duddy and John Witney, who were on an armed robbery with Harry Roberts in 1966 when he shot three cops; Wally 'Angel Face' Probyn, who was serving twelve for shooting at a policeman while on the run from Dartmoor; John McVicar, who became famous for his successful jail breaks; Dennis Bond, an armed robber; Tony Dumford, a very bright lad who was serving a double life sentence, and Roy Hall, who was sentenced with us.

Upstairs, and kept in isolation from us, was the Moors murderer Ian Brady, and David Burgess, in for murdering two young girls. We only ever caught glimpses of Brady. The prison staff tried to integrate Burgess with us, but it didn't work. Nonces, or sex offenders, are hated in prison. At one time we worked out that Johnnie Hilton's cell was directly below Brady's.

'I'm going to give him some,' Johnnie said, taking a broom into his cell. He banged on the ceiling with the broom handle. It wasn't a great idea. The following night, all night, Brady banged back at him and Johnnie got no sleep.

'I don't think I'll bother with that again,' he said.

Soon after I got to Durham I had to front up to a couple of inmates. John McVicar told me that they were badmouthing me behind my back. They didn't like Charlie, so I was lumped in with him. We came into prison with a lot of publicity about torturing people, remember. So I got hold of them when there was nobody around: 'I hear you bastards have been talking about me. You fucking got anything to say about me, fucking say it to my face.'

I must have looked as if I meant business – and I did. They backed down, and from then on I didn't get any hassle from anybody.

On the whole I never knew what people were in for, or what sentences they were serving. I never went around reading the labels outside their cells. When we were in there, as far as I was concerned, we were all in the same boat.

There were a couple of Soviet spies in with us: John Vassall, who had been a naval attaché at the British embassy in Moscow and was sentenced to eighteen years after being blackmailed into spying by the KGB because of his homosexuality (which was illegal in those days); and Frank Bossard, an air ministry official who passed details of missile technology to the Russians, and was serving twenty-one years. They had stars attached to their uniforms, signifying they were serving their first sentence, which entitled them to extra privileges, like having more time out of their cells. It was my first sentence, too, so I demanded a star. I was refused, and when I kicked up a fuss there was an inquiry which upheld the refusal. They changed the rules for me.

I learned to play bridge by watching Vassall, Bossard and a couple of others. I have played it ever since. These guys got a much easier ride from the screws, because they spoke posh and there was no risk they would be violent. Although I was patriotic, I didn't worry about them being spies. They were in that hellhole, like the rest of us. But it wasn't long before they were shipped out to more comfortable prisons.

The new governor, 'Flash' Gordon Chambers, was a hard nut, and he laid down a list of new regulations in a four-page document which was pinned up on the wing. There were petty restrictions like not allowing us to wear our own baseball boots or trainers, or our own tee shirts. The new exercise yard we had been promised had not happened, and we were only allowed out for one hour's exercise a day, never more than three inmates at a time. A workshop was about to open, and we were angry at the work we were expected to do: we'd been promised woodwork or metalwork, but they expected us to sew mailbags and paint tin soldiers. There were many other small grievances: the governor was making us jump through hoops, and he refused to negotiate. The atmosphere became explosive. Trouble was brewing for a couple of weeks, and the screws sensed it. Men with nothing ahead of them but endless years of unremitting boredom need something to look forward to, even if it is only aggro.

We kicked around a few ideas of how to protest, and in the end we decided to have a tear-up. It wasn't well planned. Johnnie Hilton came up with the idea of barricading ourselves in the assistant governor's office. Most of us felt we had nothing to lose. Witney, who was ill in his cell, wanted no part of it. But the rest of us were up for it.

It was on a Saturday evening, when we had free association time, that it kicked off. We were in the television room, close to the office, pretending to watch *The Saint*, when we got the signal from Johnnie Hilton who was keeping an eye out for the screw. There was only one screw on our landing at that time and, as he came out of the office, Johnnie copped for him, pushing him against the wall and grabbing his keys.

Instantly, all twenty of us charged to the metal gate of the AG's office – which was still unlocked – and crammed ourselves inside, carrying with us flasks of water and sandwiches we had saved for a couple of days. Adrenalin pumping, I was only vaguely aware that the sirens were wailing and that officers were pounding along the landing towards us. Hurriedly, we locked the gate behind us and began to barricade it. Filing cabinets, tables, chairs – everything we could move was stashed behind the gate creating a heavy defence. It was a desperate situation, everyone was hyped up, and the job was done in no time.

On one side of the office was a small chapel, and we ripped out the heavy wooden altar and used the wood to shore up the barricade. There was now a pack of screws outside, baying for our blood. We hurled insults at them, and they retaliated in kind. We left holes in the barricade and ripped conduit piping off the walls to poke through at them, holding them back from the gate.

Then we had a stroke of luck. I picked up the phone on the AG's desk, expecting it to have been disconnected. But the purr of the dialling tone meant that we could make calls to the outside world. Dennis Stafford knew a journalist on the *Daily Mirror* who he rang to tell what was going on. Dennis had hastily worked out what he wanted to say: 'This is Dennis Stafford, speaking from the assistant governor's office in Durham Prison. We want you to know that we have barricaded ourselves into this office as a protest against conditions in this top-security block. We want an inquiry. No one will get hurt. There will be no violence.'

It was the *Mirror*, when they splashed the story across page one the next day, who dubbed it The Durham Mutiny. The authorities would have loved to keep it out of the papers, shut it down without anyone knowing. But it took them a few hours to realise the phone was still connected and that we were using it. I managed to get a call through to my wife, Maureen, and all the others with families phoned home.

Up on the wall of the office we found a chart classifying all the prisoners on the wing in various categories of danger such as 'personal initiative', 'violence', 'likelihood of escape', 'publicity if escapes', 'notoriety', 'help on the outside', 'physical fitness'. You got points out of ten for each one. Me and Charlie were top of the class in everything, with straight tens. We got maximum points, the only two who did. We were, officially, the two most dangerous prisoners in a unit designed to hold the most dangerous prisoners in the country.

Before we pushed the filing cabinets into the barricade we had ransacked drawers to find our prison records. In the chaos, many of them were scattered across the office floor and men were scrabbling around, each trying to find his own. There was laughter as bits were read out, and furrowed brows as some men read things they had not expected to see in print. Then we ripped them up. The floor of the office was soon almost knee deep in confetti. We also read some of Brady's letters which had been suppressed (some letters are not sent out, usually because they describe prison conditions). We always called Brady and Burgess 'the animals' and I remember a little judder of shock that in his letters he referred to us as 'the animals downstairs'.

Meanwhile, the screws were gathered four deep outside the door, and they were becoming restless. We hurled abuse at them, and they hurled abuse at us. We heard dogs barking, and we learned later that there was a cordon of police cars all around the jail in case our riot was a signal for a mass breakout. We were expecting trouble, but we had taken out our own insurance policy: the press. As soon as the Home Office had been alerted by the *Mirror*, the governor at Durham was ordered to leave us alone and not precipitate any violence. They had oxyacetylene cutters on stand-by to cut through the iron bars of the gate, but this was called off. With the eyes of the country on us, the Home Office could not afford the risk of a battle between prisoners and screws that might leave anyone on either side injured or killed.

The phone was now cut off, and the heating. But with twenty of us in a small space, it was warm enough. McVicar and a couple of others wanted to give up because they thought we'd proved our point, but my brother Charlie was the main voice in there and he wanted to keep it going. We used the chapel as a lavatory. We had to use somewhere. I remember that, afterwards, the chaplain could not even look us in the eye because we had desecrated his chapel. I don't know who cleaned it up – it wasn't any of us. We all managed to get some sleep that night: we kipped on the floor and there was always someone awake, keeping an eye on what the screws were up to. A prison is a very quiet place at night, so if they had been moving around outside, we would have known.

So, it was a stand-off. Then a top dog from the Home Office arrived, a man called Alan Bainton, whose official title was Director of Prison Administration. He'd been ordered by Jim Callaghan, the

Home Secretary, to come up in person. Bainton had been a prison governor at one time, and some of the lads who knew him thought he had been a fair one. We wrote a list of our grievances and handed it out to him. Bainton told us there was no room for negotiation, so we said we would stay inside. But he assured us all our grievances would be looked into, and that there would be no violence when we left. Charlie still wanted to keep it going but we put it to the vote and there was a consensus that we should leave. We knew we would run out of water soon, so staying was only delaying the inevitable.

After twenty-five hours the barricades came down. Visiting magistrates were there to witness that we didn't get bashed by the screws as we came out. The screws didn't like it, they wanted revenge. You could see the looks on their faces, pure hatred. This was a prison where the screws were used to running it their way, and we had rocked their boat. We came out two or three at a time, had a bath, collected a meal and a mug of tea, and were then locked up in our cells. Afterwards, we were on twenty-four hour lock-up, only allowed out to collect our food and for two periods of thirty minutes a day.

While I was locked up, waiting to find out what our punishment would be for the mutiny, I had plenty of time to reflect. I thought about the chart on the wall: how had I, brought up in a loving, secure family and with my own wife and children at home, become one of the most dangerous prisoners in Britain? How had I, who had worked hard at a legitimate business, become a notorious criminal? What path had I followed that brought me to twenty-four hour lock-up in the Durham hellhole?

This book is the story of how I got there, and what happened afterwards. It may come as a surprise, but I made far more money legally in my life than I ever did from crime. But things did happen, some of them bad. If you are in an intense environment, you know that if you don't get in first, someone will get you. You have to be first, and I always was. I was afraid of nothing and nobody.

I worked hard, I played hard and I fought hard. Today, I would not like to meet the likes of me as I was then.

ONE

I REMEMBER WE GOT COWBOY SUITS ONCE

I was born three years before Hitler took Europe into the Second World War, so all my early memories are set against a backdrop of London during the Blitz. I was never afraid, I was completely unaware of the danger; to kids like me it was a huge adventure with plenty of excitement. As the bombs rearranged the area around us, we found new places to play among the rubble.

We came to recognise the noise of all the different aircraft engines, and we knew when the engines cut out on the doodlebugs that someone near us was about to cop it. If there was a local hit someone would say, 'that sounded like it was on Medlar Street,' and we'd all run round to see who had got it. I can remember when the fish shop at the top of Wyndham Road was hit and the next day we were playing in the crater. When a bomb landed really close, the windows of our flat would blow in. We couldn't wait to get outside to see what was happening. We'd collect lumps of shrapnel and take them to school the next day to show to our mates.

Immediately after the war, our favourite place to play was the bombed, burnt-out shell of a large printing works. We called it 'the thousand doors' because, even though it was a shell, there were still lots of rooms and hiding places inside and whole gangs of us all had our secret dens. We could get right up to the top and look out across the city. Sometimes we would drop stones on people queuing down below for buses. They'd curse and yell at us and sometimes the blokes would come charging like lunatics into the building, trying to find us. But we knew every inch of that place so they didn't have a hope of catching us. They'd end up hot, sweaty and angry, and have to tear off back so as not to miss their bus.

There was only one part of the war I hated, and that was when my brother Charlie and me, and thousands of other kids from London and the other big cities, were evacuated. I had to leave my warm, loving, family home. Aged only five I was too young to understand, and too young to be consoled. I sobbed my heart out every night, and longed for my own bed in my own home in Camberwell, with my mum and my grandparents.

We weren't a wealthy family, but we were very close and I grew up secure and loved. My grandmother ran a shop, and my mum helped her. It was a world where the women ran everything – they were the heads of the family. I still believe that mothers not fathers are the more natural parents to bring up children.

My grandmother, Lizzie, was a great person, very loving and warm, but she was a tough nut. She was born in Dublin, the youngest of the family, and her mother died when she was very young so she had to learn to be self-sufficient from an early age. Her family was Protestant, living in a strongly Catholic city, and her dad had changed the family name from Mackay to Mackie, the Catholic spelling, in order to be more accepted. But the religious difference wasn't as big a problem as it would have been in later years: at that time there were a lot of Protestants helping to fight for Irish independence.

When Lizzie's family moved to London she met my grandfather, Bill Allen. Bill worked for a printer as a tradesman, applying gold leaf to the lettering on expensive, leather-bound books. My mum was the eldest of their three daughters and, as we lived with or near Lizzie and Bill all my early life, these were the grandparents I knew best. The other side, my dad's lot, were part of my life, too, but we didn't see them nearly so much. My dad was the eldest boy of a huge family of thirteen kids. His father died when he was young and his mother married again, a bloke called Hummerston. So there were seven kids called Richardson and another six called Hummerston. My dad never talked about his father, apart from one thing: he used to tell us how his father had the biggest traveller's funeral there had ever been on Mitcham Common. So I guess his dad, my grandfather, was a gypsy.

We used to visit my dad's mother. I was really impressed because one of Dad's half brothers, called Nipper although he was a giant of a man, had a train set that worked with real steam. We didn't see many toys in those days and it made a real impression on me. The Hummerstons were a big breed and quite a few of them were into boxing, including my Uncle Bill who was a police champion boxer. Dad didn't like the police and always talked about Uncle Bill's boxing achievements in a way that made them sound worthless. Another uncle, Wally, was also a good boxer. Although Dad got on well with most of the Hummerstons, there was always an undercurrent of rivalry between them and the Richardson half of the family.

My dad, Charlie, was a big lump, just over six feet tall. He knew how to handle himself. I can remember him laying Wally out cold. It happened at a party at my grandparents' house, just after the war. My Auntie Gladys, mum's sister, worked at the New Zealand embassy and she brought a few of her colleagues, New Zealanders, along to the party. It was a good do: there were beer barrels with taps. Everyone got pissed, particularly Wally. He started kicking up, and by accident he kicked my grandmother. My old man said: 'Here, Wally, come outside.' It was bucketing down with rain, and Dad threw one punch at Wally and knocked him out cold. Then he went calmly back inside as if nothing had happened, leaving Wally spark out on the pavement. I can remember the New Zealanders talking about it – they were really shocked.

Dad used to box at Blackfriars ring, which was a well-known venue. You could turn up, put your name down, and they'd weigh you and find you an opponent. It wasn't all regimented like it is today. He used to fight under the name of Charlie Binks. I don't think he got much money for it, but it was something to do and, being a bit violent, he enjoyed it.

My grandparents were never happy about their daughter, Eileen, marrying my dad, but she had fallen for his good looks. He was always very smart, dapper even, and he had a twinkle in his eyes that could charm anyone. He'd lied about his age and joined the army when he was fourteen, but got into a bit of trouble for knocking out a sergeant when his regiment was in India, so he deserted and joined the merchant navy, serving at sea for the next twenty-five years. He was aged about twenty-one when he married my mum, and she was younger. When Dad got put away for two-and-a-half years for a robbery, just a few years after the marriage,

Gran and Granddad probably felt justified in their dislike of him.

Mum and Dad lived at first in Wren Road, Camberwell, and that's where I was born on 29 January 1936. I don't remember that place because when war broke out we moved to a flat in Wyndham Road – which cuts between Camberwell Road and Camberwell New Road – and that's where I was brought up, in Victoria Mansions. Gran's shop was in the same block, on the ground floor, and she and my granddad, my Auntie Gladys and my Auntie Doll lived behind it. We were in and out of their place all the time.

Charlie, my brother, was two years older than me and then, ten years after me, my brother, Alan, was born, followed six years later by my sister, Elaine. Alan and Elaine were great kids, and Elaine has grown up into a lovely, strong woman.

There was no bathroom in Victoria Mansions so, for our weekly bath, we went up to Manor Place Baths every Saturday. Sometimes there would be queues of people waiting, although there were loads of baths. You'd have a number and when they called it you could have your bath. You couldn't just run the water from the taps yourself. If you wanted it hotter or colder you had to shout out your number and then a bloke would appear with a bucket: 'More hot for number thirty-seven!' After the war they knocked down Victoria Mansions and we moved to Cameron House, a new block down the road. The shop moved, too, but it was still in the same road and, again, my grandparents lived behind it.

My grandmother ruled the family, and after her in the pecking order came my mum. They worked very hard: cooking, cleaning, running the shop, darning socks, wringing out the washing with an old-fashioned mangle. They never had a moment to themselves. During the war, and for a couple of years afterwards, Mum worked as a 'nippy', a waitress at the Lyons Corner House in Camberwell. She'd be up early to get us all washed and dressed and then she'd be off to work. When she got home she'd help in the shop then cook for us. Mum was a great cook and she made the best steak and kidney pudding I've ever tasted – it was out of this world. If she was working, Gran would feed us. She'd be busy serving customers in the shop and we'd be pestering: 'Get us our tea, Gran.' She was incredibly patient, she never once raised her voice to us. As soon as she got a break from the shop she'd start cooking for us.

The more I reflect on life, the more admiration I have for those two women. Mum was the biggest influence on my life and it is from her that I got my work ethic. She was a normal, good mum with a heart of gold. She wasn't loud and she wasn't the sort to go down the pub drinking – she had a good friend, Julie, whose husband was a docker, and a pot of tea and a chat with Julie was her main relaxation. There was no telly around during the war years, so the wireless was very important and we all used to sit round listening to it. Even after the war, when there were nine-inch screen black and white tellies, people preferred the radio.

The shop opened at seven in the morning and closed at six-thirty in the evening and was old-fashioned by today's standards. It sold sweets, tobacco, newspapers and snuff. Jam was sold by weight; Gran would put a piece of greaseproof paper on the scales then weigh out a quarter of jam; people who wanted snuff brought in their own little boxes to be filled. My gran made the best ice cream going, and in the summer there would be people queuing round the block for it. We knew we'd sell it all because she only made it if the weather was hot. She also made up her own soft drinks: coloured water made fizzy by a squirt of oxygen from a big bottle at the back of the shop. She'd put the tube from the oxygen into the bottle of water, turn on the oxygen and for a second or two let it fizz inside. You'd hear the noise of that fizz all the time in the shop in the summer, and if I ever hear a fizzing noise it takes me right back there. There was a fruit machine in the shop which attracted kids, and some of them would try to nick cigarettes – I can remember a couple of kids getting barred.

So, I was brought up to know that you had to work hard to get on and I've worked hard ever since. But I've never seen the point of doing things that you didn't need to do. After the war, when I was about eleven or twelve, I did a paper round for my gran. The last house I had to deliver to was very near my school, so I would wait until I was going to school to shove the paper through the letterbox. The bloke used to complain regularly about his paper being so late but, as far I was concerned, it saved me a lot of bother. Of course, the other paper lads might not have got away with it but, being family, I could.

But that came later, after the one really unhappy episode in my childhood. The government decided it wanted to get kids out of big cities during the bombing, they said our lives were at risk. In retrospect, I think it was a big con. They didn't give a toss about the kids, they simply wanted to get all the mothers back into the factories to do war work. Anyway, me and Charlie were sent to Piddletrenthide in Dorset. It sounds like an idyllic country village, and no doubt it is, in parts. But we were sent to a farm run by three middle-aged sisters who were making a business out of taking in evacuees.

They were ugly, and so was the regime they ran. They had about twenty of us kids, and we were billeted four or five to a room. It was brutal, unfriendly and a complete contrast to our own home. It was a real blow; I'd never known anything but love and security before. It was a good training for being in prison, though. We lived on very basic rations. Our mum would send down food, including butter, but we would never see any of it. She'd come to visit us – the long train journey took her four hours in each direction – and she'd ask if we got the things she sent, but we never had. Once she brought me down a little boat, but I tried to float it in the horse trough and it sank. I was

17

the youngest, only five, and I was sent to bed at six each evening, very early. The others, including Charlie, were allowed to stay up later.

One time, Charlie devised an escape plan – he was in charge, being the oldest – although it wasn't exactly a plan, more just a feeling of desperation and a need to get out of there. We scrambled up on to the back of a hay cart but after about three or four miles we were spotted and taken back; we were punished by being separated and not allowed to play outside. We both caught scabies, a very nasty skin infection which caused big scabs on our arms and bodies. Although it was horrible having it, it was our saviour because we were so ill that we had to be admitted to the local hospital. Mum came down and when she saw the state we were in and heard how we'd been beaten for running away, and that we had never received our food parcels, she'd had enough. She took me straight from the hospital back to London with her, leaving Charlie in hospital because the nurses said he was too sick to move.

When we got home the old man went off alarming at her for leaving Charlie down there:

'You brought one back without the other? You can't fucking do that!' he said.

He got a train down to Dorset straightaway, marched into the hospital and brought Charlie back. He was tough, but he had a strong sense of family and he wanted us all to be together.

Back in London, life returned to normal again. We'd only been away nine months but it felt much longer. I can remember the relief of being back in our own home, with our family. We were the lucky ones – some kids stayed away from London for years during the war. But then again, not all of them got horrible people to stay with like we did. For me, that was a terrible, terrible part of my life and, even now, I have to push the memories away because it was so unhappy. No spell in prison was ever as bad as that.

Everyone was wheeling and dealing back in those days. We lived in an area known for scrap-metal dealing and the roads around us had more totters with horses and carts than cars at the pavement, all loaded with things to be sold or traded. There were local characters, like Peggy Birchmore who got his name because he had a wooden leg which he would sometimes take off to wallop people with. Peggy was in his fifties, a real Camberwell character. He dealt in scrap metal, rags, paper – everything had a sale in it back then. He was very streetwise, because you had to be, dealing with totters. They were up to all sorts of little moves, like slipping their foot on to the scale when the rags were being weighed. I knew all the dealers. As a kid I enjoyed hanging around and watching them selling their bits and pieces. The old clothes were sorted, because wool was worth more than other materials, and best of all were 'breakers' – coats or suits without any breaks or tears in them – which could be resold. You could get half a crown apiece for them and, apparently, they were sold on to Poland and Africa and other places.

My dad was often away at sea and would come back after a long trip with a big ham on the bone, or something like that. It was worth a lot in those days because people couldn't get such things while food was on ration. He would give it to the butcher and then Mum would be alright for extra meat for about a month. The war corrupted the whole country. Everyone was at it – there were coupons being exchanged, goods being sold under the counter. It was how people survived, and it was unrealistic to think that the minute the war ended everyone would go back to being respectable again. There were lots of street bookies, because betting was illegal, and kids could earn money being lookouts for the bookies' runners. But then, years later, they made betting legal and all of a sudden this illegal little business that you could go to prison for became perfectly OK and respectable, just by someone signing a name on a piece of legislation.

Even as kids, me and Charlie had an eye for business. One way we found to make money was to get hold of the tarry blocks – wood covered with tar that had been used to make the road surface – which were being dug up to remake the roads with tarmac. We used to nick them, chop them up and sell them as firewood. Then there were the docks. Two thirds of everything that you could pick up on the black market came from the docks, which were about two miles from where we lived. Tinned food could be bought legit if the can was dented – let's just say it got accidentally damaged on purpose – then it was classified as damaged stock and it would end up on the markets.

We were small enough to get under the gates of the docks at Jamaica Road in Bermondsey. We'd nick anything we could, but the easiest things were coconuts, because they were not well guarded. The more valuable goods had security on them. But these were broken shells of coconuts which, I guess, were going to be taken somewhere and crushed for oil or for use in baking. We'd load as much as we could up our jumpers and wriggle back out under the gate. We sold them to other kids at school. Things like that were so rare back then. Sometimes the mums and dads would clip us round the ears because they thought we'd flogged their kids unsafe food. They didn't mind that it was stolen but they'd go off on one because the coconut was sometimes a bit bruised from lying in the sun. Mostly, however, it was pure white and beautiful, a real luxury back then, and the kids loved it. You only saw coconuts at fairs in those days.

Another of our money-making schemes was scrumping. Country kids call it scrumping when they climb into orchards to steal fruit but we had our own version of it. We still stole fruit, but off the backs of lorries. Where we lived, a lot of lorries carrying fruit from Kent would come past on their way to Covent Garden market. We worked out how to control the traffic lights and stop the trucks. The lights were connected to pressure pads in the road which, when a heavy weight ran over them, changed them to red. We had a lookout to signal when a lorry was coming, then two of us would jump on the pad to change the lights and stop the lorry, and then we'd slip round the back, jump up, nick everything we could carry, and jump off at the next red lights. We called it scrumping off lorries. But it wasn't only fruit we nicked – Charlie got caught nicking a book off one of the passing lorries and was put on probation for two years.

There never seemed to be many police around; the area where we lived, round Wyndham Road, was a bit of a no-man's land. Besides, during the war they were all off fighting. When a cop did appear he might nick someone for a bit of thieving – it could be something as basic as a few apples but they'd get three months for it. Everyone accepted it in those days.

Dad never told us much about his trips abroad but we were always very excited when he came back, mainly because he brought us presents, things you never saw in England just after the war. I remember we got cowboy suits once. He didn't talk a lot about anything: he never spoke at mealtimes, just concentrated on getting his food down. We knew he'd won the Burma Star during the war, and lots of other medals, and he told us he had manned machine guns while his convoy was being bombed, and how he was torpedoed, but he didn't dwell on it. He was never a boastful man. I've got a photograph of him with all the other officers from one of the ships he was on, all lined up in their braided uniforms looking very smart, and my dad's got four rows of medal ribbons, far more than anyone else.

The seafaring life suited him and he rose to be a second engineer, with two gold rings on his sleeve. He could have been chief engineer on a smaller ship, but he liked the long-haul runs to places like Australia and America. It gave him his freedom: he loved his family, but he liked his time away from us all, too. The shipping line paid a cheque to Mum every week, so we were always provided for.

I started school at Camberwell Grove Junior School before we were evacuated and I went back there when we returned. I started earlier than I should have done: I used to follow Charlie and hang around outside waiting for him so the teachers took pity on me and let me in to the lessons. I wasn't a star in the classroom, I've had a hearing defect since birth and I was always struggling to catch what the teachers were saying. Nowadays they'd have done something to help me, but I just had to get on with it. I can hear vowel sounds quite clearly but I can't get consonants too well, which means I often pick up what's being said halfway through a sentence when I can get the gist of it. I'm also dyslexic and to this day I'm a slow reader. What happens when you're not good at something is you tend to get worse because you avoid it, and that's probably why I didn't do well at school.

After I was eleven, I went to The Avenue Secondary Modern on John Ruskin Street, just off the Walworth Road and about ten minutes' walk from our flat. It was a new school, one of the many erected by the Labour government just after the war. It was a boys' school and there was a uniform but it wasn't compulsory because so many of the kids couldn't afford it – loads of them got coupons for free school meals. And, because there were so many, there wasn't any stigma attached – in fact, I felt a bit envious. How come they're getting it free and I'm not? Why can't I have it free? Back then, of course, we all got the government's third of a pint of milk free every day.

After Camberwell Grove Junior I was never at the same school as Charlie. He went to The Avenue, but he got sent away to approved school for three years before I joined. Charlie going away hit our mum hard but to me it was just a normal part of life; I was so busy with my own mates that I didn't really miss him. With the old man in the merchant navy it seemed normal for some of the family to be away, and I accepted it without much thought. Charlie ran away a couple of times and would turn up at home, nicking my socks and other bits of clothing. I always knew when Charlie was on his toes because my things would disappear: 'Charlie's home,' I'd say.

Just like the old man went down to rescue him from evacuation, he also helped out once with Charlie's escape from Stamford House, the remand home. It was supposed to be fairly secure but Charlie had got out. Dad went to meet him and take him some clothes. Except that he forgot to take shoes and socks, so they travelled home on the tube with Charlie wearing Dad's socks and no shoes. Charlie was trying to keep his head down so that nobody would take any notice of them, but when Dad saw some bloke staring at them he jumped up and went into one:

'What you staring at? Am I fucking well on fire, or what?' He was never shy to tell people what he was thinking. Charlie always likes to run the old man down, but when we were kids he was there for us when we needed him.

I wasn't exactly a model pupil at school. I was always involved in fights and rows. I loved it. That was part of life back then. There was bullying, so you had to be able to defend yourself, which came naturally to me. I was strong, and soon realised I could take care of myself. I didn't need much of an excuse – then or later – to get into a fight.

I loved sport, too, and I was picked to play for South London at cricket. In fact, our school team was so good, winning all the trophies, that we were chosen to represent South London against St Paul's public school. I think we beat them. I was an all-rounder, good at batting and bowling. Soccer was my great love, and we played from early childhood, whenever anyone had a ball. I would never have

23

been good enough to turn pro, but I was a good Sunday league player after I left school and in every prison I ever went to I'd be looking to join the football team.

As a kid I was a Millwall supporter. Nowadays, they seem to have a younger fan base but in those days they were the team traditionally supported by the dockers and their families. We couldn't afford tickets, so we used to go across the railway line at the back of The Den then we'd shout up and the dockers would lean over from the stands and pull us up and into the ground. We also used to watch Charlton, who were in the First Division and one of the top teams in the country at that time. We could get to their ground on a number 40 tram which took us right up to The Valley. But they were never as close to my heart as Millwall.

The headmaster of The Avenue, a man called Lynch who used to stride around with his hands deep in his jacket pockets, was never slow handing out a caning. I got the cane so much, and for such minor things, that I can't remember any of my so-called mis-demeanours, but they were usually to do with fighting. Everyone used to get it. Some teachers sent you to the head to be caned, but some enjoyed doing it themselves. There was a little guy called Clarke who used to stand on a chair in order to give us a thrashing.

I learned an important lesson from all this physical punishment: the good teachers didn't need to inflict a caning to keep discipline. Later on, I would find myself in many situations which could only be handled using violence, but far more often all that was needed was a presence – a sense of authority or respect – to impose your will.

We had a teacher called Emlyn Jones, a big Welshman who didn't stand any nonsense but could control a class without losing his rag. One day in the holidays we spotted Mr Jones at the Oval cricket ground when we were watching a game. We weren't supposed to know his first name, but it was unusual to us kids in Camberwell so we all remembered it. We started shouting 'Emlyn', and then ducking out of sight when he turned round. He knew it was kids from school, but he never did anything about it. He was a decent bloke.

I remember one day when I helped out a kid who was always being bullied. I took on the lad who was beating him up. He was much older and bigger than me, but I whipped him. Mr Jones saw the fight and asked me why I took him on.

'Because he was beating up Turkey Jones,' I said.

'But he's bigger and older than you. Didn't that bother you?'

'Nah, because he can't fight.'

Mr Jones just laughed – he thought it was amusing.

We bunked off from school a lot. It was easy, thanks to the new Labour government. They thought they were being progressive and enlightened when they introduced new ideas about kids having study periods – time when you were supposed to find a quiet place in the school library, or somewhere, and sit down to study. We loved them, we'd climb over the back gate and be away. It was one of those idealistic new measures that was completely useless because kids like us needed someone keeping an eye on us all the time. First stop outside school was the cigarette shop. We'd buy cigarettes, one at a time, for a penny each. Of course, if we were spotted smoking we'd be caned next time we were in school.

Lots of the kids from The Avenue got into trouble with the law. They were nicking lead and other stuff as soon as they were big enough to lift it. Everyone was at it, including me. I could get the lead off the roofs easily enough, but the scrap-metal yards wouldn't deal with kids. I'd have an old pram full with bits of metal and one of the totters hanging around outside the yard would say, 'Here son, I'll take that off you,' so I'd only get half its value. I didn't like it. Young as I was, I knew that I was entitled to all the money because I was the one who had put in all the effort and all the risk. I could see that the middle man had to make his cut, but it rankled with me and I was determined, even then, to get into a position where nobody could rake a percentage off me so easily.

When I was twelve or thirteen years old I notched up my first conviction. It was for stealing a torch, valued at a shilling (five pence in today's currency). I was out collecting conkers with a mate, John Daly, and another kid, Jimmy Hutton. (John Daly has gone on to become a millionaire film producer and boxing promoter. His company, Hemdale, set up with actor David Hemmings, financed *The Last Emperor* and *Platoon*. He also promoted the Muhammad Ali and George Foreman fight in Zaire, the famous 'Rumble in the Jungle'. John has never lost touch with me, writing to me when I was in prison and supporting my appeal against my last sentence.) John, Jimmy and me were up Red Post Hill, round the back of Dulwich Hamlet football club. There were loads of cars parked there and we were peering in at their speedometers to see how fast they could go. We loved cars, like most young lads do.

The car door was unlocked, the torch was on the seat, so, naturally, it found its way into my bag. We mooched along to the end of the lane and there was a police van there and we got pulled. We were carrying a sack of conkers and the police insisted on looking in it, so they found the torch. They wanted to know which car I'd taken it from. We honestly couldn't remember because we'd looked in loads, but they couldn't charge me unless someone said they'd lost it. They thought I was lying so they pulled me into the back of the van and started smacking me around the face, really knocking hell out of me. I still couldn't tell them which car it was. I was taken to the station and by the time I got home the bruises on my face had come up so that I looked like I'd gone fifteen rounds in the boxing ring.

My old man went mad. He scorched down to the police station with me in tow and shouted that he wanted to see the coward who had slapped his kid. He swore and yelled, demanding to see the bully who had beaten up his son:

'Get him out here. Let him come and see if he can slap me around the face.'

He really gave it to them, and wouldn't leave for about an hour. With his temper up, my dad was formidable. Two police sergeants came out and tried to placate him. They were saying how sorry they were – they knew this cop had taken a liberty, they weren't defending it. Eventually, the old man calmed down but he was very bitter about it. He felt that there were rules to the game and whacking a kid around the face was definitely not within those rules.

By this time, Dad had served a couple of years in prison and he didn't trust the police. As a small kid I had been brought up to believe the police were there to protect us, but my attitude towards them hardened. I no longer had any respect for them, they were just like the bullies at school – picking on the young and vulnerable. It's incidents like this which form your character, and I know this experience helped to turn me into the person I became, and helped provoke my involvement in the events you are going to read about.

Dad may not have saved me from a conviction, but we never saw the cop who beat me up around that patch again. It was about this time that Dad gave up going to sea which meant he was at home a lot more. He had enjoyed the freedom of getting away; he probably had a girl in every port. Now he was trapped at home and it didn't suit him. I remember one night when there was a terrible commotion – enough to wake me up – I got out of bed and went into the front room where I saw Dad with his hands round Mum's throat, throttling her.

I thought he was trying to murder my mum. I jumped on his back and started thumping him. He grabbed hold of me and pushed me away. 'When you get older, you'll understand,' he said. That was his explanation. What he meant was that he wasn't really trying to throttle her, just control her, shut her up. She probably started it. But I think me jumping in did stop it getting out of hand. It was tricky for me, I was only a kid of about twelve. The next morning, nothing was said about it and life was back to normal.

Dad was restless, he was always out and he used to come home really late. He was a womaniser, a real charmer, and Mum knew he was going with other women. He didn't find it difficult to pull birds. He once told me, years later, that he'd fucked every race of woman in the world apart from a half-caste Eskimo.

I said: 'Why not a half-caste Eskimo?'

'Find me one and I will,' was his reply.

Mum used to pack his suitcase and leave it outside the door, to let him know how angry she was. Usually he just picked it up and walked in and said: 'What's your game?' It was just Mum's way of letting him know that she was on to him. But one night he took the case and disappeared. We assumed he'd be back after a couple of nights, but he didn't return. We found out, later, he'd gone to Canada with a Scottish nurse called Lizzie and got a job on the railways. I've got a half brother who was born out there and to this day he has a Canadian passport, even though he lives in Spain. (He's also called Charlie: Dad, who was called Charlie, named two of his sons Charlie and later had a grandson called Charlie. It gets confusing, so I call my half-brother Chas, and my nephew Charlie Boy.) We were all for Mum, she was the one we cared about, and we thought Dad was a bastard for leaving her. She never stopped loving him, but she gave him a nickname, 'Bootnose', which we all used. It was a small, derogatory thing to say about him, and it made her feel better.

Later on, Dad was always looking for an excuse as to why he'd left home and he used to blame me and Charlie. He'd say we drove him out but that wasn't true, although when there were rows we always took Mum's side, naturally. Charlie did hit Dad over the head with a starting handle once – it was in the days when lorries needed starting handles to crank them. The old man chased him up the road but Charlie was too quick for him. Charlie was going out working with Dad's brother, Jim, collecting sacks, which they could then sell, from farms. Dad and me went out in a lorry doing the same thing, but Uncle Jimmy knew all the good farms to go to whereas we were going round blind. They always came back with half a lorry load of sacks while we only had a little parcel.

That might be what the row flared up over, because Dad did get mad about it. I can't honestly remember. I was there when it happened, just outside our flat. It was something or nothing, no great significance, and when everyone calmed down it was forgotten about.

TWO

I EVEN DROVE A BIG OLD HEARSE

The only subject I was any good at in school was drawing so, when I left, my first job was as an apprentice draughtsman at a company called Durrants in Great Dover Street. The school tried palming all of us off on all sorts of jobs, and sometimes they succeeded. I lasted about twelve months as a draughtsman. I didn't really know what I wanted to do, but I knew I didn't want to sit in an office from nine to five every day. Besides, I had to go to college one day a week and for me that was like being back at school, in a classroom, which I hated. I used to play up to the teachers, just like I did at school. I was eventually expelled from the college for bunking off, and that was the end of my formal education. I could have left school at twelve or thirteen for all the difference those last few years made.

While I was working for Durrants, all the apprentices had to spend a year in the offices and I was in the cashiers' department. They used me as a messenger, sending me down to the bank to deposit cheques and bring paperwork back. I had a little briefcase to carry everything in. Once a week, they would collect the cash to pay the wages for the staff, and the guv'nor used to get in a terrible state in case any of it got nicked. It was always a big deal, working out different routes and things like that. He was worried about being attacked and robbed – there was a lot of it going on. It did make me think about it, and how easy it would be, but robbery was never my style.

I could have stayed on at Durrants but I was going nowhere and it wasn't my kind of job. My mate, Whippet Tear, was working at Waterloo Station as a junior porter and he suggested I should join him. Whippet was my best mate from when we were very young: we were at school together, and he lived in a block of flats just down the road from us.

The boat-trains would come into Waterloo from Southampton. When we heard they'd come through Clapham Junction it meant they were five or six minutes away and all the porters would get out on to the platform. It was a bit of a bun fight: we all wanted to land the job of looking after the bags of the most generous tippers and some of the older porters did not like the way me and Whippet used to jump on the train before it stopped. We'd make our way through to first class, take the names of the likeliest looking passengers and find out how many pieces of luggage they had. Sometimes it was as many as twelve pieces, and the Americans were used to being charged for each item, so it could be lucrative. We didn't mind being treated like serfs because we were getting a few quid off these rich people. There was one particular boat-train which brought diplomats from South America who had sailed over on the SS *Andes*. It was very luxurious and the passengers were important, influential people with wallets full of money. They were richer and more generous than the Yanks.

I did that job for about twelve months then someone I knew said he was getting very good money doing stone cleaning, so I went along and got myself a job with him. A gang of us would work from cradles alongside huge buildings, spraying them and cleaning them with wire brushes. Whenever I go across London Bridge I look at a big, imposing building called Regis House, which we cleaned. Because it was a regular job, I used Charlie's National Insurance cards. He was two years older than me, so it meant I went on to the rate for a man straightaway, and Charlie was happy to have his cards stamped.

We used to go up inside the building to the roof and then climb into the cradle to come down the outside. Sometimes, if I was late, I'd climb up the ropes on the outside of the building to get to the cradle. Heights didn't bother me, not like they do some people. There was a fella I knew from the snooker halls down the Elephant and Castle, quite a well-known hard man in that area, and he said he wanted a job so I took him along with me. He got up and into the cradle and then he just froze. He couldn't stand the height. We had to get him out, so we swung the cradle against an open window, but he wouldn't take the step across into the building. It took ages to coax him to do it. It didn't do his street cred a lot of good.

Growing up in the fifties was a good time, it was when teenagers were first coming into their own. Music for kids was just taking off and I liked the big band sound, but I never got very into music because of my hearing defect. Out of school we used to go to youth clubs, where we could play table tennis, listen to records and meet girls. Girls were beginning to be a big preoccupation, and I never seemed to have a problem meeting them and getting to know them. The first girl I went with, properly, was the daughter of the caretaker ot a block of flats along the road from where we lived. I was fourteen years old. We just caught each other's eye, and it went from there. It wasn't a big romance – at that age you're just exploring things. We used to just hang around together, round the flats. What I remember most about it is that I had to have a fight with another lad over her. I won.

We mainly socialised in our own village, Camberwell, but sometimes we'd go to places like the Locarno in Streatham, which later became the Cat's Whiskers. When I was older I went to the Lyceum in the West End. I was a quiet sort of fella, I was never flash. The teddy boy fashion was in, but I never took much notice of fashions. Charlie has said that I was the King of the Teds, but that's complete rubbish. I didn't feel the need to dress up to fit into a niche, to be one of a certain crowd. I just got on with things my own way. It was a good time, I was enjoying myself, and girls were very much part of it. They were never in short supply, but Charlie didn't find chatting them up as easy as I did. I introduced him to Margaret, who he married when he was twenty-one. A girl I was going out with said she wanted to bring a mate along, so I took Charlie with me and that was it – they ended up having five children together.

We also went to boxing clubs, like the famous Fitzroy Club in the Walworth Road (which later became Fitzroy Lynn). Boxing was part of the culture, something you wanted to be a part of. I loved it then and I love it now: I've stayed involved with it all my life. It was normal in those days for dads to take their kids along on a Saturday morning, to teach them self-defence, show them how to throw a punch. Nobody round where we came from wanted their kids to grow up as weaklings, and fighting was in our blood. My dad would go with us if he was home, but often we went with my great-uncle, Harry Mackie, who lived in Trafalgar Road opposite the Fitzroy. There were loads of amateur boxing clubs, even if there wasn't anything else much for kids in those days.

When we were quite young we used to hang around outside the Sultan's Arms pub, just off Wyndham Road, on Friday or Saturday nights, because there was always a bit of fisticuffs. The totters and dealers would have a skinful, a barney would start and then they'd go outside for a 'straightener', which is what we call a fight: it straightens things out between two people. We'd watch them getting at it, that was our entertainment. We saw it in real life, not on television. Often they'd be friends again after beating hell out of each other.

One place we went, a youth club in Eltham called Clubland, was run by a chaplain. We all had to pay, which was a bit rich because the club had been given £30,000 – a massive amount of money in those days – by the famous American comedian and movie star Bob Hope, who was born in Eltham. He gave the club all the proceeds from a show he put on, like a benefit night. This chaplain still demanded a 'silver' collection from us – no copper, it had to be silver. It was supposed to be a club for kids who couldn't afford things, poor kids, so it was a right liberty. But that's how you learn things: I learned that people who seem to be good, have all the trappings of it, and get respect for it – like a chaplain – can be selfish, greedy bastards, just like you get in every other walk of life. As a kid you naively think that if someone has gone into the church he must be a good person, but you learn that good and bad are spread across every part of life. It's just that some people are hypocrites.

Charlie was a good boxer and so was I, and sometimes we would be on the same bill. The old man would come and watch. One time down at New Cross, Charlie was put against this huge geezer who towered over him. It looked like a right mismatch. At the weigh-in, the old man demanded to know what the other fella weighed, and kicked up about his son being put against someone so much heavier.

'What's your fucking game putting my son in with him? What's he weigh? Come on, what's he weigh?'

The old man was blowing up alarming, but Charlie didn't care, and while all this was going on he just went into the ring and knocked the big guy out cold. Charlie was fighting for the Evening Institute Championship, and he eventually lost out in the final. I fought on the same bill that night and it was a right tear-up for three rounds, but in the end I won on points.

I boxed as a welterweight then, by the time I was seventeen or eighteen, as a middleweight. I used to spar with a pro at the Thomas à Becket, the famous pub with boxing training rings on the upstairs floor where all the big names trained. I was going to turn pro at eighteen – I had my licence to fight professionally – but it never happened because Henry Callaghan, who was going to be my manager, lost his brother Bobby, who I used to spar with. Bobby died after a fight and it was a big blow for the whole family.

I didn't worry about not turning pro – if I'd really had the ambition I'd have found another manager. There were lots of things happening in my life then, girls and work stuff, and I didn't miss it. But I still loved the boxing world: we used to go to watch my cousin, Alan Mackie, box at Manor Place Baths where, as a nipper, I'd queued for my Saturday bath.

Most of my fighting has been of the unofficial variety. We'd go into a pub and there would be another gang of lads there and you'd end up having a stand-up. There were always fights at the Locarno on a Saturday night, it didn't take much to get one going. I was a very good fighter and I was never afraid to take anybody on. Ever since school I'd had a reputation as a scrapper, and a lot of blokes wouldn't risk a straightener with me. But there were always some who thought they could take on anyone, and had to learn a lesson. I never lost a fight, which gave me great confidence. I've taken a few punches, of course, but I've never been injured in a fight.

One of the most important fights of my life happened when I was eighteen. It was with Charlie, who was twenty. Being the older brother, he'd always been the one in charge, the leader. I didn't set out to stand up to him and teach him a lesson, it just happened. He took a coat of mine, one I'd saved up for and had never worn. I was expecting to wear it that night but when I got home from work I found he'd gone out in it. I was mad, and when he came in wearing it I had a go at him.

'That's my fucking coat. Who the fuck do you think you are, helping yourself to my things all the time?'

He didn't say anything, just came at me, nutting me, a regular little trick of his. I didn't think about it, I steamed into him. I walloped him and cut his nose, blacked his eye. I think he was shocked by my reaction – he'd expected to get away with it, as usual. But he got up off the floor and came back at me and we both wanted to fight it out. But Mum was there, screaming and hollering for us to stop, and trying to separate us. By then I was the same height as Charlie – we're both about five feet ten-and-a-half inches tall – there was nothing between us in size. He turned round and marched out of the house.

I had a little cut under my eye, but otherwise I wasn't hurt. Neither of us wore rings so we didn't cut each other badly. But it wasn't about the damage I'd done to him physically. What was important was that I'd stood up to him for the first time, and I wasn't afraid of him after that. That was the last time he ever tried to impose his will on me physically. It was a situation that had been simmering for some time, and that fight cleared the air. We never mentioned it again, but we both knew that our relationship changed that day. He never forgot that I could take him on, and it got him off my back.

Charlie had always liked to make it clear in little ways that he was the boss, and the fight sorted that out between us: he couldn't treat me as his kid brother any more.

We were rivals, in some ways. We used to argue about who had had the most girls: we were both fit, virile young men, and there was no shortage of girls around. I had him beat in that contest. But he taught me a lot of other things. Being two years older, Charlie learned how to be streetwise that bit earlier than I did, and he passed on one valuable lesson to me: a lesson which, in the end, I knew better than he did. He taught me that it's important to be sure about your associates, and I always make inquiries about people and their families. If they come from a good family, one where they've been brought up to know the score, you can feel safe with them. My brother didn't always put his own teaching into practice, which cost us all a great deal of our liberty later on.

By the time of our fight we were living in a flat in Champion Hill, a big council flat we moved to when I was about seventeen, about a mile from Wyndham Road. It had five bedrooms, so there was plenty of room for all of us.

I loved cars, from when I was a nipper. My granddad had a car, a lovely old Wolsey Wasp which he kept garaged up under some arches during the war when he couldn't get petrol. He used to take us away on holidays in it when I was a kid, down to Herne Bay. He had leg problems so he couldn't walk far, but he could drive. When I got older I offered to chauffeur him but he wasn't having it. When I was eighteen, though, he loaned me the motor to go hopping in Kent. Picking hops was a holiday for lots of people from our area, and my mate Whippet Tear's family always used to go.

I thought hopping was a good way to earn a few bob. I was probably showing off my driving, because we'd just set off to come home when Whippet suddenly grabbed the wheel. He thought I was going to hit a car that was coming towards us. We swerved into a ditch, hit a tree and turned over. I went flying through the roof, did my back in and was in hospital for three weeks. We were lucky no one got killed. My mum was in a right state, really worried about me.

Charlie acquired a car first, a Ford Consul, and I was very proud because I thought it was a beautiful motor. As soon as I was old enough to drive, I was behind the wheel. There were so many cars over the years, I can't remember them all. But some stand out: I had a real love affair with a Chevrolet Impala, which I bought brand new on HP from the Earls Court motor show when I was twenty-three. I ordered it and got it two months later – the anticipation was like being a kid waiting for Christmas. It was metallic green, with big wings, bench seats and a column gear change. People would turn round in the street when I drove past. I had a Mark Two Jaguar, 3.8 litre in racing green and, at another time, I had a pale-blue Bentley – complete with chauffeur for three months when I was banned from driving. I kept that one for about two years, but no car ever lasted longer than that with me.

I even drove a big old hearse, a Rolls-Royce with a big, outside brake. I always preferred a wonderful old car to a modern piece of tin. The brake on this hearse let me down one day – it just sprang off and the car rolled down the hill outside my house and knocked down a neighbour's garden wall. I had to get someone to rebuild it, but that caused even more grief because he left a pile of concrete – about five hundredweight – in the road, which set hard. The people who lived in that road were not pleased. The hearse was great because I could load the whole family and friends in and drive off down the coast.

I loved American motors, the bigger the better. I was driving to a football match in Herne Bay in one once, a Dodge, when I turned it over. I had a kid in the car with me – he wanted to ride with me not with his dad, a mate of mine called Arthur Baron who ended up managing the Cray Wanderers team, and who was following behind. Arthur had lived near us when we were kids, and worked with Charlie and me. (By this time Charlie had his own scrapyard, and I worked with him part time, at weekends, and then later full time.) Imagine Arthur's reaction when he saw us careering off the road and turning over. Luckily, nobody was hurt that time.

As I've said, another of the great loves of my life is sport. Even after I left school I remained very involved, particularly in football: I played for Marden Town and for Chislehurst Old Boys. Whippet was in the team with me and we played on Saturday afternoons. I'd have been working at the scrap-metal yard in Addington Square for Charlie – even when I was doing another job all week I always helped out with the metal business at weekends. I'd sometimes get to the football late, after the match had started. My brother used to delay me on purpose, to stop me getting there on time. He always said there was something important to do at the yard, even when there wasn't. Eventually, I learned to ignore him and just go. I think he was envious of my involvement with my mates, and he didn't understand the need for relaxation.

Charlie was always wound up, on the go, couldn't enjoy himself unless he was doing business. He liked controlling things and he wanted to control me – but he learned early on that he never could. I may have worked for him, but I wasn't ever going to jump just because he said jump, like some of his employees had to.

When I was aged about nineteen or twenty we took over Westminster Boys Club team, which was in the Sunday league. It was going to close down because they couldn't fulfil their commitments, so the bloke running it was happy to let us have it. Arthur Baron was older than us, and mad keen on football, so he became the manager, but I was running it at the beginning. It was good fun: it meant that me and all the lads working at the yard who enjoyed a game could turn out for the club. I was quite a ferocious player, playing at centre half, centre forward or inside right. We kept the team in the Metropolitan Sunday league, and were soon in its first division. I changed the strip from red shirts with white shorts to a full red strip, which was unique at the time. Football was my relaxation, and it was a good morale booster for the chaps working at Charlie's yard, the troops.

We used to give the refs a good time at the clubs we were running in those days, and we'd pick them up and drive them to the matches with us. I'm not exactly saying they were bent, but I think they made a lot of wise decisions in our favour. The social life attached to the team attracted some really good semi-pro players to join us, which is one reason we did so well. Norman Golding and Clive Clark, who both later played professionally, used to play with us.

Over the years, I've played everything: tennis, squash, badminton, cricket, football – lots of them while I was in prison. I play golf. I love skiing, and just lately I've joined a gym to get really fit again. I love sport, any sport, playing it or just following it.

THREE

WALKING THE PLANK

'Roll up, roll up! Treat the kids for Christmas! Bring them to meet the animals at the Christmas grotto!'

It was the most bizarre business I've ever had anything to do with. It may have only lasted a couple of weeks, but those two weeks were packed with dramas. In the run-up to Christmas 1958 we had some empty premises, a scrap-metal yard we'd moved from. It seemed a waste not to make use of it and Charlie came up with a gimmick I thought would earn us a few bob. It did – but I'm not sure it was worth the stress.

There were lots of cheap goods on the market, and we knew plenty of people who were running 'long firms', so called because it takes a long time and a bit of patience to make money out of them. They were a type of fraud that was big in those days, and it still goes on today; a mate of mine, Kenny Bloom, was king of the long firms for many years until he retired not long ago. Charlie got involved in it quite heavily.

Running a long firm means you set up a business, give it a good-sounding name and get a printed letterhead, and then start buying supplies off legit companies. For a while you pay upfront, maybe even for as long as a year, gradually increasing your orders until you are seen as a good customer and you are able to set up a credit account, paying after you receive the goods. You pass all the money through a bank account, so that the bank thinks you are a reliable company and is prepared to lend you money. Then you sting everybody, the bank and the suppliers, at the same time. You put in a huge order to all your suppliers at the same time and disappear with the goods. When they try to track you down, you've vanished. There may even have been a convenient fire or flood at your warehouse.

It takes a few weeks for the supplier to get panicky about you not paying, because you've been a good customer up to then. So you've got time to shift all the goods you've got on to markets, or to shop-keepers who don't ask too many questions. Because you haven't paid for the goods, you can sell them cheap. It's a good deal for everyone except the original supplier. Long firms were popular because nobody got hurt: it was like robbing a bank. It was only the big boys who could afford it who were being conned, you weren't robbing the man on the street or small, struggling companies.

Anyway, Charlie knew a few of the long-firm operators and he was quite happy to take a load of stock from them. We helped them set up their businesses sometimes: they'd come into the yard, give us three grand in cash, and we'd give them a cheque on our business which they could pay into the bank to help establish them as legit. There was a good profit to be made from their knock-down goods. They would let people have radios for a tenner which should have cost £15 trade price, so they could sell them for £15, giving the customer a deal and making a fair bit at the same time.

So, Charlie set up a showroom full of the stuff above the offices of the empty scrapyard at Addington Square. But he needed a way to coax customers in. We knew a woman called Dolly Legs; well, that was what she was known as – I don't know how she got the name, it can't have been because of her legs because she always wore trousers. Her old man was a coalman and they both loved animals. They had a place down Orpington way, where they kept a small menagerie. There was an African buffalo, two brown bears, ponies, ferrets and other things. They were a couple of local characters.

Charlie bunged Dolly Legs a few quid to bring some animals up to the yard. She brought a bear, the buffalo and some ferrets. I had a husky dog at the time, a beautiful animal. So we were able to set up a little zoo to attract the kids and their mums, and help persuade them to do their Christmas shopping upstairs. We built up cages for some of the animals, and the buffalo was chained up. Alan, my younger brother, was drafted in to run the whole enterprise. Alan was a really good kid, different from me and Charlie. I think we have a bad gene in us, which missed Alan. He was working with us when he left school, setting himself up to go solo and get on in life. He agreed to look after the 'zoo' and the grotto.

Well, you can imagine the chaos. The kids knew no fear and would stick their hands into the cages, and then scream when the bear sucked their fingers. The mums would be shrieking in terror, the kids would be going back for more, fighting to get near to the cages, chucking things at the animals. It worked in terms of selling stuff, because the mothers would be so relieved their kids still had all their fingers that they'd drag them upstairs and buy things. It frightened the life out of me whenever I went round there: I was really worried that a kid would get hurt.

One day Charlie took Dolly Legs's bears down to Wandsworth Road market, in a van. I can't remember what the plan was but it was something to do with advertising one of his businesses. For a laugh, Charlie told one of his mates to go to the back of the van to get something – he thought the sight of two bears in there would freak him out. It did, and as he backed away the bears managed to get out of the van and amble off through the market. Everyone ran for their lives. It was total chaos. The bears were harmless, but of course the people didn't know that: they just saw a couple of bears charging about. Luckily, Dolly Legs was around and she could control them, and she eventually got them back into the van.

Another day, back at the yard, the bear and the buffalo had a fight. There wasn't as much room at the yard as there was where they normally lived, in Orpington. For some reason, the bear leaned through its cage and with one huge paw whacked the buffalo on its behind. The buffalo whipped round and tried to butt the bear with its horns, which were big horns that grew sideways out of its head. The kids and the mums were freaking out, but luckily it all calmed down. They say you should never work with animals or children, and after that short experience of trying to work with both, I'd agree.

After my time as a porter at Waterloo and stone cleaning, I went to work with Charlie full time. That was nothing new: I'd been working with him for years at weekends. Me going to work with him full time was expected; it was just part of family life. Charlie left his approved school when he was sixteen, and set himself up in the scrap-metal business. He had started working with our Uncle Jim, collecting and selling sacks from farms, and they spotted a huge cache of aeroplane parts which they bought and then sold on for a profit. That gave Charlie enough cash to open his own yard.

After renting premises in Brixton he bought a yard in Addington Square, off Camberwell Road, about five minutes away from home. It was small, as yards go, and the offices were a ramshackle, two-storey structure tacked on to the end of a row of much taller, three-storey houses. The company was called Peckford Scrap Metal, from the address of the Brixton yard. After a little while, Mum gave up working in Gran's shop and joined the firm to run the books and man the office. She worked for Charlie for a few years until she took over the shop full time when Gran retired.

At first, when I was only doing it part time, working for Charlie involved taking a horse and cart out to collect scrap, but then I used to drive a lorry. (There was no such thing as an HGV licence in those days, and I've driven forty-ton lorries, cranes, the lot in my time.) We'd collect scrap from aerodromes, like Blackbushe in Hampshire and another one near Romford in Essex. We'd cut it up and load it up – we'd only cut it as much as we had to, so it would still be in huge pieces. It was hard work, and if I was big and strong to start with, I grew bigger and stronger. Sometimes we would take it direct to the smelters where we'd get paid for twelve-and-a-half per cent irony, which meant the iron content was twelve-and-a-half per cent. Or we could clean it up and sell it as aluminium. It was all legal: we paid for it.

But not all our metal activities were legal. A couple of times we got a tip-off from the dockers that there were some submarine torpedoes lying around on barges in the docks. The nose cones were made of copper and they weighed well over a hundredweight. The dockers would either fix us up with keys to the dock gate padlocks, or they'd cut a link in the chain – slice it almost through, so that when you looked at it you couldn't see that it had been cut. When the cops drove round looking at the chains it looked secure. Then we'd turn up in the night with a couple of lorries. The torpedo nose cones were very heavy, but I could hump them. We got a good price for copper, although we'd have to bung the dockers a fair amount.

When Charlie was called up for the army – all young men were required to do National Service for two years in those days – he couldn't stand the thought of doing as he was told for all that time and not making any money, so he deliberately made as much trouble for himself as possible, and ended up with a dishonourable discharge. He served six months in the army glasshouse at Shepton Mallet, alongside three young men who were also doing all they could to get out as fast as possible: Ronnie and Reggie Kray and Johnnie Nash.

There had to be an easier way for me to avoid doing my bit for queen and country, and Charlie helped me out. For a year or so I had managed to get out of National Service simply because I'd been using Charlie's national insurance cards, and I didn't exist on the official system. One by one, all my mates were called up, and I used to take the mickey out of them. They retorted that I'd get my papers one day – and, sure enough, they arrived when I was nineteen: I got caught out when I had to appear in court and the magistrates wondered why I wasn't in uniform doing my bit.

I was arrested when I was eighteen. I used to hang around the Elephant with my mates. There was a little phrase back then: 'using the plank'. I didn't know what it meant when a bloke I knew first mentioned it. He and his mate needed a driver, and I could drive so I agreed to go with them. First thing we did was to go to a building site and nick a scaffolding plank. Then the plan was to find a tobacconist's shop, ram the door with the plank on the bumper at the back of the motor, load up as many cigarettes as possible and drive off. We were driving around looking for a shop to do when the police spotted us. I tried to get away from them and ended up driving into a cul de sac. They found the plank in the car.

I was remanded in custody for a week to Wormwood Scrubs, which was my first little taste of prison. It livened me right up, I can tell you. On exercise in the yard you meet loads of other young men, which is why prison is not a good place to send young fellas. All of a sudden you are trying to prove yourself against these others, and you come out and get up to all sorts of villainy you would never have done had it not been for prison in the first place.

When the case came to court I didn't admit to anything, but the other two, who were both older than me, pleaded guilty – even though in court the police said we were planning to rob a jewellery shop. One of them got nine months, the other got six months and I got probation.

I was also ordered to register for National Service and my call-up papers came a few months later. That they were a couple of years late made it even worse, because by then I'd met Maureen, who soon became my wife. We were saving up to get married and, to raise the cash, I was still working at the stone cleaning as well as with Charlie.

I really didn't want two years away from real life. I heard how a mate of mine had got out of it by pretending to be what the politically correct brigade today would call educationally challenged – in other words, really stupid. So Charlie took me for my interview and explained that I was on the slow side, very slow even, and that I couldn't answer their questions. We kept the pretence up really well, with Charlie speaking for me and me just looking vacant. In the end I was classified as grade four, which meant I would only be called up in a dire emergency.

At one time, I'd probably have been sent away and given more education, but as National Service was coming to an end, they weren't bothered trying to train someone as thick as I pretended to be. So I walked out a free man. Charlie was pleased because I was still working at a straight job as a stone cleaner under his name, which meant his cards were being stamped. And I was pleased because I could get on with things.

We quickly made a name for ourselves as scrap dealers. We'd offer the best prices and we dealt very fairly with the totters who brought metal to us. But we were no pushover – we were happy to sort out anyone who thought they could put one over on us. Very quickly, the word went round that you didn't mess with the Richardsons. It was a big mistake to steal from our yard – there would be a quick 'straightener' for anyone who did.

Charlie was twenty-one when he married Margaret – she was expecting their first child. They lived at home with Mum and the rest of us at first, and that made me determined that when I married Maureen we'd buy a house of our own. Maureen was a very attractive girl and we went out together for eighteen months before we had the big white wedding at the church in Camberwell Church Street. It was a proper job: that was the way I did things. I was twenty and she was a few months younger.

Maureen's father was Irish, a smashing man who tragically died when he was in his fifties. Her mother was English. The family lived in a flat on the Old Kent Road and, before we married, Maureen worked as a shorthand typist. After we married she never worked again. I always took care of my family financially, no problem.

We moved into a semi-detached house in Sidcup Road, Eltham, as soon as we got back from our honeymoon in Herne Bay. Eighteen months later Melanie was born, followed five years later by Donna.

Soon after he came out of the army, Charlie and me took over another scrapyard in New Church Road, just around the corner from Addington Square, with an old house we used as offices. I insisted we took it because it was a much bigger yard. It became the main offices for the business from then on, even though at one time Charlie owned six yards. For a time we kept Addington Square going as a depot for rags and newspapers.

A much better idea I had was to turn the upstairs premises into a nightclub. In those days, there was a great shortage of places for drinking after the pubs closed and, besides, it gave us our own social life on the doorstep. The first club we opened was the Addington. It wasn't exactly a sophisticated venue and the clientele were mainly the blokes we did business with – the totters and the other dealers – who really enjoyed having somewhere of their own to go to, especially on a Monday which, as they worked all weekend, was traditionally their day for doing nothing and getting drunk. The street bookies and local villains used the club, too. In those days, the pubs had to close at three o'clock in the afternoon, so if you wanted to carry on drinking you had to go to a club. We'd open the Addington in the afternoons and late nights, when the pubs were closed. We employed barmaids to run it, but we'd all take a turn behind the bar – mostly Dad after he returned from Canada.

I was usually round the corner running the New Church Road yard, so if there was ever any trouble at the club it took only a minute or two to get round there and straighten it out. The barmaid would ring up if there was any nonsense brewing, mostly drunks taking a few liberties. The word soon got out that we weren't the right people to tangle with.

One afternoon I got a call from Dad that a bloke round there was causing a bit of aggravation. He was a big geezer called Buck, who went around saying he was the hardest man in Peckham. There were a lot of totters and dealers in there; they'd finished work for the day and were enjoying an afternoon drink. This Buck was throwing his weight about, causing aggravation to our regular customers. I was in my overalls, smothered in grease and dirt, in the middle of loading up a lorry, so I wasn't too pleased to get called up.

I rushed round there and as I went up the stairs I could see him with his back towards me. Three stairs from the top I leant over the banister, grabbed him by the top of his coat, pulled him over the banister and dragged him downstairs. He got up and I hit him on the chin, hard, and knocked him out. We didn't want to leave him at the bottom of the stairs, so another fella who was working for us got hold of his arms and I took his legs. We were going to dump him outside on the pavement. But before we got to the entrance he came round and started kicking out. He kicked me up the bollocks, really hard. So I jumped with all my weight on to his legs. Crack, one bone went. The other leg, the ligaments were done. We left him outside the gates of the yard, in a fair bit of pain.

I said: 'That's what you get for coming round here fucking about.'

Someone called an ambulance. He was out of action for about nine months.

The Peckham mob loved it because the bloke wasn't popular. Only a couple of months ago, an old mate from Peckham reminded me about it and had a good laugh. Buck was a bully, so he got what was coming to him.

Our next club was the Casbar, above the New Church Road offices. We did it up properly and there was a large, well-stocked bar. There were optics for the spirits, and bottled beer. There were stools at the bar and seating in the various rooms and alcoves leading off the main room. The place was carpeted and wallpapered nicely, with blinds covering the windows with scenes of Paris nightlife – cancan girls and so on – depicted on them. We got to know some nurses who lived in Kingston, and we'd pick them up in a van with seats and bring them to the Casbar. If you had a few birds in, you could have a good lark and a party.

The Casbar was not open to just anyone: it was for our own lads, the guys who worked for us, and the footballers from our team. We invited people we liked, and it had a name as a real good place to get into, everyone wanted to be part of it. Our lads worked bloody hard all week, so we liked to give them a drink and a bit of a party on a Friday night. Later on we would be called a 'gang', but we never thought of it like that. It was just that we had people we trusted around us. Our working lives and social lives spilled over into one, and the Casbar, and the offices at New Church Road, were the centre for both work and pleasure. We had a lot of great evenings there, lots of laughs. Some of our mates were real comedians.

Soon afterwards we opened the Orange club, in the Walworth Road. It was a restaurant with a club above – it was really another drinking club but we also provided some gambling. You could buy snooker tables cheap in those days, no more than £25, so we had one for dice at one end and another game, probably poker, at the other. The set-up was good: people could go out for a meal and then come upstairs afterwards to the club. There was also the Cavern, in Lordship Lane, which we ran for a short time. It was a small club which we took over and put on the map.

Licensing laws were very slack at the time. All we had to do was register the premises, pay a nominal fee and off we went with a private members' club. We had a friendly warrant officer at the police station: he wasn't crooked, but we'd give him a drink whenever he wanted. He was helpful. The clubs would get raided for after-hours drinking every so often – you simply accepted it as inevitable. The Orange was very popular, and a lot of people from north and east of the river would come there. We had a microphone and people would get up and sing – you could say we invented karaoke. It didn't matter if they were any good or not, everyone enjoyed the atmosphere.

Inevitably, the Orange lost its licence after being raided for after-hours drinking. We expected raids, as they were part of the normal business risks. After a few, you would lose the licence. But we simply renamed it the Rainbow club, re-licensed it and carried on. The licensing magistrates got a bit funny about it being in the same premises, so we swapped it over with the restaurant: restaurant upstairs, club downstairs.

We made money from the clubs, but it was mainly the excitement we enjoyed. The next one we opened was called the Shirley Anne, named after the girlfriend of the guy who ran it for us. The club was nothing more than a large garage, attached to a house in New Cross. The bloke who owned the house used to run a car-repair business at the garage, but was happy to rent the garage space out to us. We bought a club licence, did it up and we were up and running.

The Shirley Anne was a big, successful club. We didn't open it until eleven at night, when the pubs were closing. There was a small gambling area at the back, but mostly it was just a big drinking club which could take as many as a hundred people. There was such a shortage of good drinking clubs that people came from Notting Hill and all around London. We opened it every night of the week and the money flowed in. The doorman knew the regulars and was very careful who he let in: if he didn't know them personally they had to be recommended by someone we knew.

We didn't have proper drains at the Shirley Anne, so when it rained the drains would get blocked and cause a flood outside the club. The first time it happened we put down lots of blocks and planks, and the punters had to balance across them to get to the doors. They called it 'walking the plank' and they loved it. They were always disappointed if the planks weren't there – they made it a bit special.

I had to sort out the bloke who ran the club for us. He was a snide little git, and he took a liberty, running off with a few quid belonging to us. I couldn't let him get away with that, not because it was a large amount of money but because if you let one of them get away with it, everyone starts taking money from you. We didn't know where he'd gone, but I put out a few feelers and heard that he was living in the Euston area. Once we'd got an address I went round there and belted him. He deserved it, and he was expecting it. I'd always let people know when I was looking for them, take my time finding them, get them really afraid. That was important – it livened them up a bit.

When we got to him, I laid into him, wham. Afterwards I said:

'That was a right fucking liberty you took, you c***. This is what you get for being a devious bastard, thinking you can put one over on me.'

We never saw him again. It was important to take action, because clubs attract trouble, with people getting pissed and going off on one, so you need to lay down a few ground rules. If they know you will take action, they behave better.

The Shirley Anne kept going for quite a while. When the police raided it we would never let them in, so they would get in from the house next door – the bloke used to let them go through his premises. They would come mob-handed and confiscate all the booze. But the club was doing so well we could afford to write off a few losses, and I'm sure they enjoyed a drink on us when they'd carted it all away.

We had four clubs running at the same time: the Addington, the Casbar, the Rainbow and the Shirley Anne. We had people managing them, so I only popped in whenever I felt like it, to keep the staff on their toes. One night we arrived at the Shirley Anne pissed, and we decided to go through the bloke next door's house, pretending to be the cops. He let us in and told us to go straight through. He never realised it was us, but we couldn't be too heavy with him as he was renting us the premises.

The clubs were our social life. We worked very hard all day and it was important to have a safety valve, a way of relaxing. I enjoyed a glass of scotch and, like everyone in those days, I smoked. There were drugs around, although nothing much when you think of the drug scene today. We were innocents compared to the kids these days. But there were amphetamines, little blue pep pills, which we all took. Sometimes I wouldn't sleep for three nights, and the only way to keep going at that pace was on amphetamines. But I never became hooked, and I always tried to get some sleep. I'd get back to my own bed for a couple of hours' kip: even if I didn't get home until seven in the morning, I'd get an hour or two in before I had to get back to the yard. And I always stayed at home over the weekend, catching up with sleep and with my family.

It was easy to get hold of the pep pills, everyone had them. Charlie was into something else: old Tommy Knight, a chemist who had a shop in the Walworth Road, used to sell him a tonic which he took all the time. He'd drink gallons of the stuff. It had something in it to liven him up, and something in it to help him get it up – it was the equivalent of Viagra today. I think it contained strychnine. I tried it a few times, and it kept me going without sleep. It made Charlie very aggressive: he would go into one for no reason, his temper was permanently frayed. He never had a go at me – he'd learned that lesson – but he could lay into other people without much provocation.

When she was about ten years old, my sister Elaine brought an Alsatian dog home with her. She was always soppy about animals. It was a great big thing, much too big really for Mum's flat at Champion Hill, and it was always barking. Charlie, who was about twenty-eight at the time, was round at Mum's and he said: 'If you don't stop that fucking dog barking I'll throw it out of the fucking window.' When the dog started up again Charlie grabbed it, carried it out on to the balcony and threw it over. People in the flats below saw the dog going past their windows. They ran down, and so did Elaine. The dog was still alive but when they got it to the vet its legs were so badly broken it had to be put down. Mum covered up with the vet and the neighbours by saying the dog had jumped off the balcony. She and Elaine were both really upset, but what could they do? Charlie didn't worry about it. To him, it was another problem solved.

FOUR

HE CAME TOWARDS US WITH A GUN IN HIS HAND

I'm not proud of a lot of the things I did. Me, Charlie and my dad had a name as people not to be messed with, and we couldn't allow people to be disrespectful. I've mellowed a great deal over the years. As I've said, I wouldn't like to meet the likes of myself now, as I was then. I never felt any fear, I had a lot of surplus energy and I didn't give a monkey's for anyone. I hardly needed an excuse to have a row.

Back in the sixties there was a long-running, very popular television show called *Bonanza*, which was about a family of ranchers out West, father and sons, who always looked out for each other. The Peckham mob took to calling me, my dad and Charlie the Bonanza gang after an incident we were all involved in. A geezer called Bill Slack had a club in Peckham. He was a well-known villain and a hard man – you had to be pretty hard to run a club in Peckham in those days, and Bill Slack had a reputation for being a bit handy. I was out one night with a mate, Dickie Martin, who worked in the demolition business and had dealings with our yards. He suggested we go down to Bill's place. It was about midnight, and we banged on the door of the club. Nothing happened. We banged a bit louder and then, all of a sudden, the doors burst open and about ten or eleven of them poured out. They were looking for aggro. They may have recognised Dickie but I don't think they knew me.

'What the fuck do you fucking arseholes want?' one of them bawled at us.

They came tearing at us. I knocked one aside, shot round the corner, sorted out another one who was after me and then got out of the way smartish. It was ridiculous, so many of them on us. I went straight home. Charlie was there, and when I told him what happened we got ourselves a couple of tools – jemmies and coshes – and went back to the club. It was shut. Maybe they were expecting us, I don't know. Anyway, we jemmied the door open and smashed the club up. There was glass everywhere, from the mirrors and the drinking glasses and the bottles. That was the end of that club, I don't think Slack ever opened up again. If he didn't know who I was to start with, he did now. We'd left our calling card.

So now Bill Slack knew he'd got a problem. We had to find out where he lived in Peckham, and a couple of weeks went by before we tracked him down – which was probably a worrisome time for him. We went round one morning, about nine o'clock. We co-ordinated our watches, and Dad went to knock on the front door to divert him while, at the same time, me and Charlie were over the rear wall and rushing in the back way. We didn't say anything: we didn't advertise our presence like a pair of barking dogs. But Slack heard us come in and he came towards us with a gun in his hand. That didn't last long:

I smashed it out of his hand. I had a large iron bit from a pneumatic drill. I gave him such a bad beating with it that in the end it was so slippery with blood I couldn't hold on to it – it was like a sausage slipping out of my hand. After sorting him out we scarpered, and we never heard of him again.

I knew we were building a reputation, and I revelled in it. I knew we were going to be something, and I worked at it, I spent all my time on it. We were making really good money, and part of that was because we were well known. We didn't have to advertise: everyone had heard of the Richardsons. We were a family, working together, building the company up into something really good.

The clubs we ran were a nice diversion, and made money for us. But the metal business was the most important, by far. We never allowed our social times to compromise it: the yards were always opened on time. And the number of yards was expanding. We took over one in Battersea, just off Wandsworth Common. It was bought as a going concern and we put someone we trusted in to run it. It was an important move west in our expanding empire.

The most important, and the biggest, yard was always the New Church Road one. We used it as a depot: we'd send a lorry round the other yards to pick up the metal and bring it into New Church Road, where we had a weighbridge. Eventually we had six yards, and the annual turnover was £250,000 – nearly three million in today's money.

We didn't have problems from rivals. Nobody dared to interfere with our businesses. We were young, we were aggressive, we had a look on our faces that sent out the message that it wasn't wise to mess with us. Anyone who tried it on got taught a lesson, and the word went round. A few lessons were given out, but mostly people didn't provoke us. We didn't need too much of an excuse to steam in. We were easily insulted if someone tried to turn us over or said something out of turn. In we'd go, biff boff, sorted.

Of course, in that line of business we were often handling stolen property. We didn't ask questions. One guy from Middlesex supplied us with a lot of lead, and it turned out he was nicking it off people's houses. He had done loads of them, sometimes taking every drainpipe from an entire road and, apparently, the local paper had made a big song and dance about it. The police followed him to our yard, and when they turned over our piles of lead they found the pipes – they even matched the colours of the paint to the houses they'd come from. Charlie didn't take the bait when one cop offered him the chance to get out of it by bunging him a hundred quid. Instead, we went to court, and he got fined £80 and I got fined £40. It was a liberty, because it wasn't our fault – you couldn't make inquiries as to where every bit of scrap came from.

We looked after the blokes who worked for us. They got big bonuses and we took care of all their little problems. One of our drivers, Peter Hagen, who also got nicked on the drainpipe case, had a dispute with some geezer who then collected together some mates with a view to sorting him out. They met up at the Lyceum, and a whole mob of them descended on us. A lot of them were hangers on, there to see the action, but there were plenty who were looking for a fight.

They went to Addington Square first. There were about thirty of them and they had knives and a shotgun. We were at New Church Road, but as soon as we got the phone call from the other yard I took one of the lorries and shot round there, slung it up on the kerb outside the yard and drove straight at them, which scattered them. But then they came back round to New Church Road. Some member of the public rang the police, because one of the mob at the gate was brandishing a shotgun. I wasn't frightened, I can never remember being frightened. I was quite brave, maybe misguided, but I was confident about everything I did. Charlie came out with a bottle of acid and Arthur Baron yelled out: 'No, not the acid!' That put the wind up them and they were dispersing when the police cars zoomed up.

About half of them managed to get away, but the others couldn't get out without walking into the arms of the Old Bill. So I called to them to get into the yard, quick. They threw their tools into the big pile of scrap metal, and then we spread the men about a bit – a couple of them started carrying lumps of metal around, others were in the office. When the police walked in it looked like business as usual, and we told the cops that these guys were customers of ours. We looked surprised to see the police there, and I said: 'What's the problem?' The cops radioed back to their station that they were on a wild goose chase.

After the cops went, I told the blokes who had been out to get us to fuck off, and that was the end of that. I think they were glad to get out of there – they didn't win any medals that day. But you never want to see someone get nicked, so we helped them out. I didn't know him at the time, but Charlie Wilson, one of the Great Train boys, was in that mob. We talked about it when we were inside together, years later.

Another fight happened after Reggie Jones, one of our men, got a beating. Friday night was drinks night for our staff, and we'd have a bit of a party in the Casbar after a few drinks in the Masons Arms on East Street, just off the Walworth Road. It was a regular event. On this particular evening, near closing time, we went round to the Casbar but we left our driver, Reggie, to collect more supplies of booze from the pub. Once the pub closed the landlord would make up our order and pass it out through the side door: it was usually a couple of crates of light ale, some vodka, scotch, whatever. Reggie was sitting outside in the motor, waiting. Suddenly a bloke called Jimmy Brindle ran out of the pub like a lunatic and jumped into the car, frantic to get away from this mob that was after him. It seemed that Brindle had been having a row with Jackie Rosa, a well-known face. Rosa, who had a reputation as a right hard man, wanted Jimmy to drive him up to the West End, but Jimmy didn't want to. Rosa and his mates turned on Jimmy, who did a runner. Not that we knew any of this at the time.

They followed Jimmy out of the pub and dragged him and Reggie, who was nothing to do with it, out of the motor and gave them both a seeing to. So when Reggie arrived back with our drinks he had a black eye and a few bruises. He told us what had happened, and we were furious. We didn't know who they were, but there weren't many places they could have gone, and the most likely was the Newton Reform Club just off the Walworth Road, near the Elephant. So down we flew, two carloads, about eight of us – although some of them had come along for the view.

We got down there and they were standing in a little group in the middle of the floor, all happy with their night's work beating up Jimmy Brindle. Then we walked in. Charlie nutted the first one and, wallop, I hit the next one and down he went. We got stuck in and I grabbed a big champagne bottle and cracked it over Rosa's head. He fell and grabbed at the bar to hold himself up, knocking over hundreds of drinks. Just about all the local chaps from South London were in that club, watching us steam into them: anyone who was anyone was there. All of a sudden there's six of them laid out on the floor. The rest of them in there were asking, 'Who the fuckin' hell are they?' They may not have seen us before, but they knew we weren't people you would want to pick an argument with.

We walked out and went back to our party. People were coming up to us afterwards saying: 'You wanna be careful. They'll be round here with shooters.' I just said, 'Well, they know where we are. We're not hiding.' We didn't have any bother from them.

That helped us accumulate a reputation. It was good PR, although that's not what we set out to do. We just wanted to get even because Reggie had been beaten up. We didn't think about Jimmy Brindle, although by doing him a good turn and getting revenge on Rosa and Co. we were actually doing ourselves a favour, too: Jimmy's wife, Eva, was the sister of Frankie Fraser, who would later become my business partner, and it was because of this fight that we met.

On a different occasion, we helped out another employee of ours, Johnnie Lawrence. He was living with, and had a daughter with, a girl who went off with one of the Roff brothers, Mickey. Fair enough, it was up to her who she shacked up with. But Roffie broke into Johnnie's flat and nicked all the furniture, which was a right liberty. We found out that Roffie was living round Albany Road, near Burgess Park. We smashed his door in and nicked the furniture back. After this, Roffie was still on our wanted list – not one of our favourites – so we went round there one night and banged on the door, trying to get him out. We issued a few verbal threats:

'Get out here you bastard.'

After a while he ran out, jumped into his van and started to drive off. Charlie threw a stone at the van. Roffie went to the police and said he'd been shot at – he was a right grass – so Charlie got nicked for malicious shooting, which was a terrible liberty because he didn't have a gun. Johnnie Nash and Peter Hagen were also nicked, but I managed to get away: I didn't put myself on show when the police car came up, put it that way. Charlie managed to get the charge against him thrown out, but Johnnie Nash and Peter Hagen got a short stretch each for assault.

I never carried a gun or a knife, but there were always other things available. I didn't mind using a weapon, a lump of metal or something that came to hand at the time. I knew how I could get a gun if I wanted one, but I never did.

I did have a little set-to with Mickey Roff after that. I pulled up at some traffic lights and, by coincidence, he was in the car in front. When I saw him I jumped out and rushed up to his car to drag him out, but the lights changed and he pulled away. Then he went to the police, again, and made a statement that I'd attacked him with a knife. We had a policeman on the payroll at the time, and he straightened it out for me.

Charlie used to bung the police a few quid. I resented it: we were running legit businesses – apart from the odd bit of hookey metal that would come in, which couldn't be avoided. But if you didn't bung them, the police would sit outside your premises and ruin business, because people who were bringing metal in would be put off and go elsewhere. They'd rather sell for a lower rate than do their business under the watchful eyes of the cops.

Charlie had a line to a top cop. He'd ring him up, he'd sort it, and the cop car would pull away. We suspected that he deliberately used to tell them to sit there, so that he'd get his bung. Meeting bent cops was all down to the right introductions. The local bookmaker, Albert Connaught, was our conduit, because he was in touch with them all. He used to go to all the police balls and functions. You'd go to Albert and tell him what you wanted, and he'd say:

'Leave it to me, I'll have a word.' It would be sorted, and the bung money was delivered through Albert.

Charlie and me worked alongside each other all day, but we had different social lives. We never saw each other much when the gates of the yards were chained. By this time he had five kids, but he was having an affair with another woman. I didn't get on with her and I couldn't see what he saw in her, although she looked OK. She became very important in Charlie's life for a while, and she was there when one of the most shocking events of my whole life occurred. I couldn't have dreamt of anything worse. It nearly broke the whole family, and Mum was rigid with grief for months, years even, afterwards. She never fully got over it. Neither did I; it really did me in. For years I couldn't talk about it without tears welling in my eyes and I'd start crying. Even to this day it's hard for me.

Alan, our younger brother, was killed. It was the most horrific accident, but if anybody was to blame it was Charlie. Alan was eighteen, and a smashing lad – big and fit like me, but with a gentle nature. He was a good footballer, good enough to have a trial for Crystal Palace. He was a great kid to have around. But suddenly he wasn't around anymore.

Charlie had bought himself a speedboat which he used for cutting about on the Thames for pleasure. He was having his affair with this woman, Jean Goodman, and he'd bring her to the yard and they'd go upstairs together. I never warmed to her. She was small and quite attractive, and she had a young son whose father was an American serviceman. I felt she was a distraction, took his mind off the business.

One weekend Charlie decided to take Jean for a cruise up the river. He persuaded Alan to go with him. He said he wanted to give Alan a good time, speeding down the Thames, but he needed someone to help launch the boat with him, and he had to talk Alan into it. My brother Charlie is brilliant at persuading people to do what he wants.

Anyway, they were racing up the river when Charlie realised they were going to hit the wake of a pleasure steamer. He had no time to take evasive action and the speedboat flipped over and all three of them ended up in the river. A barge went past, and it seems that its underwater wake tugged the three of them under. Charlie and Jean surfaced, but Alan didn't. His body and the remains of Charlie's boat were found by the river police the next day. There was a rope from the boat tangled round Alan's leg, stopping him coming up. Our neighbour and good friend Arthur Baron had to identify the body because we were all too upset to go. The accident itself wasn't Charlie's fault: the pleasure boat should not have been where it was. But the thing that haunts me is something that our grandmother said to Charlie: 'You imposed your will on that boy.' Alan didn't want to go on the river, and he should not have been persuaded. She was right, Charlie imposed his will.

I have never confronted Charlie about it. He was as devastated as we all were. We got through by not talking about it, because it was just too upsetting. I don't allow myself to think about the life Alan might have had, the fine man he would have become. What's the point? But we made sure that when Mum died, many years later, she went into the same grave as Alan. She wanted to be with him again, and now she is, for eternity.

I've never understood why Charlie had to get involved in long firms. We had a great, profitable business, but then he started messing around with all this other stuff. He moved into the back office and left me to get on with the yards, while all these dodgy, long-firm idiots started hanging around. I thought it was unnecessary because the money being made from the metal was plenty to go round. Charlie wasn't always a good judge of people, he always wanted to control them, to use them. He didn't make friends in the way I did: I'm still close to the friends I made when I was young. If I was doing business with someone I'd make a few inquiries about them. I was the sensible one, I guess. Charlie didn't give a monkey's if he thought he could get a few quid, put something over on someone.

The trouble is, the cops put one over on him. He was caught delivering a load of dodgy metal to a factory in East London. He was charged with handling stolen metal and out on bail for two bonds of £1000, put up by two of our blokes, Reggie Rumble and Reggie Saunders. That was a fair bit of money in those days. Reggie Saunders had been delivering our milk to the yard before we offered him a job, so he was always called Reggie the Milkman.

Then, after being on bail for a couple of months, Charlie took about £25,000 out of the company and disappeared. Over the weekend, he had cashed in all the metal we had: it was a Monday morning when I discovered the yards had been cleaned out. He'd even taken money on account of more metal coming in. I had no funds at all. It was a shock. He'd dumped everyone. Jean Goodman went with him.

By then Charlie had split up with his wife, Margaret. It was never a marriage made in heaven. She relied on Charlie for everything, but they were rowing all the time and he took the kids and left her. Margaret couldn't have afforded to look after five kids. So our mum was bringing those kids up, and when Charlie went on the trot she looked after them all the time.

At first, I didn't even know where Charlie had gone. Turns out he went to Canada, to join our dad who was still working on the railways out there. Charlie set up a scrap-metal business, Target Metal, which didn't work out and he lost a lot of money running it.

I had to find the money to pay off the two Reggies who stood bail for him: that was a family debt, so it was a matter of honour to pay it. I borrowed money to keep the business going, to give me a float to buy more metal, and before long we were cracking away again with a thriving business. I sold half of the Rainbow nightclub to Patsy Callaghan, who could run it and bring his own customers in, which solved a problem for me because there was a lot to do on my own. We had soon paid everyone back. Arthur Baron was a big help to me at this time.

After about nine or ten months, Charlie showed up again. He kept a low profile for a while until he was sure the heat had died down and the charges against him had been dropped. He put a few quid about to get them scrubbed out. He was skint, and expected to pick up the reins of the business. I was so pleased to see him, and so were the rest of the family. It was like the prodigal's return, we were all making a big fuss of him; but as far as the business was concerned, everything was different. It could never be the same again. I'd sorted it out, got it back on its feet after he cleaned it out, and now he was expecting me to stand aside for him to take control. He couldn't see that the pecking order had changed. We didn't get on, and it got worse and worse.

We had a few arguments, and I tried to make him understand my point of view. I'm always very loyal to the family, I'm a family person. I didn't want to cut him out but I didn't want to be bossed around by him, either.

To ease the tension, I took a bit of time away from the yards. I tried out a new scheme: being a bookie. I travelled the country with a bookie called Patsy Hogan – I provided the backing money for all the expenses, he provided the expertise.

Patsy ran a round book, which means he took money on all the horses in a race. If someone placed a big bet, you laid it off by betting through the top man. The top man was the guy who could look down over the whole course – the members' enclosure, the silver ring, Tattersalls, the lot – and see all the tic tac men who were signalling the prices. Nowadays it's all done by mobile phone and computer. If you run a round book you don't lose, but you don't make so much money. We travelled to Ascot, Epsom, Sandown Park, Goodwood, lots of places, mostly in the south of England. It was a great experience and I loved being in the open air and meeting lots of people, making good contacts, drinking champagne. But it simply didn't make the kind of money I was used to picking up. Patsy's wife had a flower shop so he was just glad of a few days' work on top of that, and he didn't have such expensive tastes as I did.

I worked with Patsy for about three months. I have never been a gambling man myself, it doesn't make sense to me. I think being a gambler-holic is worse than being an alcoholic. An alcoholic can only spend so much in a day, but a gambler can blow thousands. Two mates of mine got paid £8000 from some job involving skulduggery. That would be at least £90,000 today, but they blew the lot in a betting shop, came out with nothing. To me, gambling's a mug's game.

Later on, when I went to the races for a day out, I'd have a flutter, say, £30 a race. If you won it was a bonus, but if you lost it was affordable, just part of the day's expenses. I used to place my bets with Neville Berry, who at one time ran the tote. He was a nice man. He lost a lot when a guy placed a bet for nearly two hundred grand and the tote had an inquiry. He had to go back to being a bookie on the rails. I never even asked him the prices when I bet with him because I knew he would always give me the best price for my horse. After old Neville died his son took over the business.

It was easy in those days to nobble horses, because there wasn't the security or the drug testing that there is today. I was never directly involved, but I sometimes made a few quid from hearing what was going on. Dogs used to get nobbled, too, and I did get involved but I lost money. I was approached because I had the cash to finance it, and also because they wanted my reputation around them, to stop them being ripped off. The girls who worked at the kennels were supposed to take care of things, slip the right drug to the right dog. But once they got to the track things would happen that were outside our control, and often the wrong dog would be nobbled. And even if you nobbled the favourite, you had to still pick the winner to back. It just wasn't worth it for me. It still goes on today, of course it does. There are also jockeys who are up to no good – they just have to be more careful now, that's all.

I was still working with Charlie at this time, but the atmosphere was bad, and at the end of 1962 I walked out with nothing. We weren't enemies or anything like that, but we both realised we couldn't work closely together and I felt it was time to go solo. I'm a proud man and I asked for nothing from him, despite the fact that I'd made the business a success. I wasn't worried about money: I've always been capable of making a living.

My next venture was a shop called the Walk Round Bargain Store, in Deptford High Road. I was in partnership with a mate of mine, Larry Stone. I was later described in court as a wholesale chemist, but it wasn't a pharmacy. I was simply buying up lots of long-firm stock – razor blades, cosmetics, shampoo, stuff like that – and selling it at a good profit. I bought the company off the peg. We paid a peppercorn rent for the place because it needed decorating, so there wasn't too much outlay. It was a nice little earner and it kept me going for a while.

Charlie was still pulling his long-firm tricks. He had to organise a fire in a huge warehouse he had in the City with some mates so that they could tell the suppliers that all the stock had gone up in smoke when, in fact, they'd sold it. Unfortunately, the toe-rags he employed to carry out the arson overdid it and the whole place went up in seconds. It was an enormous fire, and of course the police were on to it.

They investigated it but they couldn't prove anything. Charlie had a copper he was bunging to keep an eye on that building: thankfully for Charlie, he kept a cool head and his mouth shut.

Not too long after I started my shop, Frankie Fraser walked into my life, and our partnership was formed.

F I V E

WE LAID THE LOT OF
THEM OUT

One visit I made to prison was not to serve time, but to play football. One day, we got the word from someone we knew in Parkhurst that the prison had allowed a team from a bank to go in and play the prisoners' team. So we decided it would be a real laugh if we could get in. Me and my mate Leslie McCarthy borrowed some headed notepaper from Lonsdales, the sports equipment company, who had just set up in Berwick Street, Soho. Calling ourselves the Lonsdale football team, we wrote to the prison governor saying that we had heard from our friends on the bank team what a good match they'd had at Parkhurst, and we got a letter back saying they'd like us to come down for a game.

Off we went. We put Arthur Baron up front as our manager – he was older, a bit bald, and he looked the part. In the team, with me and

Leslie, were: Terry Spinks, the boxer; Ronnie Jeffreys, an old mate of ours; Terry Murphy, an ex-boxer whose son, Glen, starred in *London's Burning* years later and Frankie Fraser. Quite a few of the team had served time.

We went across on the ferry and drove up to the prison gates in our coach. There was no problem, we were waved straight in. Some of the lads inside knew we were coming, but nobody let on that they recognised us. We got changed into our strip and went out on to the pitch. All the prisoners were out on exercise so they all came to watch. We kept up the pretence until half time, when they all swarmed on to the pitch to shake hands and chat with us. We had lots of tobacco and cigarettes in our bags to give them, and they were all stuffing letters into our hands to take out with us. Of course, the screws knew then what was going on, but there was little they could do. They let us play the second half, because they couldn't really stop it.

The prison team took it seriously – they beat us 3–1. Football is a serious occupation inside, where there's nothing much else going on. The prison staff had laid on a tea for us afterwards, but there was no way they were going to let us stay a minute longer than they could avoid and we were hustled out as soon as we got changed after the match. After we'd gone, the whole nick was spun (searched) because there were rumours that we had taken in a gun for someone. It wasn't true. But spinning was just the screws' way of giving it back to the prisoners for us having put one over them.

Football was an important part of life and we loved mixing with the real thing, with footballers who were at the top of the game. In 1962 me and Frankie Fraser – who is a mad Arsenal fan – took the entire Arsenal side out to lunch in Soho, all the big names, including Don Howe, George Armstrong and Terry Neill. It was just a social thing: we knew one of their trainers and we asked if the boys would like to be treated to a meal. They didn't get anything like the money they get today, and they were pleased to take up the invite. We hired the whole restaurant and we had a large table down the middle. Everyone had a good drink, good food and a bit of a laugh. No strings attached, just a bit of hospitality from us to them.

At one time, me and Leslie McCarthy got a football team together, calling it the Soho Ramblers, to play a team of sport swriters from the national and sporting press. A few well-known villains were in our team, and Albert Dimes, a well-known face, and the actor Stanley Baker – both of whom I got to know really well – came along to support us. That was our only fixture.

Frankie Fraser is a very polite sort of guy, very polite. He came to the shop in Deptford to thank me for helping out in the Jimmy Brindle affair. Jimmy had told him how we'd sorted out the other mob, and Frankie was grateful. He was very close to his sister, Eva, who was married to Jimmy. It was ironic, because we hadn't pitched in for Brindle's sake but for our driver's, Reggie Jones.

Frankie was just out of jail after a long stretch, one of several he had served. He was very well known in criminal circles in London – in fact, he was well known to criminals across the country, because he had served time in so many nicks. He'd spent some time in Broadmoor, so he already had the nickname 'Mad' Frankie, but it's not something I ever called him. He always did his sentences the hard way, being in chokey (solitary) much of the time, and losing all his remission. He refused to allow the system to beat him.

Much later, when he stood in the dock alongside me at the 'torture trial', he was also very well known to the general public – just as me and Charlie were. But that was in the future. When Frankie came to see me, none of us had any idea what lay ahead.

We hit it off and we talked about all sorts of different things. He told me he still had a half share, with Joey Wilkins, in some fruit machines. So I suggested we went to see Joey and get his share back. I knew Joey Wilkins's uncle, Bert, who was a regular customer at our yard. Bert had connections: he'd served time for manslaughter and was at one stage in partnership with Billy Hill, a well-known face who knew everybody. By the time I met him, Bert was a straight businessman, he didn't touch anything illegal.

Joey Wilkins was not all that happy to give Frankie his share of the business back and Frankie felt a bit embarrassed because Joe had been doing all the work. But Joey agreed. I formed a company and called it Atlantic Machines, which gave it a nice, American sort of feel, and we found ourselves some premises in Windmill Street, off Tottenham Court Road. Leslie McCarthy agreed to be a director and had a lot of input in forming the company. We needed a respectable name for the letterhead, so I spoke to a drunken old solicitor's clerk called Leaworthy who introduced Leslie to Sir Noel Dryden. He'd been an actor and a BBC announcer, but the main love affair of his life was with the bottle, so he was happy to become a board member for a regular retainer.

There were loads of these posh guys back then with no money. Life was a struggle, especially if they were boozers, so they were happy to sign up to firms like ours, no questions asked. We didn't pay Sir Noel a lot of money, just a few quid, but it was money for nothing and he got it regularly. I met him a couple of times, but he certainly wasn't involved in running the business.

We needed money to buy more machines. I had all the contacts, and knew where to get the machines (we bought them from Ruffler and Walker) and we found good guys to service and empty them. I had a few thousand to put up, but we needed more. We went to see Billy Hill, who, in the early fifties, pulled off two huge robberies netting what would in today's terms be at least £6 million, and he didn't really need to work. He was a master card sharp, and he operated card scams all over the place. The club owners would allow him in and take a huge cut of his proceeds – he never operated without their permission. Billy used to play cards at top gambling clubs, like Aspinall's in Berkeley Square, which was owned by John Aspinall. I heard a rumour that he took Kerry Packer, the Australian newspaper magnate, for half a million there.

We went to Billy's flat in Moscow Road, Bayswater, a lovely place, and he was wearing his dressing-gown when he met us. There was a large Capo di Monte ornament of four scruffy kids playing cards, one of them with a card between his toes which he was hooking to his mate. The owner of one of the clubs had given it to Billy. Billy knew Frankie. Frankie and Albert Dimes were both on a 'pension' from Billy, which meant he paid them regularly to be on call for him whenever he needed a bit of help. I could tell he was weighing me up. He said he thought the machines were hard work, but I told him they were regular money.

'The problem is getting the money to buy more machines, because they are in so much demand,' I said. 'We've got more sites than we've got machines.'

'I might be able to help you there, lads,' he said.

He walked across the room, opened a drawer, and took out £5000. He had plenty of money and he could afford to do it, but it was a way of saying that he wanted to be our friend. He knew who to look after, and he liked helping out an up and coming young man like me. I was never called on to do anything for him but I would have done, and he knew it. He was a gentleman.

I started with the sites that Frankie already had, and built them up pretty rapidly, adding lots of places in the West End. Because he knew everyone, Albert Dimes was really helpful. He was a big guy, over six feet tall, and he had a presence. He was like the League of Nations in Soho, everyone took their problems to Albert to sort out.

The Greeks had an argument with the Turks, or the Italians, or the Maltese, or anyone – they all went to Albert. He used to hold court in his betting shop in Frith Street, but he had staff running it so he'd take you to the Italian restaurant next door, Bianca's, where they made a big fuss of him. He was a true diplomat.

So if we found a place, a club or a pub, that looked like it was taking a lot of money for someone else's machines, we'd tell Albert and he'd get on to them. 'I've got a couple of good friends who'd like to put a new machine in for you,' he'd say. It was easy, they were always keen to have our machines. We never had to lean on club owners to get them in.

We soon had more clubs asking for our machines than we could supply. Our name counted for a lot, but it was always purely a business deal: we offered the club a better percentage of the take from the machines. The machines took sixpences, and some of them earned us £100 a week, which would be about £1100 today, so it was a great business. We had counting machines to sort out the cash. The staff working for us were all blokes we knew, like Patsy Fleming. He was a mate of Fraser's and they'd first met when they were kids in approved school. One time, Patsy escaped from prison with the notorious escaper, Alfie Hinds. Patsy was a real nice guy and when he came out of prison we gave him a job as a mechanic.

We also employed Jimmy Andrews, another face who had done a lot of time with Frankie, and Roy Porritt, who was a friend of mine. Our best mechanic was a young lad I recruited, straight, who could do anything with a broken machine.

The club owners certainly benefited from their connection with us, and not just because we ran the machines efficiently and gave them a good rake off. They liked having us popping in and out. We never expected free drinks from the clubs where our machines were, we'd never sink to that. We'd always buy our drinks when we popped in for a chat with the guv'nor. The clubs used to use our names: if they had a few tearaways causing trouble, they'd drop in their association with us and that was all it took to sort it out. If there was a machine that wasn't taking much money and we decided to remove it, the club owners would beg us to keep it there.

We rarely had to resort to physical violence. Sometimes we were credited with things we didn't do. Years later, when I was in Parkhurst, a huge guy came up to me, he must have weighed about twenty stone. He shook my hand and thanked me for doing him over. He thought me and Frankie had beaten him up in the Starlight club. I was there that night, just walking in when it happened. He reckoned he deserved what he got, and I reckon he did too. He was in the fish business, selling jellied eels and seafood – that was his legit business. But he'd taken a liberty with someone and he was spotted the minute he went into the Starlight. He was plotted up and they got him on the way out. He got a right beating in a recess by the stairwell. He's convinced it was me and Fraser who did it, and that has given him a bit of a lift. Not that the people who did do it were nobodies: they were a couple of faces. But when he said to me:

'Ed, I know it was you beat me up, but I did deserve it. I must say you was right,' I was just pleased to leave it at that. It helped him justify it, and gave him a tale to tell.

Soho was really buzzing back then. It was cracking. I'm an adaptable sort of fella, and if there's a few quid to be made I'll fall into anything. The machines were a good earner and Frankie and I were both getting a nice amount to take home. I liked the social life up West, too. We spent our evenings in the Stork Room, the Astor, the Latin Quarter or the Pigalle – where Shirley Bassey used to sing. It was in the Astor that I first met Diana Dors. She was a stunningly beautiful young girl in those days. (I met her several times, years later, when she was unwell. She'd be with her husband, Alan Lake, and Alex Steene, the boxing promoter. It was a shame to see what illness had done to her.) The Astor was run by Bertie Green, who operated a theatrical agency there during the day, which provided acts for all the clubs.

We'd often start our rounds at the Log Cabin, in Wardour Street, which was owned by a mate, Tommy McCarthy. It was a small club, no live music, and it didn't stay open late. We used it to meet up before visiting one or two other clubs. We had a few fights in the Astor, little incidents, nothing significant. One night, something went off with some Scots guys. Patsy Fleming, who worked for us, was just sitting there and he got striped with a razor on his head. It was a mistake, they thought he was someone else, and we didn't get involved because it was a genuine mistake and they apologised.

I don't want to give the impression that we were always fighting. We had a lot of fun. Tommy Clark was a mate of mine and he was a real character. You'd arrange to meet him and he'd turn up wearing a bowler hat and carrying a rolled umbrella, looking like a barrister, just for a laugh. One night we were drinking in the Stork Room, which was owned by Al Burnett – he was a famous entertainer in those days. Al also owned the Pigalle and he had another club just down the road, the Society, which he liked to keep very exclusive: people like Princess Margaret used to go there.

The Society was difficult to get into because they tried to keep riff-raff like us out, but I conned Al into letting me go there now and again for a quiet drink. So, on this night, I took Clarkie in with me, and it was going alright until Clarkie went off to the gents. While he was gone the floor show started and a chorus line of dancing girls came on stage – high heels, high-kicking, high plumes on their heads – real high-class stuff. And who's on the end of them, kicking his legs up? Tommy Clark. Everyone in the place collapsed laughing, but I don't think Al allowed me back in there again.

Tommy was one of those characters, a real lunatic, who was always popping up. He worked for Charlie. He was always welcome when he turned up because he made you laugh. He died recently.

We met a lot of interesting people, especially through Albert Dimes. Through him I met an American who was dodging a warrant out for his extradition back there. He was on his toes over here, moving about Europe, living in Spain and Switzerland.

He introduced us to a bank in Liechtenstein. In those days huge sums of money would come over to Europe from America, particularly from the Las Vegas casinos, to be banked in Liechtenstein where no questions were ever asked. It would, literally, come over in bags. I met one man who used to bring suitcases through, and later, when I was inside, I heard that he ran away with one. What an idiot – you don't normally risk upsetting the big boys from America by doing things like that. It was about £15,000 he got away with, around £175,000 in today's money. He survived because they had a million other problems to deal with and he was small fry. He's still here to this day.

Anyway, the introduction to the Liechtenstein bank was going to be useful for some skulduggery I was planning with the commodities market. I had a guy in place working for a big company, and he was going to push a lot of deals through the Liechtenstein account. He was on a third of the take, I was on a third, and another pal was on a third. It had just started going through when the geezer on the inside got the sack. I did a deal and got out.

Looking after people from other countries was all part of a kind of reciprocal service. Another mate of mine had a restaurant in Miami. I could send people over there and he'd always treat them well, and I'd do the same with the Americans he sent to me. They weren't all villains, they were often straight people: lawyers, maybe someone's wife, nice folk. I'd always take them to the Ritz, which they loved.

Occasionally, we'd look after a villain who was on his toes and we'd find him somewhere to stay, take care of his expenses. It was the done thing. When Ronnie Biggs escaped from Wandsworth in July 1965, it was his name that made all the headlines. But three others got out with him: Eric Flowers, from London, a Scotsman called Andy Anderson and a bloke called Doyle. The escape plan had been made for Biggs and Flowers, the other two just took their chances. Anderson had done time with a bloke who worked for us as a mechanic and, when Anderson said he was going to escape, our mate told him to ring Atlantic Machines if he needed help.

Anderson remembered the address and turned up there. The guys who organised the escape had given him a suit and £2, but he'd had to buy himself a shirt so he was skint. Frankie found him waiting in our car park at the offices in Tottenham Court Road. He brought him inside, where I and a few others were chatting with Stanley Baker, the actor who starred in the film *Zulu*. Stanley was a mate: I'd met up with him a few times in Soho through Albert Dimes. He was a man's man, and he liked hanging around with hard men. He knew that 'There but for the grace of God, go I.' He told me that if his acting career hadn't taken off the way it did, he could easily have been a villain.

I once went down to Wales with him and Donald Houston, another famous actor, to Stan's village of Ferndale, in the Rhondda valley. Stan drove us all down in his Bentley. It was a good laugh, and we had quite a few drinks. Stan was very popular because he had arranged for the miners from Ferndale to sing the chorus on the *Zulu* soundtrack, and they got enough money out of that to build a new village hall. When we walked into the hall they all started singing the theme from *Zulu*. Stan did a show for them, a really good song and

My grandparents. Lizzie, my mother's
mother, ruled the family

Mum and Dad on their wedding day

My dad Charlie *(standing, third from right)* served in the merchant navy for twenty-five
years and was decorated during the war

My mother Eileen, the biggest influence on my life

Aged about thirteen, with my mum

Outside our shop in Wyndham Road. *Left to right:* me, Maureen, Alan, Aunt Dorothy, my grandmother (holding one of Charlie's kids) and grandfather, Margaret, Mum and Elaine

Maureen and I got married at the church in Camberwell Church Street, and spent our honeymoon in Herne Bay. We were both barely out of our teens

Our two beautiful girls, Melanie and Donna

Dad (*right*) with his brother Jim. Brother Charlie worked with Uncle Jimmy before opening his own scrapyard

Me and Harry Rawlings soak up the sights, and other delights, in Paris. I even painted a picture based on this photo *(below)*

Harry and I are still great mates. He and Della set their wedding date for when I came out of prison so that I could be best man

I was always keen on football. Soho Rangers FC: *back row, left to right* – Stanley Baker, Billy Rawlings, Reggie Saunders, George Wisbey, Danny Pembroke, Bill Staynton, Tommy McCarthy, Albert Dimes, Frankie Fraser; *front row* – Bert McCarthy, me, Peter Warner, Ronnie Jeffreys, Ronnie Oliver

Me and the lads always enjoyed a night out at the boxing. *Left to right:* Harry Rawlings, me, Leslie McCarthy, Ronnie Jeffreys and Martin O'Day

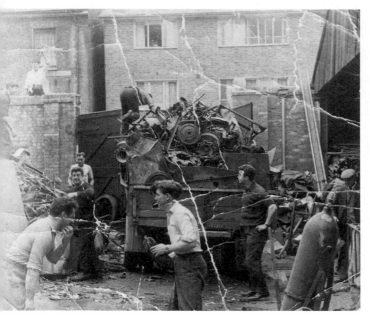

At work in our scrapyard. Reggie the Milkman is
in the centre foreground and I'm behind him to
the right

We had a look on our
faces… people soon learned
not to mess with us

K.W.P. Metals was the company I bought after I came out of prison

With my old mate Alan Martin, the manager of my metal yard, at a do in the late seventies

Boxing has always been part of my life: here I am with world middleweight champion Terry Downes (*centre*) and Charlie Rumble

The *Oceana*. After one or two hairy moments at sea I decided boat ownership was not for me

I didn't want to go at first but I took to skiing straightaway. This is me in Austria, about to hit the slopes

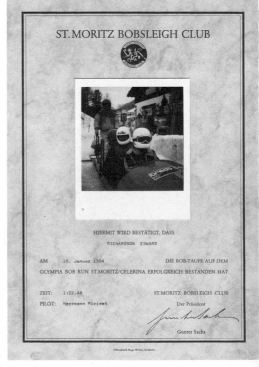

ST. MORITZ BOBSLEIGH CLUB

HIERMIT WIRD BESTÄTIGT, DASS

RICHARDSON EDWARD

AM   19. Januar 1984   DIE BOB-TAUFE AUF DEM

OLYMPIA BOB RUN ST.MORITZ/CELERINA ERFOLGREICH BESTANDEN HAT

ZEIT: 1:22.48   ST.MORITZ BOBSLEIGH CLUB

PILOT: Herrmann Müriset   Der Präsident

                                     Gunter Sachs

I love bobsleighing too and took part in this run at St Moritz in 1984. That's me in the middle in the 'kiwi' helmet dance act. It surprised me because I didn't realise what an all-round entertainer he was. Donald Houston did a turn as well and while he was performing many of the miners carried on playing cards. It wasn't disrespectful, it was just their tradition. When Stan told them he had a couple of pals from England with him, they stood up at the end and sang *God Save the Queen*, which they would not normally have done. I don't give a stuff about the queen, but I was honoured that they did it for us. We stayed in Porthcawl, where Stan also had to see a few people.

Stan once did us a huge favour, really put himself on the line for us. Our Atlantic Machines premises were raided one time and the cops found all these thunder flashes in the cellar. They were raiding the premises looking for stolen fruit machines, but we never had to steal anyone else's equipment. I had no knowledge of the thunder flashes, didn't know they were there – you didn't go round searching your own cellars. My guess is Jimmy Andrews, who worked for us, was storing them there for some villainy. But the only people allowed to have them were the War Office (the Ministry of Defence today) and film producers, who were allowed to use them for filming. So Stan got a colleague of his from the film industry to say that he was storing them there. It worked, and the law had to back off.

When Frankie brought Andy Anderson in I knew who it was – although no names had been given, I'd heard a news report that four men had got out of Wandsworth. We had a whip round and raised a few hundred for him. Frankie took Andy to stay that night at his mother's flat and I got on to Arthur Thompson, a good mate who ruled the roost in Glasgow. We figured that Andy would be safer up there, as he had a broad Scottish accent. He was taken care of brilliantly in Scotland, and then after three or four months he went to Manchester where my mate Bobby McDermott, who hired all the barrows out to the barrowboys and knew everyone, took him on.

After he'd been on his toes for about eight months Andy was recaptured, when he was queuing to get a coach back to Glasgow for the weekend.

It worked both ways. On one occasion, my mate Harry Rawlings and I had to disappear for a week or two and I was looked after in Paris by a Frenchman, Robert, who we met in Southport. We came to be up in Southport after hooking up with George James, who owned a few casinos around the country, including Charlie Chester's, in London. There was a Yank going into Charlie Chester's and winning loads of money. He was obviously cheating, and I was asked if I could help sort it out. I approached Albert Dimes, who was happy to help me and, at the same time, to protect Billy Hill's interests. We told the American we had a cheque for him, got him out the back into the offices and sat him down.

Albert had already sussed what he was up to. The organisation he worked for had sold hundreds of packs of cards to the casino cheap. They were nice cards, but they were marked with luminous ink that could only be seen with special glasses. The geezer tried to protest his innocence, so Albert forced his head down on to the table and grabbed him by the throat. Albert was a big bloke, over six feet, imposing. Me and Frank were hemming him in. We gave him some strong verbals.

'Listen mate, we don't want any crap from you. We fucking know what you've been up to. Who the fuck do you think you are?'

We told him he wasn't going to get a penny of his winnings, and he was lucky to be walking out and not going out on a stretcher. He'd already made a few quid out of it but it had come on top, and he accepted he had to get out. We never saw him again.

After that we were 'on a pension' from Charlie Chester's, picking up a regular wage just to be helpful. This was just the first of a few favours we did for George. He liked having 'the boys', as he called us, around. He was happy to put our machines in his clubs, including the one in Southport. At this time we were expanding out of London and had machines in clubs in Cardiff, Manchester, Liverpool, all over the place. We had machines in over fifty clubs. The ones outside London weren't as profitable as the clubs in the capital and the cost of sending people out to service them was greater. But we were still making a lot of money from them, and there were plenty of punters who were happy to pump in a pile of sixpences in the hope of winning the jackpot.

The clubs in Wales belonged to George James, and he used to get us to go down there. He'd introduce us to people as big London gamblers. If they knew we were coming it would bring the punters in. He'd give me a load of chips and sit me down at a table. One time it was baccarat, which I didn't know how to play. He kept saying, 'It don't matter, it don't matter, just lose the money.' But I had plenty of help behind me because the spectators were all looking and muttering: 'He should stick on that', so I did what they said. I couldn't wait to get rid of the money. What George wanted was for a story to go round about big London gamblers losing thousands – it put his club on the map.

One night in Swansea I was on the roulette table and I just couldn't lose, even though I wanted to. George's wife was next to me and she was losing everything, so I kept pushing chips to her. Stanley Baker was there that night.

George's club on the seafront in Southport, the King's Head, was very popular, because there were no casinos in Manchester back then so the gamblers would drive over for a good night at the tables. The baccarat tables were run by the Frenchman I mentioned, Robert, who had met George through their mutual love for rugby. Robert had the best pair of hands with a pack of cards I have ever seen. He could shuffle eight packs on the table so quickly.

We went up there one night, checked into our hotel and made our way to the King's Head. Outside, we were told there was real trouble from a bunch of blokes who were out there arguing with the staff. Frankie and me and another mate went inside, where we heard they'd been heavy with Robert. I ripped one of the iron bars off the edge of the roulette table, and we went back outside and steamed into them. We laid the lot of them out. They were local tearaways, so they didn't scream too much. Afterwards Robert took us out for a meal, to thank us.

In the end, Robert's gratitude cost him a lot more than one meal. As I've said, when Harry Rawlings and I had to escape the heat in London for a while we went to Paris, where Robert was living again, and he looked after us royally. But we'll come to that later.

We had another spot of bother in Southport, at a club called the Horseshoe. There was a geezer called Peter the Greek, or Peter Joannides to give him his full name, who thought he ran the place. He gave me a bit of lip and a fight started. I glassed him, and suddenly all the big guys in the club turned on us. Fraser and me had to get out. We ran at speed and leapt into our motor. We were ahead of all the blokes coming after us, but there was this big Alsatian which was also chasing us, barking its head off. As Fraser opened the car door to pile in, it followed him in. Once inside the car, it completely calmed down, stopped barking, not even a whimper, and wasn't a bit aggressive. I was driving, and after twenty miles or so I stopped and we shoved the dog out. It hadn't been any bother, but we didn't want it as a souvenir from the seaside. The dog made its way home, but it took three or four days to get there. Just as well it did make it, though, as the owner of the club had been really upset about the dog going.

Peter the Greek had gone to the police and given them my car number. I was arrested in London and some cops came down from

Southport to take me back up there, where I was charged with grievous bodily harm (GBH). Those coppers loved it, going to London to arrest a gangster. It was probably the most exciting job of their career, and when I was held in the cells they wanted me to live up to the image. When I asked for a meal they brought me the menus from all the local restaurants and fetched me a nice bit of steak and half a bottle of wine. They enjoyed having me there, but it wasn't for long because I managed to get bail – for a massive £15,000.

The case got thrown out at the magistrates' court committal stage. Nobody could identify me. Even Joannides, who'd laid the charges against me, said he was too under the influence of alcohol to know who had hit him. I'd had all the witnesses squared away by Bobby McDermott from Manchester, the King of the Barrowboys, who had helped us out when Andy Anderson was on the run. Bobby had good contacts and was well respected. He could get things done, and he didn't mind putting himself about for me. It wasn't unusual to get out of things if you had a few quid. The witnesses got paid – they might as well take a few quid as not. The police made out that the witnesses had been intimidated, and there were questions in the House of Commons and a call for an investigation, but it all blew over.

The machines weren't the only business I had with Fraser. A well-known old villain, Ruby Sparks, mentioned the London (now Heathrow) airport car park scam to Frankie. Ruby had been around for years and knew everyone. He got his nickname, Ruby, because when he was a young man he stole a load of rubies from an Indian maharajah. Anyway, he introduced me and Frankie to a guy who was involved in a scam going on at London airport. This bloke wanted to increase his cut, so he asked us to help him out and take a share ourselves. At first I thought it sounded dodgy. I didn't have a lot of faith in the scam, but we ended up getting good money out of it and we were never nicked. This was in 1964, and the bloke in charge of the scam let us have a piece of it: I can't say he was happy, but he didn't have much choice – he'd been getting loads of crooked money out of it for years. He had to let us have a corner, which gave us plenty, and it also meant that he was safe from others trying to muscle in. His men operated the whole thing for us, we just took our money.

It was a great scam, we were all getting a good whack out of it. The men taking the money at the car park gates were all disabled or ex-servicemen. They used to fiddle the figures, only putting through the tills some of the money they took and they could change the time stamp on the tickets. It was dead easy to do, and we picked up a grand or so every week. I went down one time in the pale-blue Bentley to pick up some money, with a chauffeur at the wheel. I had lost my licence, a three-month ban for careless driving after I jumped the lights at Victoria Bridge as they were on the change, and there was traffic screaming the other way towards me. One driver took my number and that was it. I decided that I would be off the road in style. So I employed a chauffeur, Alan Tear, who was Whippet Tear's brother, and I acquired the posh motor. After a while, though, we used to let them deliver the money to us.

Another little enterprise we tried out was porn film clubs. As we went about our fruit machine business in Soho, we noticed that film clubs showing porn movies were springing up around the place. At that time the whole of Soho was run by three people: Maltese Frank Mifsud, Bernie Silver and Jimmy Humphries. They had the police sorted. If anyone else tried to set up they were nicked, all their stock was confiscated, and then it was flogged cheap to those three. No one could get in there.

But they didn't seem to be bothering with these film clubs. So we went to Maltese Frank and asked if he or the other two minded if we took over these clubs. He said to go ahead. We realised that to control the clubs we had to control the touts on the street who were drumming up the business They were the ones who brought the customers in, in return for a percentage. It still works the same way today.

So we raided the clubs, six or seven handed, all blokes who were on the firm. We burst in, put all the lights on, told all the customers to line up against the wall. They were all very obedient. After all, they'd been caught in a seedy place watching porn movies, so they weren't going to give us any trouble. They thought we were the police. The owners were in no doubt as to who we were: we confiscated all their equipment and told them if they opened up again they would be badly hurt. We gave them a wallop to drive the message home, nothing too severe. Just enough to make the point. By the time we had done eight or ten of them, we had control of the film clubs and the touts had to work for us because there was nobody else operating.

We never regarded the Krays as rivals: they weren't in our league, and they never dared confront us.

The Krays would have liked to have become involved in the West End club scene, but they knew that me and Frank were in there and they didn't have the bottle to challenge us. There was never any direct threat from them: as far as we were concerned they were small-time blokes who thought themselves a lot bigger than they were. They were playing at being gangsters, like you see in the movies.

We had a meeting with them once at the Elephant and Castle, arranged by Johnnie Nash, one of the Nash brothers – a good family who come from Islington. We had a drink, shook hands, and to be honest I didn't hang about long. It didn't mean anything: they weren't significant. They didn't want to get entangled with us, they knew we were harder than they were.

The Krays read books about gangsters in America and they wanted to be in the same league, but they didn't have the brains. We were businessmen who could make money legitimately. All they had was a little collection of blokes around them who made them feel good. They opened a club, but other people had to run it because they didn't have a clue. They just sat around their mum's house in Vallance Road, talking themselves up.

They wanted to muscle in on our porn film trade in Soho, and they came round to the offices of Atlantic Machines to ask if we would mind them opening a blue movie club. We said we would mind very much, because we had a monopoly and we didn't want them or anyone else creaming off any of the money. They took the news alright, and we all smiled and shook hands. But I've heard since that Ronnie was very aggravated by our attitude, and that's part of the reason he went after one of Charlie's blokes, George Cornell, and murdered him.

One night me and Frankie went down the Astor club, had a few drinks and were leaving when a fight broke out between a couple of Scottish guys. Nothing to do with us, leave 'em to sort it out. Someone called the police. We paid our tab and left the back way – we had no desire to bump into the Old Bill. As we were going out we met a geezer called Eric Mason, a bloke from West London way. Fraser knew him. As far as we were concerned he was just an acquaintance, and we would have said hello and left it at that. But he was wound up about the fight which he seemed to think was something to do with us.

'The twins won't like this,' he said.

'You fuckin' what?' I said. 'Why do I care what the fuckin' twins like?'

We grabbed hold of him and steered him to our motor. I said: 'I think you had better come with us, Eric.'

We took him to the basement of our offices in Windmill Street, just off Tottenham Court Road. We were very polite, the perfect hosts.

'After you, Eric. Down we go, Eric. Turn left at the bottom of the stairs, Eric.'

Then we started on him.

I said: 'Who do you think you fuckin' are? That we'd be worried by the fuckin' twins?'

Frank got hold of a chopper and he went off on one.

'Take that back to Vallance Road,' he said.

He gave Mason a terrible beating. There was blood gushing from his forehead and, as far as I was concerned, he'd had plenty. It wasn't worth killing a guy – or nearly killing him – for saying, 'The twins won't like this,' even though it was a bad mistake to say it.

We bundled him up in a blanket, carried him to the motor and dropped him off on the steps of Charing Cross Hospital. He didn't run to the police: he knew the score. But when he got out of hospital after a few days, he went round to the Krays in Vallance Road. He thought because he was on their firm they'd take us on in revenge. But we were too strong for that little mob. I heard they gave him a few quid and told him to go away. Years later I had a drink with him, and his attitude was that he'd made a mistake and been punished for it. I believe he lives in Manchester now.

I don't care what people think about that attack on Mason. It put down a marker, and it was the end of any threatening behaviour from the Kray mob. It wasn't until we were in nick – and Charlie was in South Africa – that they turned on George Cornell. They wouldn't have dared if we'd been out.

I didn't have much to do with Cornell. He worked for Charlie, and we didn't share the same interests. Cornell was one of Charlie's hard men, one of his enforcers in the long-firm businesses. Charlie would say, 'George, go round and see this arsehole', and George would do it. Charlie was good at using people. He had people like Roy Hall, who had been working with him since he was a kid when his father was killed on the railway. Roy made some nice bits of money with me but he never got two bob out of Charlie, yet the minute Charlie wanted him to do something, Roy was there.

Charlie inspired that kind of loyalty, and George Cornell was one of his lot. George had been brought up with the twins and came from their part of London. He knew them well, knew their strength, and was always slagging them off, calling them a 'pair of poofs', and Ronnie a 'fat poof'. In the end, he paid a very heavy price for it. But that came after me and Charlie were under arrest.

SIX

A RARE PRIZE FOR THE COPS

lthough I wasn't working with Charlie, we were still close, and we saw each other a fair bit. He was always trying to involve me in his work and sometimes I was happy enough to go along, particularly if it involved a bit of travel. I popped round the yard a bit, and I was loyal and always there when needed. I went to Italy a couple of times for Charlie, to sort out business deals for him and a slippery toad he got himself involved with, Jack Duval.

Duval was the cause of a great deal of trouble that came our way. If Charlie had never teamed up with him, there would probably never have been the infamous torture trial, although I dare say the police would have tried to pin something else on us. But Jack Duval was our personal nemesis. He was a very skilful, major league conman, who lived in great style, constantly taking money off Peter to pay Paul – in the nick of time, to avoid arrest or a bullet through his brain. He was a slippery character and I never liked or trusted him, but Charlie was impressed by him. He'd greet me as though he'd known me forever, pinching my cheek and making a great fuss, real over the top stuff. He could speak several languages, but he never told the truth in any of them.

It stood out a mile to me: if he was conning everybody else, he was probably conning Charlie, too. Charlie thought he could control Duval and all the others he met in that line of work, but it was like trying to control a train load of monkeys. That was one of Charlie's big mistakes, and the one that cost all of us years of our liberty. These weren't our kind of people. We dealt with villains, of course we did, but everyone knew the score and played by the same rules, and rule number one is that you don't rip off your own. Blokes like Duval would con their own mothers, cheat their grannies and sell their sisters into the white slave trade. They had no morals whatsoever.

Duval had a long firm running, 'buying' stockings from Milan. It was easy, because the Italian government were working hard to encourage exports and were guaranteeing to pay half the money to the local firms who sold abroad. Even though it was nearly twenty years after the war, silk stockings were hard to come by and expensive, and because Charlie could sell them cheap they were a very popular line. For a time it was lucrative, but when the supply dried up Charlie asked me to go out to Milan to find out from Duval what was going on.

When I got there I found that the sneaky little git had bigger fish to fry than Charlie's stockings: he was smuggling diamonds out of Switzerland for the Mafia. And he had involved me. At first I thought Duval was being a good host when he took me over to Switzerland, to Lugano, to visit the casinos and get some duty-free shopping. It didn't take me long to suss out that he was smuggling something, because he always had a meet with someone. When I got it out of him what he was up to I sorted him out in the way we understand in my world: he was pulled up and disciplined. I put a strong paw over him for doing that without me knowing the risk I was running. Let's just say I left him with a bit of a sore head.

'That's for putting me at risk, you fucker,' I said as I whacked him.

'And that's a reminder that you owe Charlie a load of stockings,' I said as I whacked him again. Like all those slithering little conmen, he was a coward, and he just whined a bit, never put up any resistance. Years later, I heard that the Mafia sorted him out properly.

When we were in Milan we had a good time – eating in the sunshine, enjoying a drink. We had to visit the factories where all the hosiery was being made, so if I didn't have Duval with me I hired an interpreter. She gave me a bit of a dressing-down once, because she said we British were all warmongers:

'In Italy we are more concerned about living a nice life,' she said.

We had a big discussion about the merits of Britain versus Italy, and she slaughtered me. She was good in an argument, better than a lot of barristers I've known.

To my amazement, and against my advice, Charlie continued to do business with the creepy little Duval. After Duval had been pursued around Europe by the police, the Mafia and all the angry businessmen he'd conned, he sneaked back into Britain where, immediately, Charlie was after him. Duval was hiding out in Brighton, and one of Charlie's long-firm associates, Tommy Costello, unwittingly told him where Duval was. After a 'straightener', which left Duval with another sore head, he and Charlie were back in business running long firms. Needless to say, after a few months Duval was on his toes with the money, bouncing cheques left, right and centre and leaving Charlie with a different kind of sore head – and with a thirst for revenge.

I went out to Milan a couple more times to tie up deals for Charlie. I went with one of Charlie's long-firm blokes, Ken Neal, an educated man with a cut-glass accent. He killed himself a few years later, because he couldn't take doing time in prison. Some blokes just can't do prison.

Charlie's next offer of foreign travel for me was even more enticing: he wanted me to go to South Africa to look at his business interests out there. Just as I never understood why he got involved in long firms, I never understood why he got entangled in the South African mining business. He reckoned it was going to make huge money, but instead it cost him a small fortune, and I believe it was behind all our problems. Charlie was recruited for a very different ball game to any that we had played on the streets of South London, and in my opinion it was his involvement in the dirty world of South African politics that ultimately made us such targets for the law over here.

For me it was just a great chance to see a bit of the world and have a few holidays somewhere hot and beautiful. I had no interest, financial or otherwise, in Charlie's business out there, but from his verbals it sounded as though he could be on to a winner. I hoped he was going to make a few quid; I was doing very well in London, and I certainly didn't want a piece of anything he had going in South Africa. But I was more than happy to go on excursions to the sun with Charlie paying, or rather 'sorting out' the fares and hotel bills – one of his fraudulent businesses was in airline tickets which were never paid for.

It all began when Charlie heard about a business opportunity, going into a partnership with a bloke called Thomas Waldeck who owned a huge amount of land in South Africa. Apparently, the land was rich in minerals, precious and semi-precious stones – so many opals that you could pick them up off the ground as you walked along. The most valuable commodity, however, was perlite, a mineral in much demand for building and insulation. Waldeck needed money to get a mining company up and running, and Charlie was hooked. He flew out there, signed on the dotted line with Waldeck, and began to get the business side of it sorted.

There were loads of problems to be taken care of, like getting rid of some of the South African sleeping partners who Waldeck had involved in the scheme, but Charlie reckoned he had it all under control. He was even offered a huge amount by an American company who wanted to buy him out, but he turned it down because he believed he had found his crock of gold, the business opportunity that would take care of him for the rest of his life. There were lots of bribes he had to put in place: if you thought London was corrupt, you soon realised it was a boy's game compared to South Africa.

There was an organisation called the Broederbond, the Band of Brothers, a secret white supremacist association which was like a sinister version of the Masons, but with less emphasis on the social side and a lot more emphasis on keeping things financially sweet for its members. It was a very powerful organisation which literally ran South Africa, albeit covertly. Large sums had to change hands regularly, but Charlie was used to bunging the police so he accepted it as normal.

It was on his first visit to South Africa that Charlie met a man called Gordon Winter, a journalist who worked for BOSS, the notorious South African secret police – although, of course, Winter didn't advertise this fact. His wife, a good-looking woman called Jean La Grange, was also involved: her uncle was very high up in BOSS. Gordon Winter was a creepy bloke who liked to ingratiate himself with people. When I met him, all my instincts told me he was bad news and I warned Charlie off him. But by then Charlie was having an affair with Jean La Grange, and nothing would call him off.

Winter didn't seem to mind Charlie giving his wife one and, looking back, I can see it suited his devious purposes.

I knew nothing about all this political stuff, and I didn't care. I didn't like Winter, but that assessment was made on the same basis I'd size up a fella I met in South London: pure instinct. I knew Winter and his wife were involved with South Africa's equivalent of our Special Branch, but as I wasn't doing anything illegal and I wasn't concerned with Charlie's business, I didn't worry about it. To me, South Africa was a beautiful place for holidays and a bit of fun and adventure, and there was plenty of all that.

Gordon Winter was so keen to get alongside Charlie and me that on one of my visits he took me on a tour of Johannesburg. His connections meant he could get permits to go more or less anywhere, even the township of Soweto, which wasn't exactly on the tourist map, and a place you weren't normally allowed to go. He asked if I wanted to meet Mrs Winnie Mandela, whose husband Nelson Mandela had recently been jailed on Robben Island. I wasn't interested in politics at all, but when he asked me I said: 'Yeah, I don't mind.'

As we drove into Soweto, what surprised me was the large number of big houses. I'd imagined it would be a shanty town with everyone living in rundown shacks. There were loads of those, but there were also big, well-set-up houses with nice gardens. When I asked Winter who lived in them he pointed them out one by one: 'That's where the doctor lives, that's where the guy who runs the garage lives . . .' There was a pecking order, just like everywhere else.

Mrs Mandela had a reasonable house – not one of the big, impressive ones, but a lot more than a shack. There was no security, and when we knocked she answered the door herself. She was extremely polite, but very suspicious – with good reason, as you needed to get permission to visit Soweto and you didn't see many white faces. Winter introduced me as, 'Eddie, my friend from London.' He didn't explain any more than that, and he didn't give her any reason for our visit. She didn't make much impression on me and I certainly had no feeling that she would become a big player on the world stage.

One night I was out drinking with Winter and a few other blokes, and in the bar I met a very attractive girl who seemed to think the same way about me. We ended up spending the night together, having a nice little session. The next day Jean La Grange told me she was a spy, and that I'd been set up by BOSS who wanted to find out what I was up to. I wasn't up to anything, so I just laughed. Charlie said, 'You don't understand, they slipped her into you.' I said, 'In that case, I wish they'd slip in a few more like that.'

Drink flowed freely in South Africa. One night I met up with some people who Charlie was involved with. They had a fishing business and the boat they used was the corvette which had been the main boat used in the film *The Cruel Sea*. They asked if we wanted to see it, which we did, and it was interesting to sit in the old cabin. When we were in the port they took us aboard a Japanese canning ship – canning was really big business out there. We were shown around and saw how they were using sonic waves to detect the shoals of fish. This was state of the art equipment. The Japanese got on well with our South African fishing mates, who said the Japs would mark their card for where the fish were.

Then we went to the boardroom for a drink. I asked for a whisky and dry ginger but they persuaded me to try sake, mixed with scotch. I was a big drinker in those days. When I picked up the glass with my left hand they dubbed me 'the left-hand man': apparently it was a bit of a challenge if you used your left arm, and they'd link an arm through yours and down the drink with you. It was a drinking competition and everyone got completely drunk, including the

South Africans who had taken me there. The Japanese were literally under the table. As we tried to leave the docks there was an argument with the customs people – they wanted to lock us up. Somehow we talked our way out of it, probably Winter's dubious connections again.

Most of the times I went to South Africa it was just to drop some money off for Charlie. I wasn't into all the rubbish that went with his business, but I did have some fun. On one occasion I flew out with a film director called Richard Aubrey, who knew a few people out there and was the one who introduced Charlie to Waldeck. He turned out to be a real pain in the arse. On the flight out he complained about everything: the food, his seat, the lot. He was doing the big 'I am', letting everybody know he was a writer and into making movies. He was an irritating little Welshman.

But we did come up with a great scheme. We made up a plot for a film which we called *Jungle Girl*, and Aubrey got in touch with a casting agent who sent around a load of young actresses to our hotel. The agent thought it was all gen, he had no idea that it was a load of bollocks and that all we wanted was to get to grips with some girls. Aubrey had loads of front: he even told one girl to take her jumper off for the audition. Turns out she had plenty of front, too. They were all desperate to be in our film. We finished up taking two of them out to dinner and entertaining them for the rest of the night. I'm afraid they didn't get starring roles in a film, though they were stars that night.

I flew to South Africa for another fabulous trip with Stanley Baker who, after the success of *Zulu*, was going out there to make another film, *Sands of the Kalahari*, with Susannah York and Nigel Davenport, as well as all the technicians and camera crew, and they had chartered a plane, a Boeing 707. There were plenty of spare seats, so I went along with my mate Harry Rawlings as guests of Stan. Charlie wanted me to pay some money to somebody out there, so it fitted in perfectly. We flew to Johannesburg. The film set was at Windhoek, up beyond the Kalahari Desert, and the actors and crew had to transfer to a smaller plane. We split from them, with an agreement to meet up on the film set later – after I'd done my job, delivering Charlie's money to a guy called Jimmy Collins, a big Liverpudlian who was working for him.

We had to take it to a place called Mkuze, in Natal, where Charlie and his partner Tom Waldeck owned land, so Stan gave me a contact for a mate of his who ran a hotel in Durban, a guy called Sol Kerzner, who has since made millions from the gambling haven Sun City. It was a superb hotel, and Harry, on his first trip to Africa, was well impressed. When we rang room service and asked for some fruit, two huge black guys appeared with massive bowls of it on their shoulders.

We chartered a small plane to take us out to Mkuze. Jimmy Collins, who was lonely and desperate for company, was driving a four-wheel-drive vehicle alongside the plane as we landed on the strip there, trying to see who was on board. When he saw it was me and Harry he was well pleased. We both knew him from back in London. He had about forty black blokes working out there, digging holes for the geologists to sample the mineral deposits. Jimmy took us to the local town, near the Ghost Mountains where Rider Haggard based his famous book, *King Solomon's Mines*.

The next day Jimmy paid all his workers with the money we delivered. His assistant was one of the local chief's sons, and he told Jimmy how much each man had to be paid. Jimmy had to rely on him. The poor sods were only on about £1 a week. Jimmy said:

'Come on, I'll show you something.'

He had a line of them, and he got them to march up and down for us, chanting the only words they knew in English: 'Eggs and bacon, eggs and bacon.' Jimmy had taught them out of boredom.

After a couple of days, we left Mkuze and flew back to Johannesburg and from there we set off to go to Windhoek, in South West Africa (now Namibia), to meet up with Stan Baker. We decided to drive, so we borrowed a brand-new Ford from Tommy Costello, a long-firm man from London who was on the trot from the British police. By coincidence, it was Tommy who had introduced Charlie to Jack Duval – but I can't blame Tommy for that. He'd only just taken delivery of this car, and agreed to let us have it because it was a holiday time and we couldn't get a hire car for love nor money. We paid him the going rate. About a hundred miles out from Durban the bloody car blew up. We managed to walk to a golf club, and from there we phoned the local Ford agent. He towed the car in, stripped it down, and discovered the piston had gone. He couldn't repair it because he needed to order the new piston. Poor old Tommy had to sort it out, but he ended up getting a new car out of Ford. Nowadays, Tommy is straight and owns restaurants in South London.

We booked into a hotel, and explained our predicament to the staff. One of them knew a local farmer, who agreed to fly us to Windhoek. It suited him as he could visit some family there and then fly us back a few days later. He charged £10 a flying hour, and it was an eight-hour flight, so we were happy.

On one of my earlier trips to South Africa I met a bloke called Steinbeck who had a fish-canning business. He gave me his card and told me to look him up, as he had a family farm up in Windhoek, which had a shooting lodge. We fancied the idea of taking a pop at a lot of wildlife, so I gave him a call. He wasn't there, but his brother was and he arranged to meet us in Windhoek. He was very hospitable, although I'm sure he found us a real pain as we weren't the kind of people he was used to. He was a schoolteacher, so he was a lot more educated than we were.

He had to drive us for a few hours to the shooting lodge, stopping on the way to pick up provisions. The next day he unlocked the armoury, a room attached to the lodge, and we saw the most amazing array of guns. We were kitted out with rifles, hand guns, choppers and snake serum – we were the real thing. We went out in a truck, driven by a coloured guy, with another one riding shotgun at the back. There were so many coloured workers, and it was hard for us to let them do everything for us, but that was the way of it. I must admit, it didn't seem right, but there was no way we cared about the political situation. We were out for a good time.

As we were driving along, our host, Steinbeck, spotted a herd of donkeys grazing in the bush. We couldn't see them at first because our eyes were not attuned to the bright light. But he tapped the roof of the van and told us where to look, and made it clear that we should shoot them.

'What, donkeys?' I said in surprise. Donkeys were sad animals that trundled up and down the beaches of Britain with kids on their backs. It didn't seem right to shoot them.

'Yeah, they roam wild, breed prolifically and eat all the grass we need for our cattle. We have to cull them every year, so you'd be lending us a hand if you shot a few.'

We didn't need telling twice, we were happy to oblige. It wasn't exactly brilliant sport, as they weren't very fast and agile. But after the first shot they started a bit of a stampede, and we had a bit more fun trying to get them in our sights and bring them down. Steinbeck explained that because their farms are so massive, they were in a constant struggle to keep marauding animals out. Donkeys weren't exactly predators, but there were too many of them, depleting the precious resources of water and grass. We also shot some small antelopes, steenboks, which were more what we had imagined seeing in Africa. We even shot at some monkeys. The farm land was next to a game reserve, and this little posse of monkeys strayed on to the farm. We didn't know in those days that there was anything wrong with shooting them.

The next day we spotted a vulture. I shot it as it flew overhead and it finally flapped down to the ground with a wallop, injured. We jumped off the back of the open-back truck, ran to the bird and pumped about thirty rounds into it. We were on a high, firing away at its dead carcass. Then we had photos taken of us holding its wings out – it had a wingspan of about ten feet. We were delighted with our day's work: we were like lunatics, ready to take a pop at anything.

While we were at the farm, we also went riding. Africa was a fantastic place. The outdoor life really suited me. There was no television there at that time, but who needed it? Social life was all outdoors, with garden parties and barbecues.

We'd had such a good time on safari that there was no time left for going to the film set. We had to get back to Johannesburg, so we met up with the pilot. The only trouble was the weather: it was the rainy season and it was coming down in sheets. Little dry trenches turned into rivers in a matter of minutes. It was two days before the pilot got permission to take off. I wanted to take a chance and go, but the pilot insisted on having clearance. It drove me mad, but I can see his point now, as he would have lost his licence to fly if he'd defied instructions.

I wasn't famous for my patience in those days. When, eventually, we did take off the weather closed in again, and there was a range of mountains ahead which we had to get over. The pilot knew that we couldn't do it, so we had to look out of the window to see if we could spot somewhere to land. We saw a road, and he managed to put the plane down safely. We were in the middle of nowhere, near a remote farmhouse. The farmer came out and welcomed us, and he and his big Boer wife put us up for the night, cooked us a good meal and gave us plenty of beer. The farmer had photos of his Boer ancestors all round the walls. We sat round the fire in the evening talking, and they offered us some biltong, which is dried meat. You cut little strips off with your knife. I'd never seen it before, and cut myself a big piece which I stuffed into my mouth. I finished up with a mouthful of meat that I was still chewing at bedtime.

Next day, the pilot was able to get us off the ground and we flew to Johannesburg and from there back to England.

Back in London, Charlie needed money. The scrapyards were still earning very nicely, but he needed big sums of capital to invest out in South Africa. The Great Train Robbery had happened the year before and, although some of the GTR men were inside, I knew someone who had been involved and who was never nicked. He was looking after some of the others' money. I will always regret taking Charlie to meet this bloke, because he ended up investing £25,000 (nearly £300,000 today) in Charlie's schemes. Charlie gave him some right spiel.

He isn't a fool, my brother, he can sell anything. He told this bloke that once the business cracked off they'd get double their money back. Unfortunately, they never got a penny back. It happened to them with other investments, too. People still talk about it to this day. Tommy Wisbey mentioned it to me recently. But at least they know that it was nothing to do with me. I made the introduction, that's all.

I knew most of the train robbers from before they went inside for the train: Tommy Wisbey, Jimmy Hussey, Bobby Welch and Roy James. I'd met Gordon Goody, Charlie Wilson and Bruce Reynolds, but didn't know them well – when I was inside I got to know most of them a lot better.

It was a diabolical liberty, the sentences they got. I asked my friend Stan Baker to start a petition against their sentences and he got 100,000 signatures. They robbed a train and they knocked out the driver . . . and it opened London up to armed robbery. If they could be given thirty years when they weren't carrying guns, what was the point in not being armed? Guns reduced the risk of being caught, and if you did get caught, they couldn't give you longer than thirty years. There was nothing to lose.

I believe the train driver's injuries were exaggerated by the authorities, because the great train robbers were so popular. When we heard about it we all thought, good luck to them. And that's what the rest of the population was feeling, too, so the judiciary had to stop them becoming folk heroes.

My trip to Paris with Harry Rawlings where we hooked up with Robert, the brilliant croupier we met in Southport, was triggered by a small act of violence that later got magnified a thousand times and made into the main plank of evidence against me at the torture trial. At the time, it was just a bit of necessary housekeeping, a business matter that needed to be sorted. Benny Coulston had it coming, and he knew it.

My mate Harry had a wholesale business in Lambeth Walk, and he sometimes left his kid brother, Billy, in charge of it. Billy was aged only twenty-three, a straight young man. Coulston turned him over by going in with a large case of cigarettes to sell. Billy paid £650 for them, and would have turned a nice quick profit except, of course, that the case was stuffed with paper under one layer of cigarettes. Coulston was a dirty rat for pulling a stunt like that, and we were looking for him.

Charlie got hold of him first. Charlie knew Coulston was on the wanted list and got him round to his office. Then he rang me to say he was there. As far as I was concerned, it was a bit of natural justice, and I was doing it as a favour to my mate Harry. I took Fraser with me. We didn't really hurt him, just knocked him about a bit. But then Fraser grabbed hold of a company stamp off the desk and whacked him with that. It cut his head open, but it wasn't a serious injury. We rolled him up in a carpet and tied both ends.

'Which bridge shall we drop him off?' I asked, and we had a discussion about the best place to drop him into the Thames. It was just to frighten him, liven him up. He was shouting:

'I'll pay you back. I'll get the money. I'll give you more . . .' We just enjoyed hearing him crawl to us.

When we let him go, Coulston went to hospital where they wanted to keep him in overnight for observation because he had a slight head injury. But he dived out of the hospital window and disappeared, only to turn up eighteen months later giving evidence against us. The cut did leave a small scar, which made Coulston a rare prize for the cops who were out to get us: he was the only one of the so-called torture victims to have a scar of any sort, or any evidence of a visit to a hospital or a doctor, to prove he had an injury.

Anyway, because Coulston was such a little rat, Harry and me decided it would be a good idea to lie low for a while, in case he'd gone to the police and they were looking for us. The truth is, we weren't too worried about the police, but it was a good excuse to get away for a little holiday – and our instincts about Coulston were right, because he was a police informer who ended up landing me with a ten-year sentence. He cost Harry even more: Harry's brother Billy, a really nice kid, was so upset about being turned over by Coulston that he later committed suicide. When Harry married and had kids, he called his oldest boy Billy, in his memory.

We'd never been to Paris, so we thought it would be a great adventure. We flew over and booked into a hotel that was recommended to us by George James. That first evening, we went out to hit the town, feeling confident that we'd find our way about in no time. Harry asked the cab driver where we could go to meet some girls, meaning a nightclub like the ones in London – the Astor, the Pigalle, the Stork Room – where there were hostesses who would sit and drink with you and entertain you for the evening. It cost, and if you wanted to take a girl home at the end of the evening it cost more, but it was a pleasant, sociable way to pass an evening.

So when this cab driver dropped us off, we thought we were going into a nightclub. We walked inside, and the woman on the door told us how many francs we would have to pay if we liked one of the girls. We said 'no problem', because we still thought she meant it was the cost of a girl sitting with us. But when we went through the next door there was a line of girls standing there. We were in a brothel. It's not what we expected at all, but we looked at each other, shrugged our shoulders and decided it was too late to turn back. The girls were very tasty looking, so we picked out one each and went off to their rooms with them.

The one with me took lots of time over it. She washed me in the bidet, and then she set about seducing me. I must say, French women know what they are doing, and they are very feminine, with a little bit of chic about them. This girl took such a long time and really seemed to be enjoying it all – not what you expect from a prostitute. One wall of the room was a mirror, and years later, when I was in the porn industry, I realised that it must have been a two-way mirror, and that there were voyeurs on the other side paying to watch my performance, and probably giving me marks out of ten. That's why she was in no hurry.

The following morning, we realised we were going to find it harder than we'd imagined to find the right places to go, especially as we didn't speak any French. I said: 'Harry, we'll ring Robert. He'll show us the right places to go.'

He was round in a flash, and from then on he insisted on paying for everything. It must have cost him a fortune. We went to Maxims, we had a top table at the Lido, we were drinking Dom Perignon champagne – me and Harry were sitting there with glasses full of the stuff. And Robert gave us a lesson in drinking champagne: little but often. Only pour a little into the glass and keep putting the bottle back in the ice bucket, and then you are always drinking it ice cold. He's dead right, and I've always remembered that.

He took us sightseeing to the Eiffel Tower, and the Arc de Triomphe where we went for a meal in a restaurant owned by one of his friends. We had oysters, the works. We kept trying to pay, but Robert wasn't having any of it. He wouldn't even let us pay for souvenirs to take home to the kids. Another day he took us to lots of little clubs in the market area, introducing us to loads of people. Everyone seemed to know Robert, and everyone treated him with respect. He was always immaculately smart. His English was good, but a little bit broken.

We were getting embarrassed by never paying for anything. We knew we were costing a lot of money. When we were in one bar, Robert told us that a man who was in there with his little boy had done seven years in prison. I said to Harry:

'This is our chance to repay a bit of the hospitality, put our hands in our pockets for once.'

Back at home, when someone comes out of jail we always have a bit of a collection to help them get back on their feet. So we called the little boy over and put a fair few quid in his hat. Robert came back to us, with the money, looking puzzled.

'What are you doing?'

'We're just trying to help out a guy who's done seven years, just trying to be sociable.'

That's when Robert told us that the seven years was ten years ago.

Oops, we got it wrong again. We're not doing too well at understanding the French culture. Robert managed to explain it away.

Eventually, we told him that what we would enjoy would be a nice evening in a club, where we could talk to the girls, have a drink with them, and then see what happens. A relaxing evening with a bit of female company. Robert picked us up in his motor and drove us to this big house. We went up to a room at the top where there were comfortable sofas, soft music, and drinks laid on – scotch, vodka, whatever you fancied. Then three girls came in. Blimey! We realised we were in another brothel, just a very high-class one. Anyway, we weren't about to walk out, were we? So we got chatting and laughing with the girls, and Harry said to one of them:

'Take something off.' She took her skirt off. They found it amusing, and we found it amusing, and the evening just got better and better. It must have cost Robert a fortune – three girls, all that time – but he didn't blink an eyelid. It was a really good night, a lot of laughs, a few drinks and pretty girls – even if it wasn't what we'd had in mind.

After seven days or so we were in touch back home and we got the word that nobody was looking for us over Coulston, so it was time to go back to London. Robert was probably glad to see the back of us, but he gave us parting gifts of classy ties with handkerchiefs. We wanted to repay him for at least some of the amazing hospitality. We didn't feel we could buy him a present, so we decided to get something really good for his wife, Jenny. We saw a gold Dupont cigarette lighter, which we thought was perfect. We had it gift wrapped, but when she opened it Robert said: *'Elle ne fume pas.'* She doesn't smoke. It was an easy mistake to make, as everyone smoked in those days. But even that parting gift we managed to get wrong.

'We didn't get anything right, did we?' Harry asked as we flew home.

'No, but we had the fucking best time of our lives,' I said.

I never heard from Robert again, and I bet he's glad he never heard from me again.

Boxing continued to play an important part in my life. I loved being around the sport, being part of the boxing world. I used to go to clubs with a lot of people from the boxing world. Gil Clancy, who managed Emile Griffith, was a mate. Albert Dimes introduced me to Angelo Dundee, Muhammad Ali's manager. One of the last big nights out before my arrest was to go to Wembley to see Henry Cooper fight Ali. Albert had been told by Dundee that Ali (he was boxing under his real name of Cassius Clay back then) was a very fast, tidy, heavyweight, and that Cooper didn't stand a chance. Then Cooper knocked him down. It was a great moment. But after that Ali never let him get a look in. Mickey Duff was a ringside bookie back then, taking bets.

I became good friends with the boxing manager, Bert McCarthy (his brother Leslie used to work with me), and I used to travel around to support his fighters, even going over to Ireland a few times. One time we chartered a plane from Luton airport to take about thirty of us to support his boxer, Pat Dwyer. When we got to the airport the plane wasn't ready so, of course, we all went into the bar. We could see a plane out on the runway, and there was a bloke underneath it with a screwdriver, so we were all joking that this was our plane. Well, after an hour and-a-half delay, it turns out it *was* our plane, so some of the blokes wouldn't get on it. Billy Gentry, a well-known face, was one of those who got a cab back to London.

Anyway, by the time we got to Ireland there was no time for a meal, and of course we were all drinking some more at the boxing venue. Afterwards, Barney Eastwood – a big bookie in Northern Ireland who later managed Barry McGuigan – had laid on a place in

Carrickfergus for us to have a meal, but the food wasn't served until 11pm, because they didn't know what time the boxing would be over. Naturally, we ordered more drinks. I ordered a couple of cases of champagne, so by the time the food arrived we were, you might say, past it. When we got back to the hotels there were a few incidents – men running around the corridors bollock naked, that kind of thing. It was a good night, lots of laughs and lots of incidents.

Another time, I went to Ireland with Bert McCarthy and the English boxers were pasted 10–0 by the Irish fighters. We were the only English people there and the whole crowd took the piss out of us, in a friendly way. Nevertheless, it seemed a shame that, because there was no Irish Boxing Board of Control, Irish boxers had to come over here because there were no Irish titles. So we made plans to set up the Boxing Club of Ireland, which would have been a charity organisation to benefit young Irish fighters and Irish charities.

We went to see the people previously on the original Irish Board of Control, and they were very co-operative, because they wanted to see it restarted. We spent a lot of time and money on this project. We were in discussions with Eamonn Andrews to be the chairman: he was a boxing commentator before he became a big star, and he had an involvement in the main television station in Dublin. He was up for it, and we were negotiating with his television company. Barney Eastwood, the promoter, was involved, and Terry Goodwin, a sports writer from the *Daily Telegraph*, was going to do the PR.

We'd sorted out a venue for the fights: the Intercontinental Hotel in Dublin, where there was a large, suitable room. We would have made the fights really posh affairs – dicky bows, evening dress, the lot. In Dublin there are embassies from around the world, so we were going to invite all the ambassadors to support Irish sport by having tables.

We were well on the way to having it up and running, but then I got arrested and put inside. The whole deal collapsed later, while I was inside. I think they would have found it hard to carry on, because of the name I acquired thanks to the Mr Smith's trial and the torture trial.

I kept my family life very separate from my business life. Maureen knew nothing about my work. When we first married we bought a semi on the Sidcup bypass, with a ninety per cent mortgage from the Woolwich. I took care of all the bills and gave Maureen cash for the housekeeping.

One day I saw a house in Chislehurst for sale, a lovely architect-designed house with seven bedrooms and a big garden. I had a bit of money at the time, so I put down a deposit and we moved in: we stayed there for about thirty years. It cost about £12,000 and it's now worth about two-and-a-half million.

Maureen was an excellent wife and mother, I have nothing but good to say about her. She brought Melanie and Donna up superbly, they're a real credit. In the early days I think Maureen complained a bit about the hours I kept. I remember her trying to persuade me to emigrate to Australia, because she thought we'd be closer as a family out there. But then she accepted the way I was.

I was the problem in our marriage, I admit it. I was a hard, macho man, with a very traditional view of married life. I always got home, even if only for half an hour in the morning, but I wasn't a devoted husband. I paid for everything, and they wanted for nothing. Donna had private dance and ballet lessons, Melanie went through university, they lived well. Not that I ever minded: it was my pleasure to provide for my family. You had to be a getter, though, to bring in the money.

But I wasn't around a great deal. I had a flat in Park Crescent, a lovely sweep of Georgian buildings near Regent's Park: it's one of the most prestigious addresses in London. It was only a one-bedroom flat, and I mainly had it for entertaining. I bought it off an American journalist who was going out to Vietnam. I can remember the porters being a bit snotty with me, because I wasn't the kind of tenant they wanted, even though I did bung them good tips. They probably thought I was abusing it, going in at four o'clock in the morning and coming out again, three hours later. I had a lovely Irish girlfriend who came back there with me on a regular basis. After I went to prison she wrote to me, but I never wrote back because I was keeping in close touch with my family.

SEVEN

LIKE SOMETHING OUT OF THE WILD WEST

The storm clouds were gathering, but I had no idea. Lots of things happened at roughly the same time, all of them unrelated except for one common factor: the name of Richardson. It was the unfortunate conjunction of all of them that led to me, at least, getting such a long and disproportionate sentence at the torture trial.

The fight at Mr Smith's should never have happened, and it took me by surprise. It should have been a normal bit of business, the kind we were used to, but it ended with one man dead and several people in hospital, including me. It was also the catalyst that led to the torture trial arrests: with me and Frankie Fraser both out of action with our injuries, those slimy little rats who Charlie knocked about with were all the more willing to do deals with the police, making up all sorts of nonsense to get themselves off the charges that were hanging over them. And it also led to the murder of George Cornell, which ultimately brought the Krays down – if we'd been about, they would never have dared to kill George.

Mr Smith and the Witchdoctor was a club at Catford, owned by two blokes from Manchester. It was a reasonable size, as the building had originally been a cinema. There was a raised area with tables for eating, a dance floor, and a stage where there would be floor shows. Bertie Green, our mate who owned the Astor, provided the dancing girls and the singers.

The owners ran a couple of successful clubs up north and were quite handy fellas, but they obviously could not be around all the time to supervise Mr Smith's. They wanted to get a gambling licence, so they needed to show that the club was safe and well run. They knew the London scene well enough to turn to Billy Hill and Albert Dimes for help, and naturally our names came up. It was suggested to them that, in return for letting us have a couple of our machines in the club, we would supply the doormen. We had a meeting at Billy Hill's flat and it was all agreed. They didn't tell us exactly what kind of trouble they were having in the club, and no names were mentioned, but we gathered there were some local tearaways abusing the place and lowering the tone, which was putting off other customers.

'No problem,' we said. We were happy to help out, and they were going to pay us £100 a week (£1100 today) to cover the door, so there was a nice little profit in it. We worked out which blokes we would use on the door, and went down to the club for a recce that afternoon, 7 March 1966. It was the first time we'd been there, but it looked a good club and we were confident we could help out. We were invited to stay on for a meal, but we had other business to see to, so we agreed we'd go back later on, about ten o'clock, for a drink to seal the deal. It was a Monday night so the club wasn't too busy.

A little group if us went down: me, Frank Fraser, Harry Rawlings, Ronnie Jeffreys and Billy Staynton. We went in and saw a group of men we knew, including Billy Haward (whose brother, 'Flash' Harry Haward, was a well-known face and was inside at the time), Peter Hennessy, who was one of a number of brothers I knew slightly, Billy Gardiner and Henry Botton, a minor villain. We knew them well enough to drink with, and I was sure there wouldn't be a problem with them. They knew the score, like we did.

Another friend of ours, Jimmy Moody, happened to come in that night. He wasn't with us, but obviously, when he saw us, he came over for a chat. I didn't know him very well, but he was a mate of Harry's. I got to know him better when we were all on remand together, and he was a sound bloke.

By the early hours of the morning most of the straight customers had drifted off to their beds, and we were told by the club management that there was a problem getting Haward and his crew to leave. I didn't know it at the time, but apparently they thought we had come over to Mr Smith's to dig Billy Haward out, because he was having an affair with the wife of Roy Porritt, who worked for us at Atlantic Machines. In fact, I didn't know about the affair, and if I had I wouldn't have got involved. What happens between blokes and their wives is up to them, unless it interferes with business.

The other thing I didn't know was that, after they saw us come into the club, they sent out for guns. Haward and Dickie Hart both had them. I didn't know Hart: he'd only recently come out of prison. We were all sitting around a big table and I turned to Haward.

'They want to shut up now, so it's time to be on your way,' I said.

'What the fuck's it got to do with you?' he asked.

'I'm running the door here from tonight, there'll be my blokes on the door from now on.'

Peter Hennessy, a big lump of a bloke, went off on one. He jumped up, and Haward and Hart pulled their guns out, a .45 revolver and a sawn-off shotgun. It kicked off. Harry Rawlings leaned across to grab the shotgun – he hit Haward over the head with it, there was a scuffle and Hart shot Harry in the arm with the revolver. The bullet hit an artery and the blood spurted out of him like a fountain, up into the air.

At the same moment Hennessy yelled at me: 'You, I'm gonna have a fuckin' straightener with you!'

'You wanna straightener, you can have one,' I said.

The guns were out, and I thought I would get shot in the back while I was sorting Hennessy out. I figured I couldn't win. But we went on to the dance floor and I really went for him. He landed a couple of good punches on me, but when the adrenalin is pumping you don't notice it. I thumped him and he went down. I sat astride him and I wanted to punch his head through the floorboards. He was screaming, 'I've had enough, I've had enough.' Even though I was in a no-win situation with the guns, I'd still won the fight. It was over quickly: street fights never last long, because you go all out from the off.

I looked around and there was a bit of a rush going on towards the back door. Hennessy was finished, so I made a run for the door, too. There was a fight going on there. Hart was struggling to hold on to his gun, with two or three men trying to get it off him. Fraser was shot through the leg by Hart's gun, the .45, a big gun. His thigh bone was broken and he was out of the game. Somehow, in the struggle that was still going on, Dickie Hart's gun was turned on him and he was shot. I know who did it, but even after all this time I'm not prepared to say. The fight had moved outside to the back of the club, and as I went out to make one I was peppered with shotgun pellets in the back of my leg. It didn't slow me down: in the heat of the battle I hardly felt it.

Jimmy Moody and Ronnie Jeffreys were trying to get Harry Rawlings out – Moody had tied a tourniquet round his arm, which probably saved his life. Ronnie was also hit by pellets sprayed from the shotgun, in his thigh, groin and stomach.

Moody, who had only bumped into us by chance, helped me pull Harry into his Jag and we got out of there. You can't hang around: all the lights in the houses in the street were going on and there must have been loads of calls to the police. Jimmy Moody drove us to East Dulwich Hospital, a fair way from the fight. That was deliberate: you don't get dropped on the doorstep from where it happened. After he helped to get Harry inside, and made sure that he was being seen by medical staff, Jimmy left.

Harry was immediately put on a drip. He'd lost so much blood he was in real trouble. In the meantime, an ambulance took Dickie Hart and Frankie to Lewisham Hospital. Ronnie Jeffreys was also in Lewisham, with multiple shotgun pellet wounds.

We didn't give our real names – Harry was in no condition to say anything anyway. We were put on a side ward, just the two of us. The law came to see us the next day: they were already on to Frankie Fraser and Ronnie Jeffreys, because they were in the same hospital where Hart died. But they must have heard of us from the hospital staff. They put a guard on the ward door, two cops. They were worried about us doing a runner, but we weren't even thinking of it because we were the victims. We weren't expecting to be arrested. We were the ones who'd got shot. Besides, we wouldn't have been able to run far, Harry with his drip and me with my leg swollen up and black. If you pushed your fingers into it, you left a dent: it was lead poisoning, from the pellets, which are still inside me to this day.

The cops didn't have any evidence because nobody was saying anything. A police inspector came to interview us. I refused to speak to him. I made a point of stating, in front of a doctor, that I was not saying anything to the police in case I got verballed (words put into my mouth). The doctor didn't want to know, but I needed him to hear me say it, to cover me.

Then the inspector said to Harry, who was in the next bed with the curtains round him, and still dangerously ill:

'You're dying. You're not going to walk out of here. So tell us what happened. We need to know who shot you. It won't cause you any bother because you're dying anyway.'

Harry just said: 'Well, fuck off and let me die, then.'

Luckily, he didn't die, but it was touch and go for a while.

After two or three days they took us down to Brixton nick and interviewed us. I still didn't believe I could be charged, as I hadn't had a gun and the other lot were the aggressors. But they came up with a charge of 'making an affray', an old charge, and we were remanded in custody. Frankie Fraser was charged with the murder of Dickie Hart, and he was held in the hospital wing at Wandsworth, but the rest of us were together in Brixton: Ronnie Jeffreys, Billy Haward, Jimmy Moody, Harry Rawlings and Henry Botton were all there. Peter Hennessy and Billy Gardiner were never charged.

Botton made a statement, which he should never have done. It's a basic rule: you never make a statement. Without his statement no one would have known anything. He tried to withdraw it later, but it was too late.

We were all remanded in custody at first – not surprising when the prosecution said when they opposed bail that the fight at Mr Smith's was like something out of the Wild West. This made headlines in the newspapers, which didn't help.

There was a surprise when I got to Brixton: I bumped into the owner of Chez Victor, a famous restaurant in Wardour Street where I used to eat regularly. He was known to everyone as Victor, although that wasn't his real name. He picked up hundreds of parking fines because he insisted on parking outside his restaurant, and when he refused to pay them he was jailed for a short spell. He was very indignant about the fines – and I don't think he was too impressed with the menu in there.

Fraser was tried separately from the rest of us, accused of murdering Hart. He'd been found in a garden in the road at the back of Mr Smith's. When Fraser's trial came up later that year, two officers claimed the gun was found near his head, with a track in the soil showing where he had pushed it away from himself. But two other policemen, the ones who had helped load him into the ambulance, gave evidence that he was picked up from a different garden, and as he was unable to move he couldn't possibly have had the gun. The cops destroyed their own case, and eventually Fraser got five years for affray.

When we came up for committal in April we were given bail, because, as my barrister Victor Duran pointed out, there was no evidence. He was bullying the prosecution to produce evidence, and they had none. I didn't know it at the time, but when I walked out of that court I was enjoying my last few weeks of freedom for a long time.

The evening after the fight at Mr Smith's, George Cornell was murdered by Ronnie Kray. Cornell was cocky, had a bit of a sway about him. He'd grown up with the Kray twins and he wasn't impressed by them, he knew the strength of them. He had publicly called Ronnie 'that fat poof'. Ronnie did prefer the company of pretty boys to that of pretty girls, but he tried to keep it secret. He didn't like being mocked for it. Cornell was always taking the piss out of Ronnie, and he thought he knew how far to push it. He misjudged it, though, and he was killed for that misjudgement.

He'd gone to the Blind Beggar pub in Stepney for a drink after visiting a mate of ours, Jimmy Andrews, who was in hospital. Jimmy had been shot in the leg, and some people have tried to link it to the Krays. But it wasn't them: he was shot over a domestic matter. Jimmy worked for Atlantic Machines: he was a good friend of Fraser's and we'd given him a job a few months earlier when he came out of nick. He lost part of his leg in the shooting, and died shortly afterwards from cancer. His widow remarried, to Reggie Kray's brother-in-law, Frankie Shea. Jimmy's daughter married Tony Adams, the Arsenal footballer, but they are divorced now. In recent years she got heavily into drugs and became involved in a scandal when another heroin addict died in the back of her car.

Anyway, with all of us out of action, Ronnie Kray knew the coast was clear. Me, Frankie and the rest were in nick and Charlie was in South Africa when Ronnie shot Cornell dead in the Blind Beggar. Ronnie and one of his men, Ian Barrie, pumped a lot of bullets around in a frenzy, and at the end of it George was dead. With it coming so close to the death of Dickie Hart, the two got lumped together and there was a wave of stories in the press about gang warfare and gang executions, none of which was very helpful when it came to getting a fair trial.

Eventually, the Kray twins were done for two murders: George Cornell and Jack 'the Hat' McVitie. They, too, were nearing the end of their lives as free men: it would be another two years before they were arrested, but from that day on they would spend the rest of their lives in prison.

George Cornell's widow, Olive, eventually married Alan Tear, the brother of my childhood mate, Whippet, and the guy who acted as my chauffeur when I lost my licence. Whippet died a few years ago, in a tragic accident at the print works where he worked. He fell into one of the machines. They were an unlucky family: there were thirteen or fourteen of them when we were growing up, but when I went to Alan's funeral in 2003 there were only three of them left.

Out in South Africa, Charlie's business unravelled spectacularly when his partner, Tom Waldeck, was murdered. Charlie had employed one of his associates, a bloke called Johnnie Bradbury (who I knew as John West, because that was an alias he used back in London), to do some work for him there. I'm not even sure to this day what exactly Bradbury did. As I said, I had no interest in Charlie's business out there. But I did meet Bradbury a few times in London. He was tall, over six feet, and wiry. He was good looking – at least, women seemed to find him attractive. He caused Charlie a few problems on that score. First of all, he had an affair with Tom Waldeck's wife, which didn't go down well. Charlie had to sack Bradbury, no choice – it was more important to keep his partner, Waldeck, sweet than to cater for Bradbury's bedroom activities.

Bradbury stayed out in Africa, and one night chatted up a model in a bar in Johannesburg by telling her that he was Charlie Wilson, the great train robber. There were lots of stories in the press at the time about the escape of the train robbers from prison, so he must have thought it was a good line to spin. But when he ended the affair with the model, she went to a newspaper, the *South African Sunday Times*, and they published a picture and a story about Charlie Wilson being in Johannesburg. Only, of course, the bloke in the picture was Bradbury. It could have caused a lot of problems for my brother Charlie with the respectable companies he was trying to interest in his perlite mine, because although Bradbury no longer worked for him, some of his straight business contacts had met him. But through his contact with Gordon Winter he managed to get the story squashed.

Bradbury was still a loose cannon, getting pissed and causing trouble, and one night in June 1965 he turned up at Tom Waldeck's house and shot him dead. After the murder, Charlie asked me to go to the funeral. I didn't understand all the implications, I thought I was just going out there to pay our respects to someone Charlie had been in business with: he's very persuasive, and the thought of another holiday in South Africa made it sound attractive. But I regretted going. Some of Waldeck's relations were in the Rhodesian police, and they were all very suspicious of me. They blamed Charlie for Waldeck's death and there was a real atmosphere. At that time, nobody had been arrested for the murder. I had to go back to the Waldeck house for the wake, and I tried to tell them that I was not involved in the business in any way, but I don't think they believed me.

This was quite a long time before our main problems began, but it took a while for Bradbury to be arrested, and he was finally tried, found guilty and sentenced to death in Johannesburg in May 1966 – while I was on bail for the Mr Smith's charge and just when things were getting hot for us in London. (Bradbury's sentence was later commuted to life imprisonment, and I've no idea what happened to him, except that ten years later I read a newspaper story about how, while in prison, he had an affair with a social worker who was supposed to be helping him – so he was still at it.)

There are people to this day who think Charlie was behind the killing of Waldeck, and my first reaction when I heard of Waldeck's death was that he might have had something to do with it. But it wouldn't have made any sense because, without his respectable South African partner, Charlie's business more or less collapsed. He hung on to it until a week or two after Bradbury's sentence, and then he sold out. But it is possible, I suppose, that Charlie just wanted Waldeck – who was probably conning him all the time – to be frightened, not murdered, and Bradbury lost his head and went too far.

It was Bradbury's trial that first started the idea of 'torture' in the minds of the police over here, and the public. On trial for his life, Bradbury made all sorts of lurid allegations. Charlie's name was plastered all over the newspapers out there. He was described as a London gang boss who did things like nailing people to the floor, and holding mock trials which ended in punishments like electric shocks and even death. Bradbury had nothing to lose, he could say what he liked. He said he was ordered to take part in Waldeck's murder or his wife and children would be killed. He even made a pathetic attempt at killing himself during the trial, which gave it all a bit more drama.

Naturally, the newspapers back here picked up the story, and Charlie had to issue denials. He gave a long interview to the *Sunday Times*, explaining his business. The police naturally took a big interest, and one or two British officers got a nice trip out to the sunshine to collect 'evidence'.

I had no idea how deep my brother was into this South African business. All I knew was that it cost a fortune, his money and other people's: he had some of the great train money, and he also had over £50,000 (that's about a million in today's money) from Alf Berman, an old friend of his. I have found out a lot more since, but Charlie never confided in me about his work for BOSS. He was way out of his league, but Charlie always had grandiose ideas, thought he could mess around with politics and things like that. The murder of Waldeck brought everything crashing down around him. He struggled to keep hold of his Africa business, his mining rights, but without Waldeck he had no chance. He was still heavily involved with Jean La Grange, and she was going backwards and forwards between London and South Africa to try to sort things out.

Over here, Charlie was being manipulated by her: she was using him to obtain information for her spy bosses. There are stories of break-ins, foiled assassination plots, the bugging of prime ministers and his being asked to supply arms. It all sounds a bit over the top, and I have no idea whether or not any of it is true. Nothing about my brother would surprise me, but at the time I had no clue what Charlie was up to. We led completely separate lives as far as business was concerned, and it wasn't until years later that I found out more about it.

My life was going well, I was making a lot of money, having a good time. Until the little matter of the fight at Mr Smith's came along to spoil everything.

While all these things were going on, some of the evil little cowards Charlie did business with were snivelling to the police, in return for getting the charges they were being questioned about either dropped or considerably reduced. Instead of doing their bird like anyone else would have done, they started making up all sorts of things about 'the Richardson gang'.

I'm not saying there wasn't torture. Charlie used to enjoy keeping people for hours when he was sorting them out, terrifying them and humiliating them. There was more humiliation than physical damage done, but could it be called torture? I wasn't part of all that: if I had a problem with someone I would sort it out pretty quickly. Biff, boff, that's that. I wasn't shy about giving people what they deserved, but I wouldn't keep them prisoner for hours. But I certainly saw Charlie doing it. A lot was made at the trial of Charlie sending out for food in the middle of these 'torture' sessions. He was keeping people for a few hours, so naturally he'd have to get some fish and chips or sandwiches in. Charlie liked to stretch it out.

Once, when I came back from South Africa and went round to his offices in Rotherhithe, he had one of his long-firm conmen in there, being given the third degree. It was Bunny Bridges, who came from our manor, Camberwell, and who had occasionally been drinking in the Addington club. He was the one that 'hid' Duval at his bungalow down in Brighton, when Charlie was looking for him the first time. Like the rest of the long-firm mob, he used different names to keep ahead of the law. He was a smart little smoothie, but I heard he would rather spend money on a sharp suit than on his family. He was always well dressed – except that when I saw him that day he wasn't dressed at all. He was naked, and Charlie and Roy Hall had worked him over. There was blood, and he'd obviously been there for quite a while. It was nothing to do with me, and I just wanted to get off home. I was there at the tail end of the session, because he was cleaned up, given a new shirt and sent off to Manchester to do an errand for Charlie, who was still trying to locate Duval. He couldn't get out of there fast enough.

The most famous exhibit at the trial was 'the black box', which was made to sound very sinister. It did exist. It was a piece of junk that had come into the scrapyard with a load of metal. It had two leads and a handle, and when you cranked the handle you could get an electric shock from the leads. It wasn't strong: I've held the leads in my hand and felt it. It was no stronger than the electrified fences used to keep animals in fields, and quite harmless. I don't know what it would have originally been used for – maybe something to do with testing spark plugs. We used to get all sorts of odd things in the yard.

That's not to say that it wasn't unpleasant, especially as Charlie liked to wire it up to blokes' bollocks. I saw him use it once. Alfie Berman, who lent him a load of money for the South Africa business, had a personal problem: his wife was having an affair with an Irish fella. Charlie offered to help out. He kidnapped the Irish guy and wired him up. Berman was called down to the offices at the same time, to watch him doing it. It was partly to do Berman a good turn, but it was more to keep Berman under control. It was a veiled threat: this was the sort of thing that could happen. Berman didn't want any part of it, you could tell he didn't like witnessing it. The pain was not that great, but the humiliation of being stripped and wired up was worse. Roy Hall was in charge of turning the handle, and the faster he turned it the stronger the shock. They said at the trial it was strong enough to burn the victims – but if that was the case, why didn't they produce any medical evidence?

The other really sensational bit of evidence they trotted out at the trial was that Frankie Fraser pulled out one of Benny Coulston's teeth with pliers, and that George Green's toes were broken with pliers. Green did get a pasting, and went to hospital later that night, but he never complained about his feet. If his toes had been broken, I think he would have mentioned it, and there would have been medical evidence to support his claim. As for Benny Coulston's tooth – if you have ever had a tooth removed by a dentist you will know it is a very difficult thing to do, even when you are co-operating and numbed by a local anaesthetic. Imagine trying to do it to someone who did not want it done. We even produced dental experts and dental records at the trial to try to show that the gap in Coulston's mouth was the result of him losing a tooth years before. But that didn't make headlines – what made headlines, and still has people talking to this day, was that he had a tooth pulled out with pliers. Fraser cashes in on it: he goes around with a small pair of gold pliers in his pocket. But he'll tell you, if you ask him, that it never actually happened.

The Mr Smith's trial started on 28 June 1966. My brother Charlie had been making himself busy, trying to sort out the witnesses and the jury members. In those days you needed a unanimous jury decision: today you can be convicted on a substantial majority, but back then all twelve had to be in agreement.

A mate of Charlie's, Johnnie Longman, sat in the public gallery and afterwards he followed members of the jury to find out where they lived, and started ringing them. I didn't know about this, although it was accepted that squaring people away was part of the game. But one day, soon after it started, the case was held up for a couple of hours after one of the jurors reported having a bottle with a note in it thrown through his window. The note read, 'Bring them in guilty or else.' People said it was meant to confuse the man, and throw the police off the scent because they would think it was someone who was against us who was trying to nobble the jurors. We thought the police did it.

Unfortunately, at that time, Longman was living with a woman who heard a lot of what was going on. She later gave evidence against him and Charlie, when they were charged with trying to pervert the course of justice. But that case was a year away, and by then we were all inside anyway.

The Mr Smith's trial lasted a month, and it was a good result for Harry Rawlings and Ronnie Jeffreys: they were both acquitted. That was justice, as we were not the ones who started the whole thing. In the same way, Billy Haward and Henry Botton were both found guilty of affray, and Haward was also convicted of carrying a loaded shotgun. The girls who worked at the club gave evidence about the guns, and who had them. Botton convicted himself: if he hadn't made a statement, nobody would have put him there. Years later Botton got his deserts. He was shot on his own doorstep, after helping the police, again. Peter Hennessy also died an unnatural death: he was stabbed after a fight – we'll come to that later.

For me, Jimmy Moody and Billy Staynton the trial had a strange result: the jury could not agree and a retrial was ordered. This was better than a guilty verdict – it meant we would have another chance to slug it out in court, and there were obviously real doubts about convicting us. We were remanded in custody, but my brief said he

131

would apply for bail. I was confident I would get it as I'd been out on bail before the case.

But then everything changed. As dawn broke on 30 July 1966, the day that England would win the World Cup and the whole of Britain would be in a frenzy of celebration, ninety cops swooped on addresses all over London, and Charlie and seventeen other people were arrested on the torture trial charges.

It would be many years before I would walk the streets of London again.

EIGHT

CHARLIE AND THE FRAUD MONGRELS

I heard about the arrests that day, on the radio. The report didn't give names, and it wasn't until later that I knew Charlie and all the others had been pulled in. We were all held in Brixton (today we'd have been held at Belmarsh, but it wasn't built back then). There were literally hundreds of charges against all sorts of people: GBH, assault, breaking and entering, fraud, robbery, demanding money by force, demanding money with menaces. Jean Goodman was the only woman charged – with fraud and with being involved in one of the GBH charges. After I broke away from Charlie, she was working in the office at the scrapyard. She had split up from Charlie by the time of the arrests, over his affair with Jean La Grange.

The reason the police pulled so many people in, and put the

frighteners on so many others, was so that we had fewer people on the outside who could run around and sort things out for us.

The committal proceedings began in August. Committals are heard before a magistrates' court, and the purpose is to decide whether or not there is a case to be answered. If there is, it is referred on to a higher court. Because it is about whether or not a full case will be heard, the only evidence given at a committal is prosecution evidence. Back in those days, committals could be fully reported in the press, which meant, in a case like ours, day after day of massive coverage in all the newspapers, all of it of the most sensational evidence against us.

Not long after, the law on committals was changed, and it's now only possible to publish it if the defendant agrees. It was, everyone now says, a great travesty of justice that masses of prosecution evidence could be splashed all over the newspapers without the other side being given or any of the allegations proved.

In my case, there was an even more serious injustice. The committal proceedings were actually halted while I was retried on the Mr Smith's affray case. How on earth could I get a fair trial when the jury members had for weeks been reading about torture, beatings, electric shocks, teeth being pulled out with pliers? I was not involved in most of these charges, but that didn't matter: the name Richardson was all over the media.

It was grossly unfair, and afterwards my local MP for Chislehurst, Alistair MacDonald, took the matter up and was part of the campaign to get committal hearings held without press coverage. My wife Maureen went to see him several times, and I wrote to him from prison.

The committal was a farce. Every day we were brought to court with sirens flashing and police outriders, all adding to the drama. There was a massive police presence outside the court, fuelling the idea that we were dangerous people. Everyone going into the court was searched – routine enough nowadays with all the terrorist threats, but unheard of in those days.

It was the longest committal ever, and because of the break for the Mr Smith's trial, it was held in two separate magistrates' courts: the first half at Clerkenwell and the second half at Bow Street. The dock at Clerkenwell had to be specially extended, and there were sixteen policemen positioned around it.

There were so many of us in the dock that at one time they suggested we should wear numbers round our necks. We all refused, and when they forced us to wear them we changed positions in the dock to deliberately stall the proceedings. Naturally, with so many people all trying to sort out the evidence against themselves, it was a bit noisy at times. The magistrate seemed as confused about the charges as we were. He kept telling us all to behave, and eventually a policeman was ordered to sit in the dock with us – making it even more overcrowded.

There were a few outbursts, naturally. When Charlie called the slimy Jack Duval 'a filthy bastard' the magistrate ordered that his comment should be recorded, so Jimmy Moody yelled out: 'This is a Gestapo court, put that on the record as well.' Afterwards, he'd give the Nazi salute when he entered the courtroom. On another occasion, Frankie Fraser shouted out that the evidence Jimmy Taggart was giving against him was 'like writing a James Bond book'.

When we were taken down to the cells for the lunch break, some days we'd have a good singsong, just to keep our spirits up. Because we were not convicted criminals we should have been allowed to have our own food brought in. Our wives delivered it, but we were not given it. In the early days there was often no provision for lunch, and we'd be lucky to get bread and cheese. The women were so angry at the way we were being treated they caused a protest in court one day, and the magistrate ordered the public gallery to be cleared.

Jimmy Moody got roughed up by the cops in a corridor leading from the court and managed to nut a sergeant, breaking his nose. Jimmy was then charged with causing grievous bodily harm, and for a couple of days after that he came into court handcuffed to policemen on both sides.

It was the torture allegations that grabbed the headlines, even though most of them were untrue and there was very little evidence to back them up. There were tales of electric shocks, cold baths, victims stripped of their clothes and even having to mop up their own blood with their underpants. There was evidence about choppers, hammers, shotguns, coshes, clubs and knives all being used.

What didn't come out, of course, was that all the people giving evidence against us were villains themselves, and lying like mad to save their own skins. The police had them on other charges: Jack Duval came to court from prison where he was serving three years for fraud, and Benny Coulston was also in custody. Most of the others had the charges against them dropped in return for being witnesses against us.

We didn't expect them to give evidence against us. In our day, you got beaten up but you didn't run to the police. You didn't get someone sent to prison. It just didn't happen. Most of the people we had dealings with were villains themselves, and they were the last people to run to the law. We lived by the law of the jungle, sorting out our own problems.

That's why Charlie should never have got mixed up with all these fraud mongrels. They weren't our kind of villain and, as he learned to his cost, you just couldn't trust them. The cop in charge of the case, Assistant Chief Constable Gerald McArthur from Hertfordshire Police, used Duval to orchestrate the whole case against us: Duval would be taken from prison to a police station where all the other conmen who were appearing as witnesses against us – Lucien Harris, Benny Wajcenberg, Christopher Glinski – would be brought to be given their stories by Duval. Remember, these blokes were accomplished fraudsters, so they were all good actors, and could put on a good show in court. If you can con business people out of thousands of pounds, conning a jury isn't difficult. Duval was telling his cohorts that when they were accused of anything illegal, they could get out of it by saying they were working for Charlie, that they were scared of him so they had to do it.

Rehearsing witnesses is illegal, but nothing stood in the way of getting us convicted. When Duval came up for airline ticket fraud, who was a witness for his defence? None other that ACC McArthur. McArthur used to tell people he was working on direct orders from the Home Office to put us away, which I am sure was because of Charlie's South African connections. Special Branch members sat in court throughout our trial.

They made a big thing of having to protect the witnesses, and our mate Arthur Baron was actually charged, along with Charlie and Alfie Fraser (no relation to Frankie), with trying to prevent a witness giving evidence in criminal proceedings.

After a few days I sacked my barrister, because I reckoned I could do a better job defending myself. (Strangely, none of our first-choice barristers were available to represent us.) This meant I could cross-examine the witnesses in the charges against me. I did pretty well: I was charged initially with GBH on George Green, a shifty little villain who Charlie took on to work in his long-firm frauds just after Green got out of prison. Green was in the witness box for eleven hours, and when it was my turn to cross-examine him he admitted that I had neither been involved in any attack on him, nor had he seen or heard of me attacking Lucien Harris or Jack Duval. He said that when I walked in I told Charlie to 'turn it up', meaning to stop it. I took the opportunity, while I was on my feet questioning him, to say to the court: 'I don't know what I am doing on this charge. I've done nothing, and the witness admits I didn't participate. There is no evidence against me, the only evidence is that I tried to stop it.'

The magistrate told me to stop making a speech but I said: 'I am only interested in seeing justice done.' But I achieved what I set out to do: the charges against me of assaulting Green were eventually rejected by the jury at the main trial, after I reminded the court of what he had said at committal.

I also got to question Bennie Coulston, who had to admit to having eight criminal convictions for dishonesty in the past eight years. I asked him if he was a police informer, but of course he denied it. It was made clear in his evidence, though, that he had told a different story when he first complained that he had been assaulted, and he failed to name any of us who were accused of attacking him. In his evidence Coulston did not say I put one finger on him. In fact, the only time he mentioned me was to say that after being beaten up by Charlie and Frank Fraser I gave him a glass of whisky.

All the time, new charges were being added, new defendants were being charged, others were being allowed home with the charges against them dropped. It was a circus, the whole thing. The police were running around trying to find more witnesses, and even approaching defendants to see if they would turn Queen's Evidence against us. They approached Roy Hall, who turned them down flat.

In the middle of all these committal proceedings, I came up in front of the Old Bailey for the retrial of the Mr Smith's affray charge. It was, as I said, totally impossible for me to have a fair trial: because of the newspaper coverage, not one of the jurors can have been unaware of what was going on in the committal proceedings. I was tried and found guilty of having the name Richardson. The same evidence against the other two up for retrial, Jimmy Moody and Billy Staynton, brought them a not guilty.

The police played a masterstroke. They had already made a big thing about having all the jurors under police protection, with special phone numbers for them to ring if they were approached or threatened, and in one case a policeman was actually sleeping in the juror's home, until the court stopped it. Halfway through the trial, it was going well for me, and my barrister was going to apply to have the case thrown out. Then one morning my barrister told me that the prosecution were going to make an application to have one of the jurors removed, because the police claimed that he had been seen talking in a betting shop with an associate of mine. This was nonsense – a lot of my associates were behind bars, in custody for the torture trial committal.

The police never said who it was, and if it had really happened, why didn't they arrest whoever did it? In my view it was a total fit-up. My barrister agreed that it could well be a stitch up, but there was nothing we could do. If we objected to the removal of the juror it would look as though we had a particular reason for wanting to keep him there. Anyway, as my barrister said, the court would probably allow the prosecution's application to remove him. So we didn't object to it, although we stated that it was a load of rubbish.

But it was a clever move, because the seed was sown in the minds of the jury that we were the kind of people who would intimidate and bribe jurors. Also, because they were guarding the jurors and obviously getting to know what kind of people they were, the police would have chosen one who was likely to be on my side. This, coupled with all the torture trial evidence the jurors had been reading, made it a sure-fire thing I would get convicted. The evidence in the case, and justice, had nothing to do with it: I had been painted as a very bad person because I was associated with allegations of torture and brutality. After the juror was removed the whole atmosphere changed, because it looked as if he had been got at.

My barrister, Jeremy Hutchinson, a first-class brief, advised me not to go into the witness box, as he said they had to prove a case against me, and there was not one. But I insisted I should, because I felt I had nothing to hide. I held my own under cross-examination, stressing the point that we didn't have the guns, and we didn't start the fight. But Hutchinson was probably right: it would have made the point better if I hadn't.

I was given five years for affray, the same amount as Frankie Fraser and Henry Botton. Billy Haward got eight. Frankie and Henry Botton both had very long criminal records, and Haward had been clearly identified as one of the ones with a gun. Considering I had neither a gun nor a criminal record for any violence, I think I was badly treated.

Bill Staynton and Jimmy Moody were acquitted. Jimmy had been an innocent bystander at the trouble in Mr Smith's, and his only involvement was helping get Harry to hospital. He had a barrister who really believed in him, and fought hard, and in his case at least, justice was done.

So now it was the turn of the Mr Smith's publicity to be prejudicial to the torture trial. It was a no-win situation. I believe the two trials were deliberately run in conjunction in order to get me convicted, and it would not happen today. There would be so many protests about the infringement of my rights. But back then, there was one common purpose: to get the Richardsons behind bars.

After the Mr Smith's conviction I was held in the 'chokey block' (solitary confinement) in Wandsworth, away from all the other defendants and other prisoners. I was never given any reason for being kept in solitary, except that I was on Rule 43 – where a prisoner is held apart from the others either because he has requested it or because the authorities deem it in his interests – for my own protection. But there was never any need to protect me in prison, so it was obviously just part of the plan to break me. I spent six months in twenty-three-hour-a-day solitary, apart from the days I was attending court.

Wandsworth was a disgusting regime, run by black-hearted screws. They were really nasty, hateful men who would do anything to get at you. They'd come by and miss me out for a hot drink in the evening. I'd hear them take it to the cell next door and then they'd walk past mine, so I'd be ringing the bell but they would ignore it. When they did eventually come they'd say: 'Never got your cocoa? Are you sure?' Then they'd say it was too late to get any.

Letters were a lifeline in there, and they always arrived about noon. They'd come along the row of cells and they'd unlock me, so I'd get up to go and take the letter and they would grin and say 'nothing for you' and slam the door. It was a real wind-up.

Wandsworth had a terrible name at that time, and I soon found out it deserved it. The governor was a right bastard. If you made an application to go in front of him, you had to walk past two lines of screws, one on each side, and they glared at you menacingly. I went before him to ask for a proper knife and fork – they were making me use the plastic ones that were only for suicide risk cases, or prisoners who might attack someone. I also went before him to get off Rule 43, but I was turned down. They were gloating over me, and I couldn't work out why they were trying to dig me out.

One crooked screw even attempted to get into me, trying to persuade me he could smuggle things in for me. I didn't want anything, and he got the needle because I wouldn't do deals with him. But I had nobody there I could trust, and I wasn't going to take any more risks. It was a low point for me, being in the chokey block.

I'd never been banged up on my own before. I lost a lot of weight. Remember, prison was all new to me. Years later I'd have handled six months' chokey much more easily, but it was a very brutal way to start my time inside. I felt very low: I had always taken care of my family and provided for them, and there is a terrible sense of powerlessness when you can't do anything for them.

The only one of us who was out was Jean Goodman. She was given bail two days before Christmas 1966, on condition she had no contact with Charlie. As they were no longer together, the police reckoned she was 'no longer under Richardson's influence'.

Going to court for the torture trial, which started in April 1967, was more of the same treatment that we'd had at committal: police outriders, sirens screeching, traffic cleared off the roads, different routes to court each day. I was transported on my own as I was the only one in Wandsworth.

It took a long time to swear in the jury, as we were each allowed to challenge seven jurors without cause, which we did, on principle. Altogether we challenged fifty of them, and the prosecution challenged another thirty-five. Soon afterwards they changed the law, so that now you can only challenge with a good reason. As soon as the jurors were sworn in the judge told them they would have a twenty-four-hour guard on them in order, he said, 'to make certain you are not pestered or influenced by anyone who ought not to have contact with you'. They, like the witnesses, were given a special phone number to call the police and they were told 'a police patrol car will be on the scene in minutes'.

All this security stuff was a pretty clear signal to them from day one that we were a dangerous and unsavoury bunch, no matter what the evidence said. I believe it was embracery, which is the crime of influencing a jury – they claimed it was to stop *us* doing it, but they were actually doing it themselves.

There were nine of us left in the dock after the committal, with Brian Mottram allowed to go home because of medical evidence that he had a bad heart. In fact, he had a pacemaker fitted and survived for another fourteen years. Mottram was an old schoolfriend of Charlie's, and up to his ears in the long-firm frauds with Charlie and the others.

The opening address for the prosecution was great for the reporters in court: Sebag Shaw, QC, threw in as many lurid details as he could. He said it was not a case about dishonesty and fraud, it was a case about 'violence and threats of violence, not sudden violence committed on the spur of the moment, but brutal violence, systematically carried out with utter and callous ruthlessness'. He said victims were trussed up and beaten, and pliers were used on their toenails and teeth. He talked of cigarettes being stubbed out on their bodies, the victims being stripped naked and electrodes applied, and threats made to dump them in the marshes or throw them in the river. He proudly showed the court the black box, although it wasn't the actual one that Charlie used. Altogether, he said there were eleven serious charges of assault.

You can imagine the headlines the next day – and for the rest of the trial, which lasted ten weeks. What we didn't get were headlines supporting our rebuttals of the charges. The public gallery at our trial became one of London's hot tickets, with queues to get a seat. Among those who got in on various days were Cardinal Heenan, the actor Kenneth More, the pianist Leslie 'Hutch' Hutchinson, and the Director of Public Prosecutions, Sir Norman Skelhorn.

The charges against Jean Goodman were thrown out three weeks after the case began, when George Green admitted that she had not been present when he was beaten up. Three months later she married another guy, a painter and decorator, and I've never heard about her since.

Duval was the main problem, because it was through him that almost all of the prosecution witnesses had become involved with Charlie. His little band of long-firm fraudsters were our undoing. Of the ten main prosecution witnesses, seven were associates of Duval. Some of them, like Benny Wajcenberg and Christopher Glinski, I had never seen until the committal. I wasn't charged with anything to do with them. Frankie Fraser knew Glinski, because he'd given evidence against Billy Hill years ago. He was charged with perjury at that time, but acquitted. Still, it should have been enough to warn Charlie off him.

Glinski claimed Frankie's nephew, Jimmy, was in on the beating up he received. Jimmy was one of the ones who came up at committal with us. He was at work on the day Glinski was done, and he had a lot of witnesses to prove it. The prosecution offered him a deal: plead guilty and go home straightaway. Jimmy accepted the deal, even though he could have proved he was innocent. I wasn't happy that he did it, but I can see he was under pressure, and there was so much rubbish going on he just wanted to get home. He could see how other good defence evidence was being ignored, and he didn't want to take a chance in such a loaded trial.

Jimmy Blore and Frank Prater were just another couple of long-firm blokes who were introduced to Charlie by Duval, and they didn't give evidence against me. I knew Lucien Harris, who was Duval's sidekick. He was a well-spoken, educated man who used to compile crosswords in his spare time. He was involved with Charlie in importing hosiery from Milan, so I met him a couple of times, but that was all.

Jimmy Taggart, the first of the bunch to go to the police, said in court that Charlie and Frankie Fraser did him over. They did throw a punch or two at him – he owed money to Alfie Berman, and Charlie was doing it as a favour to Berman. But he must have been a police informer anyway, why else did he tell the cops? Alfie Berman was in the dock with us, but when it came to it he turned Queen's Evidence, and confirmed everything Taggart said about Charlie. Berman had already been shifted to a different prison, so we guessed something was going on. It was a blow having him turn against Charlie.

He wasn't the only one of Charlie's mates who were charged with us who did that. Jimmy Kensit, the father of the actress Patsy Kensit, was up with us at the committal, and he got shifted to a cushier prison, which meant the cops had got into him. He made a statement against Charlie, in return for which charges against him were dropped. Kensit was one of Charlie's men, and a pickpocket by trade. I am always very suspicious of pickpockets: they can only operate by bunging the police, otherwise they'd be nicked every time they went out. The police give them a sort of 'licence' to operate, and that means they are always close to the cops.

George Green, Bennie Coulston and Norman Bickers were the three witnesses who weren't Duval's men. Green was running a long firm round the corner from Charlie's offices, and Charlie had dealings with him. On the charge that I assaulted him, I got a not guilty, and I was never charged with anything to do with Bickers, a villain who Charlie gave a job running one of the long firms.

I never thought anyone would believe the rubbish that came out of the mouth of Bennie Coulston. I was expecting the judge to overrule and strike out a lot of what he said, but Lord Justice Lawton was only too keen to help tidy things up and build the strongest possible case against us. Coulston's evidence was so outrageous that you might have been forgiven for thinking he was trying to help us, knowing none of it was really admissible. But the judge allowed it to stand.

Coulston was different from Duval and all the other fraud lot. He was a lower-bred bloke from round Lambeth way, small with dark hair. He'd never moved away from his South London roots, he was just an evil little mongrel. He didn't have the smoothness of the other conmen, and you would have thought the jury would have seen right through him.

I produced a cast-iron alibi to prove that I was in Dublin on one of the days I was supposed to have been beating up Coulston, but it didn't do me any good.

Duval's evidence was that I laid into him and said: 'You do what Charlie tells you.' I wasn't even working for Charlie at the time. Duval said I hit him with golf clubs. It's obvious that golf clubs wouldn't be good weapons, why would I use golf clubs? It was said in court that he had a black eye, but when he was asked if anyone had seen him and could testify to it, he said he was too afraid to go out so nobody saw it. It was supposed to have happened five years earlier. How could I defend it? They didn't even have a specific date; it had allegedly happened between October and December. I couldn't give an alibi for a whole three months. The charge was reduced from GBH to actual bodily harm (ABH), but it should have been thrown out. There were two other charges of assault on Duval which were chucked out halfway through the trial – that should have told the jury what an untrustworthy witness he was.

He claimed in court that Charlie stabbed him in the stomach, and he even had a small scar to show. But even his mate Prater has since claimed that the scar was a medical one, incurred when Duval – whose taste for good food and wine showed in his waistline – had an operation to remove fat from his stomach, an early version of liposuction, I suppose. Duval admitted in court that he frequently wore wigs and glasses as a disguise. The list of surnames he used included Duval, Oliver, Brabin, Longman, Rumble, Levin and Foster. There must have been at least one more: the real name he was born under in Russia.

Charlie let us down when he came to give evidence. They asked him if he would like to sit down. It sounds so polite, so considerate: 'Would you like a seat, Mr Richardson?' Charlie said yes, but he should have stood up, like I did. It demeans you, sitting down; they are patronising you, making you out to be insignificant. He was hopeless in the box, terrible. Makes me feel sick when I think of it. I think he was suffering from depression at the time.

The judge, Sir Frederick Lawton, was famous as a hard judge. His father was a prison governor, and Frankie Fraser had a real reason to hate Lawton senior, as he'd been governor of Wandsworth prison while Frank was in there, and there had been a few run-ins between them. When Frank had spotted his son, the judge, at Victoria railway station, he'd had a go at him, and would have laid him out if Frankie's wife Doreen hadn't intervened. So to liven things up at the trial Frank got his brief to remind Mr Justice Lawton of the occasion. At first Lawton said it had never happened, but later that day he made a statement to the court saying he had remembered it, but that he thought the person who accosted him was just a drunken oaf. Frank had applied for the trial to be heard by a different judge, but Lawton wouldn't have it.

Lawton had it in for me. I can remember his face when it came out in court that I drove a Bentley.

'A Bentley?' he thundered, going red in the face and looking as though he was going to have a fit. 'A Bentley, did you say?'

He reacted the same way when it was stated that I was earning £4000 a year – which I was, legitimately, from the shop in Deptford. At that time, the average salary was only just over a thousand a year, and I don't suppose His Honour the Judge was on much more than me. I think, in his eyes, the greatest crime I committed was to have a good salary and an expensive car.

When the jury went out at the end of the trial, we knew we were on a hiding. The whole trial had been rigged to present us in the worst possible light, and to ignore how discreditable and discredited the witnesses were. We were taken into the dock one at a time to hear the verdicts, and then we were sentenced the next day.

Charlie was sentenced first, and got twenty-five years. It was a shock: after all, he hadn't killed anybody. But I suppose, after the Great Train Robbery sentences, we shouldn't have been surprised. He was convicted of four counts of GBH, two of ABH, one of robbery with violence and two of demanding money with menaces.

The judge said: 'One is ashamed to live in a society with men like you. There is no known penal system to cure you. You must be kept under lock and key. You terrorised those who crossed your path, and you terrorised them in a way that was vicious, sadistic and a disgrace to society.'

I got ten years for GBH on Coulston, and two for ABH on Duval, to run concurrently. Although I now had the Mr Smith's conviction against me, I still had a very clean record. Yet I got the same amount of bird as Frank Fraser, who was convicted on two charges of GBH and demanding money with menaces, and who had a notorious record. I am not saying I didn't do bad things and that I wasn't involved in violence, but I do think the sentence I got was disproportionate, and was all to do with me having the same name as Charlie.

Sentencing me the judge said: 'I am satisfied that from time to time your services were available to your brother when he required them.'

Roy Hall got ten years for four counts of assault and GBH, Tommy Clark got eight years for GBH and demanding money with menaces, Johnnie Longman was acquitted, so was Jimmy Moody. The jury could not agree about Alf Berman, who had given evidence against us. The judge decided to accept his plea of not guilty to the serious charges of GBH that he faced, and he was released.

Apparently when the case was over, old Lawton, the judge, personally thanked the detectives involved 'for breaking up one of the most dangerous gangs I have ever heard of'. It would be laughable if it hadn't just cost me a long stretch of my liberty.

In the end, I believe that the accusations against us were politically motivated. Charlie's dealings with South Africa meant that the government wanted him out of the way, and Special Branch was out to get him. The rest of us were just pawns in that game, we were dragged into it because of Charlie. I was a particular target, because I shared the same name as him. Once they'd decided to get him, nothing could stand in their way.

After the trial, eighty-two policemen were kept on 'torture trial' duty, guarding the witnesses. Apparently, Benny Coulston had seven cops working round the clock looking after him. Six other policemen were sacked or took early retirement – they had been named as being in Charlie's pay.

It wasn't quite all over. Charlie and Johnnie Longman still had to stand trial for attempting to pervert the course of justice in my Mr Smith's case. More importantly, Frank Fraser's sister, Eva Brindle, and Charlie's secretary, Josie Shaer, along with Albie Woods, were all sentenced to two years for trying to bribe Benny Coulston to drop his evidence. It was a fit-up. Leslie McCarthy and Arthur Baron also got eighteen months for attempting to get into the jury. Anyone who was around us was fitted up.

My name came up in court again six months later, but I wasn't in the dock. The London (Heathrow) airport scam finally unravelled, and twelve men were convicted of operating a fraud which took £200,000 in four years. The judge said: 'A large proportion of the stolen money went to the Richardsons.' In fact, Charlie had nothing to do with it.

I never saw any of the toe-rags who gave evidence against us in the torture trial, and it's just as well for them. Duval got done for fraud again a few years later: he was in business in a long firm with Brian Mottram. Mottram had wriggled out of being on trial with Charlie on health grounds but he didn't wriggle out of his next sentence – he got eight years. It shows you just what kind of people Charlie's long-firm fraudsters were, that Mottram could pal up with Duval after everything he did to us. The last I heard of Duval, he was running a ladies' dress shop in North London.

Coulston dropped out of sight, although Frank Fraser heard a rumour that he and his wife were running a social club in Essex. Frank saw Bunny Bridges years later, quite by chance, somewhere near New Cross. He chased him, but Bridges had a good start and disappeared.

For me, the years in prison stretched ahead. I had a fifteen-year tariff altogether, with the Mr Smith's conviction. It seemed like an eternity. But nothing could be as bad as the chokey block at Wandsworth.

N I N E

THE THUD OF HEAVY BOOTS

At the end of the torture trial, when the judge weighed us off one by one, we were being held in individual cells beneath the Old Bailey. Charlie managed to signal to the rest of us that he had been given twenty-five years. It didn't make my fifteen feel any better. At thirty-one years old, it felt like the rest of my life, stretching ahead forever, would be behind bars. The only relief was that I would no longer be in the chokey block at Wandsworth.

We had a short session with our lawyers and then Charlie, Frank, Roy Hall and me were taken to the security wing at Durham, a place with a reputation that went before it. We knew we were on our way to the toughest regime in the British penal system. It was also as far away from London as possible, which meant that anyone who wanted to visit us had a seven-hour journey to get there by train. We were shipped up there in a convoy, each of us in a separate van, with police outriders – the police vehicles changing as we crossed the boundaries from one force to the next.

We were on E wing, the special high-security wing in the middle of the prison, constructed on the orders of Roy Jenkins – then Labour's Home Secretary – after the spy George Blake had escaped from Wormwood Scrubs in October 1966. Jenkins was a so-called liberal, but he was also an ambitious politician, and there had been calls for his resignation over Blake's escape. He didn't want to risk the scandal of another high-profile prisoner getting out, so he ordered that ultra-secure units be installed in six prisons, using the latest technology. Only three of them were up and running at this stage: Durham, Leicester and Parkhurst, with Cheltenham coming on stream later. Durham was renowned as the worst, and because there were so many big-name prisoners there (the train robbers had been there before we arrived and Ian Brady was there) it was a focus of interest for crime reporters, who even had a special tie made for anyone who joined the exclusive club of journalists who had three stories about E Wing in print.

Infrared cameras, walkie-talkies, razor wire around all the walls: there were constant reminders of the high security. We could see the surveillance nests which had been manned by soldiers with machine guns during the train robbers' time, after the chief constable claimed to have got wind of a plot to bust them out with a tank loaded with atomic weapons. How anyone could believe that I don't know, but it shows the hysteria surrounding high-profile prisoners. By the time I was there, the soldiers and the machine guns were gone, and so were the train robbers.

The screws were renowned as the toughest in the prison system, and they hated southerners. We stuck together, and whenever there was football on telly we'd support any London team. You'd hear huge cheers when teams like Crystal Palace, who I wouldn't normally support, got a goal – it was a way of winding up the Geordie screws.

There were about thirty prisoners in the high-security wing. I never knew what people were in for, and half the time I didn't even know their names. I never went around reading the little cards on the doors of people's cells. I judged people on how I found them. It can be a bit embarrassing years later, when people come up to me and remind me that they did time with me, or say things like, 'you knew my dad when you were in Parkhurst', or wherever, and I don't remember them at all. But to me it was the right way to do time.

The secure unit at Durham was supposed to be impregnable, but later, after I'd been shipped out, John McVicar got out, and Wally Probyn also very nearly made it on the same breakout attempt.

After the George Blake escape the Home Office had also introduced the system of categorising prisoners. Category A were prisoners with long sentences who had committed serious crimes and were regarded as dangerous. I was Double Cat A, which meant I was also an escape risk, and that if I did escape it would create a lot of bad publicity for the prison service.

When I first arrived at Durham I bumped into an old friend from my childhood, Tony Reuter, who was one of the lads I knew from the Elephant and Castle. Except that Tony wasn't actually there: there was a papier mâché head modelled to look just like him, and with a large pair of dark-rimmed glasses, just like the ones he wore, perched on its nose. There was a notice underneath which read: 'No, I don't want to see the visiting magistrate.'

In Durham everybody applied to see the visiting magistrates: they were magistrates who came round to hear our complaints, and they were our only official way of making a point about the conditions we were being held under. On a point of principle, we all applied to see them. Except Tony, who had been in there shortly before I arrived. Apparently he never wanted to see them, and so the others had made the model and stuck the label on. Applying to see the magistrates was just one way of sticking together – some people applied before they even arrived in Durham.

It wasn't only magistrates who came round. At one time in Durham the Labour MP Joan Lestor came to visit. The governor had laid it all on for her, and the screws were all rushing around making sure it went smoothly. We didn't take it seriously: there had been a bit of a stink about the conditions in the high-security units and people like her took an interest, but we never seriously thought they'd make any difference for us. So for a laugh we all hid. She'd come to see the prisoners in the high-security unit, and there weren't any to see, because we were all crammed under the stairs. The screws were stomping about trying to find us. Then we all swooped out, eight or ten of us, all firing questions at her. She looked startled at first, but she took it in her stride. We just wanted to mess the visit up for the screws, who were supposed to be accountable for us.

It was eight months after I arrived in that hellhole, in February 1968, that the new prison governor arrived, 'Flash' Gordon Chambers. We also got a new assistant governor for our wing, Alan Greene, who was a reasonable and fair bloke. He had joined the prison service from the navy, and was not indoctrinated into thinking of us as untameable animals, but the system didn't allow him much flexibility. When Chambers introduced his list of draconian new restrictions Greene tried to intercede, but Chambers would not compromise.

We had other grievances, apart from the new ones Chambers introduced about the workshop (where, rather than woodwork or metalwork, we had to sew mailbags and paint tin soldiers) and the uniform (we were no longer allowed to wear our own tee shirts and trainers). We were being given the appalling food that was normally only served to short-term prisoners. In most nicks, lifers and those with long tariffs were given better food because they were going to have to survive on it for many years. For a brief time we had been allowed cookery classes, given by the main chef from the prison, who enjoyed teaching us. For us, there was the major benefit of being able to eat the food we prepared ourselves, but the screws objected to the classes on the ground that we had access to knives, and Chambers stopped them.

It was this atmosphere which led to the riot and our twenty-five hours barricaded in the assistant governor's office, described at the beginning of this book. When we came out we were on twenty-four hour lock-up, only allowed out to collect our food and for two periods of thirty minutes a day. We had to go in front of the adjudication panel, made up of magistrates with the governor present, and there was no point pleading not guilty. To everybody's surprise, we didn't lose any remission, but we were given forty-two days' lock-up and loss of earnings. The best bit for me was that I knew there was a good chance I'd be moved. Usually, after any major disturbance, the main protagonists are separated.

Maureen was visiting me once a month at this time, travelling up with Jean La Grange, Charlie's girlfriend. Jean La Grange was living at my house in Chislehurst, then, as she had nowhere else to stay in Britain. Later, I put my foot down and wrote a letter to her, telling her to get out. I felt she wasn't a good influence on my daughters: I knew Melanie didn't like her, and I wanted to get rid of her. But I still had no idea of the political stuff she was involved in, and when the police spun off my house a couple of times, I was outraged. They said they were looking for jewellery. Maureen complained to our MP about it. It was only later that I put two and two together and realised it was because of Jean being a spy that they were searching – when she left the spins stopped.

When the mutiny was on, Maureen had reporters on the doorstep, asking her what was going on. She was very supportive. She told them:

'Eddie feels very bitter about his conviction and sentence. He should never be in that top-security wing. He is a first offender and should have more freedom.'

She travelled up for a visit the day after the mutiny ended, again with Jean La Grange, but they weren't sure they would be allowed in. They were: Maureen had told the press she was coming, and there would have been more bad publicity for the prison authorities if she'd been denied a visit. Afterwards she told the reporters:

'It's worse than hell on earth in there. They are cooped up like animals. It is inhuman. For people to say they are pampered prisoners is ridiculous. The only way they could think of attracting public attention to their complaints was by this demonstration.'

Jean La Grange visited Charlie for a while, and she even gave an interview to a newspaper saying she would wait seventy-seven years for him if necessary. Her visa to stay in Britain ran out that summer, and she was refused a work permit, so she married a British citizen, a middle-aged caretaker who was roped in to do it in order to get her a visa to stay. Coincidentally, his name was Frank Fraser, but he was no relation to Frankie. The relationship between Charlie and Jean didn't last, and as far as I know she went back to South Africa.

Two weeks after the mutiny, our appeal applications began. Me, Charlie, Frankie Fraser, Roy Hall, Tommy Clark and Johnnie Longman all petitioned for the right to appeal, and also for our sentences to be reduced. It took a week for the Court of Appeal to turn us down, but I wasn't exactly holding my breath. I didn't think I'd got a fair trial and I was pretty sure I wouldn't get a fair chance to appeal. I was right. It wasn't a bad blow, because you can apply again. In prison, hope springs eternal, and you go from one thing to the next. You know you've got a chance of parole after a third of your sentence, which in my case was five years, and what with the time I served in custody before the trial I was more than two years through. You hang on to the hope of an appeal overturning the sentence. There's always something coming up that might change things for you, and you pin your hopes on it.

Despite the massive publicity for the mutiny, conditions didn't improve at Durham. The screws found lots of little ways of getting back at us because their revenge had been thwarted. They decided that, because we were all so dangerous, we would never be let out of our cells more than three at a time to collect our meals or for exercise (we weren't allowed out for anything else, anyway). This meant that serving a meal took ages. We had to go downstairs, collect it from the hotplate, and take it back upstairs to be locked in before anyone else could get theirs. The food, which was bad at the best of times, was now dried up and cold before we got it, and the screws would stand around gloating, talking about the meal they had the day before, or what they were going to eat when they got off duty.

We decided to have another go at airing our grievances, this time by going on hunger strike. Just a month after the mutiny there were twenty prisoners left on E Wing, not counting the nonces upstairs, and nineteen of us went on hunger strike. We were carried away by the publicity of the mutiny, and we thought we were more important than we were. In fact, nobody gave a monkey's about us. The screws love it when you are on hunger strike, they like to see you doing it. They pretend they're concerned, when they don't really care.

We stayed off food for ten days. It was a terrible time: mentally you become very stressed out. I would never do it again, but I was naïve back then. When they came to open the door at mealtimes, you just refused to go. Once again, McVicar wanted to cave in very quickly – and he did give in before the rest of us – but Charlie was keen to keep going. We finally packed it up when two of our mates became dangerously ill. I was very weak and could barely stand up, and when I did accept food for the first time I couldn't eat it. When they weighed us we'd all lost a lot of weight, more than a stone-and-a-half. I'd become fit and strong doing weights in my first few months at Durham, after losing so much weight in Wandsworth, but now I was back at square one.

Perhaps our protests did pay off, because in May, four weeks after the hunger strike, I was shanghaied out of Durham. It happened, as it usually does, at half past five in the morning. They hope they are going to take you by surprise, while you are still asleep, to minimise any resistance. But I wasn't asleep. I had the light on in my cell: we had wires running from our cells to the light switches outside, so that we could read all night if we wanted to. I was always up late. That night, I couldn't sleep because I had a feeling something was about to happen.

I could hear noises out on the wing, the thud of heavy boots, security gates opening and closing. Everything echoes in prison because of the hard, cold surfaces everywhere. Small noises become loud, doubling in volume as they echo up and down the wings. I could tell the boots were on my landing, heading towards my door. It could have been another prisoner they were coming for, but I tensed up because I sensed it was me they were after. Sure enough, the key turned in my lock and the heavy brigade piled in. There were six of them, and more out on the landing.

I was hustled down to the main reception, without any of my belongings. When you are shanghaied your things are supposed to follow you – you usually get some of them. Downstairs I was double cuffed: my hands were cuffed together and I was cuffed to a screw. I was bundled outside into a van, with one screw driving and two others with me, including the one I was attached to. There were two decoy vans, a police car back and front and police motorcycle outriders. Even the keys to unlock my van and my cuffs were carried in another van, as an extra precaution. It was always like this with a shanghai, and while I remained on Cat A it would be the only way I was transported.

The screws loved all the excitement, it was a day out for them. Some prisoners got a buzz from it, too, enjoying the feeling of being so hard and dangerous that a substantial part of the police budget had to be thrown at guarding them. I didn't care. I didn't need a police escort to make me feel important. But I was pleased to be moved: I'd heard better reports about the other secure units and, besides, everywhere from Durham was south, which meant it would be nearer for my family to come on visits.

I never demeaned myself by asking the POs (prison officers) where we were going, but I had a strong feeling it was Leicester, and I was right. I knew it could not be as bad as Durham. It was another four years before that hellish unit at Durham was finally closed down, after a Home Office report branded it 'inhumane'.

Thank God, my time there was over.

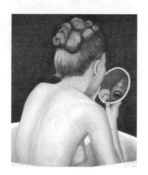

TEN

I GAVE HIM SOME FIERCE VERBALS

It was a relief to get to Leicester. I met up again with some mates, like Tommy Wisbey and Bobby Welch from the Great Train Robbery. Tommy Wisbey had been told to sweep a cell out for a new prisoner, and he was really pleased when it turned out to be me. One of the first things I did was to go in to see Bobby Welch, and he told me not to have my tea that night. I went round to his cell and we had jellied eels and strawberries and cream. It was fantastic: you can't believe how good it tasted after the food at Durham. There was a much better atmosphere, the screws were better and the work was more interesting. Joey Martin, who was serving a double life sentence and had been at Durham with me, was making table tennis tables for local youth clubs and other community projects, a little job organised for him by the chaplain,

Simon Beasley, who was a great fellow. Beasley was a volunteer chaplain, not on the prison staff.

There was a television room, where we mainly voted to watch sport. But sometimes there were only a couple of people in there, so you could more or less choose what you wanted to see. There was a snooker table, table tennis table and weights, plus a decent exercise yard. I began to get fit and strong again.

Visits were very lax in those early days at Leicester. I could buy a tray of tea and coffee and carry it across to the table where Maureen was sitting, and there would be a cloth covering the tray. It was easy for something, like a packet of bacon, some sausages, or some tobacco, to be slipped under the cloth. It meant that we had a few luxuries, and those little things do make life much easier. Nowadays, with all the problems of drugs in prison, they have to be a lot stricter.

The high-security unit was very small: there were only ever a few of us in it. Arthur Hosein, who was serving thirty years for the kidnap and murder of Muriel McKay, the wife of a top executive in Rupert Murdoch's business which owned the *Sun* and the *News of the World*, was there. Arthur and his brother thought they were getting Murdoch's wife, but they made a mistake. When it all started to come on top they got rid of her, but her body was never found and it is believed they fed her to the pigs on their farm. He was a tailor by trade, which came in very handy for altering prison trousers and shirts.

Another prisoner I met in there was Harry Johnson, who was otherwise known as Hate 'Em All Harry. The name says it all. I found him very amusing because he hated everyone without exception, although most of his anger was directed at the staff. He was volatile and difficult to handle, so they shoved him into the special unit with us hard cases so that he wouldn't be able to bully anyone. He was like a big version of Alf Garnett in *Till Death Us Do Part*: he was thick-set (five feet ten inches tall, about thirteen stone) and with wild, staring eyes. He could be extremely violent when the mood took him.

Snooker was very popular, and we had a rule that if you were waiting for a game you played the winner of the game before. One evening Arthur Hosein had won the previous game and the next person waiting was Hate 'Em All Harry, who, among all his other charms, was a real right-wing racist.

So the balls were set up and Hosein broke them and the game started. Hate 'Em All expected to win, because he played a tidy game of snooker, but he was having a bad run of luck. He was a lot of points behind, and when the brown ball was potted by Hosein it looked like Harry was on a sure beating. You could see the annoyance on his face: losing was bad enough, but losing to a 'Paki' was even more humiliating. As Hosein was bending over the table to play the blue ball, Harry walked up behind him and struck him on the head with the cue. It was a heavy blow, and Hosein fell to the floor. Harry walked away.

'What the fuck did you do that for?' I asked him.

'He was laughing at me.'

'No he wasn't,' I said. Then Harry came out with a classic that I've never forgotten:

'His eyes were laughing.'

Hosein and Harry were both moved soon afterwards and there were seven of us left in the secure unit, including Joey's brother-in-law, George Elliot, and Ron Brown. I called the unit The Submarine because it was so small and compact, and claustrophobic. I'd been reading an article in a newspaper about the stress sailors suffer from being in tight confinement on submarines, and it seemed to me that we were in a very similar situation.

Like Durham, it was a prison within a prison, the idea being that if anyone escaped the unit they would still have to get out of the prison. Of course, being so closely confined with people always jars after a few months. I learned on my tour around the British prison system that the first few weeks in a new place are always the best, as you catch up with old mates and enjoy a few new privileges. But eventually the company begins to grate. Some people have annoying little habits, and it gets so that you know what they are going to do before they do it. It's not conducive to good mental health. Being so small, the special unit at Leicester was the worst for this.

I soon realised that there was bad feeling between Tommy Wisbey and Joey Martin. They'd had a quarrel over something stupid and I had to intervene and get them together, because Joey had devised a really good escape plan, and he wanted to cut Tommy out of it. It would have been a disaster to leave him out: we needed all the help we could get. Joey's brother-in-law didn't want to risk it, he didn't have long left to serve, but he was happy to keep schtum while the rest of us went.

The layout of the high-security unit was an oblong with two rows of cells, then a kitchen area, and a television room along one side of the open area where the snooker table stood, and another row of cells and a woodwork room along the other side. On the top wall there was the screws' office, with a glass front so that they could look out on us the whole time. Leading off their office was a cell which was used as a laundry room. You had to go through the screws' office to get clothes, which we enjoyed doing because we could have a look round, lark about, drive them mad when they were supposed to be writing reports or were just trying to get a rest, and it meant they had to lock and unlock doors to let us in and out. The laundry room contained great piles of clothes – shirts, trousers, vests, pants – all split up into different sizes.

Cameras were trained on every inch of the wing, except our cells. There was a microphone on the wall, to pick up any noise, but we would take a radio out to the exercise yard with us and point it, at full volume, at the mike, or we'd shout and swear down it. So the screws kept it switched off. To get to the exercise yard you had to go through one of the cells, which was obviously never used for a prisoner. Then you went through an electronically controlled door into a short corridor, with another electronic gate at the end which led out into the yard.

The exercise yard was a good size, and was surrounded by a strong, mesh fence about twenty-six feet high. It was constructed with concrete posts at intervals, each forking into a V at the top, with coils of barbed wire passing between the Vs. It was surrounded by another yard: our compound had been specially hived off from a bigger yard, the outside edge of which was the prison wall. Leicester, famously, has the highest wall in any British prison, with a forty-feet drop from the outside to the ground. From the inside, however, it was roughly the same height as our wire fence.

When Joey first came to me with the idea to build a cabinet, it sounded a bit far-fetched, but as he explained it I could see it was a really good plan.

The first thing we did was to suggest moving the laundry to the empty cell we had to go through to get to the exercise yard, and where we stored our gym weights – we used to take them outside to weight-train in the summer. Joey, who was busy every day in the woodwork room making table tennis tables, volunteered to make shelves to store the clothes neatly. The screws thought it was a good idea – it would tidy up the problem with the clothes and give Joey and the rest of us something to keep us busy.

The cell was thirteen feet long by six feet wide, so Joey constructed a cabinet which stretched along the length of one wall and, above, two rows of shelves split into compartments for all the different items of clothing. The cabinet was meant to have a solid base that would take the weight of our gym weights, but Joey made it with a top that could be taken off. The two sections of shelves, each thirteen feet long, were brilliantly constructed: they were divided into pigeonholes, each with a neatly painted label for the different sizes of shirts, trousers, pants, socks and so on. But they could also be slotted together into one, twenty-six-foot ladder, which would get us to the top of the mesh enclosure round our yard.

We also constructed two 'runners' made of strong plywood, which, when joined together, would get us across from the top of the wire mesh to the top of the prison wall. It was vital that we knew how long these runners needed to be, and for that we needed a measurement of the distance between our compound and the outer wall.

When we were out on exercise there would always be a screw outside the wire, standing near the outer wall, so we'd find some pretext to call him over to speak to us through the wire.

'Can you give us a light?' we'd say, for example.

As he came across to us we'd count his steps, then try to work out from his size what the length of each step would be. We'd try it again, with a different screw, but it was very hit and miss. I tried pacing it out along the corridor between the cells, to try and get an idea of it, but it was only a very rough guess.

Then we came up with a better idea. There were always people wandering around the outer yard – barrow parties doing clean ups, blokes pushing brooms. So we came up with a plan to tie a cigarette on to a piece of cotton, and lob it through into the outer yard. Then, when the cleaner came to pick it up, we'd yank on the cotton and whip it back, and all fall about laughing as if it was the funniest thing we'd ever seen. The screws in the outer yard laughed as well. They liked to see us happy. Remember, they all thought we were far worse than we actually were.

So then we asked the screw to put it further out into the yard for us. Eventually, after a couple of days of it, we said:

'Do us a favour, mate. Put this right over by the far wall this time, for a laugh.'

The screw did it, thinking he was joining in the fun. Magic. We whipped it in when the cleaner came, and we had a piece of cotton that gave us an exact measurement, nineteen feet and a few inches. I don't know whose idea it was, we were all plotting together all the time. It worked, and that's all that mattered. We even made an allowance for the wall being three to four feet thicker at the base than at the top.

Joey had all the plywood, but we needed some special bits and pieces – nuts and bolts and things – to join together the two ladders and the two runners. Joey would let me know the specifications, and I'd get what we needed. There were crooked screws who would bring things in: for the first five or six years of my sentence, until security tightened, I always had a Coke bottle filled with brandy brought in by a screw. But we didn't dare ask the bent officers for the extra bits for the ladders. They, unwittingly, helped by taking out stiffs – that's prison slang for letters which are smuggled out and posted outside. I'd give details of exactly what we needed, and it would come in.

The runners were made of two layers of five-ply, with holes here and there along it. We stored them inside Joey's cabinet, which was painted blue. We all used to go and chat to Joey while he was in the woodwork room building the ladders and the runners, and screws used to talk to him, too. He kept his cool. Ron Brown made a rope of plaited sheets – easy, because we could collect our own sheets, and we could always take more than we needed. The first time he experimented with plaiting them together the rope broke when we tested it, so we had to add more sheets. It would only have got us halfway down the wall, but we were all fit, young blokes and we figured we could easily drop twenty feet.

All this time we were having regular searches of our cells, but the screws were so confident in the security of the submarine, with its surveillance cameras and electronic doors, that they didn't put themselves out – and, besides, all the incriminating evidence was in the laundry cell.

The routine drill when we were on exercise was that two officers were required to bring us in from the yard. One had to be a senior, white collar officer, and the other was just a screw. As we came in they would lock the door behind us, then we'd put all our weights down, and then they would open the opposite door. The two doors were never opened at the same time. Then we'd put the weights away and collect anything we needed from the laundry store.

As part of the plot, I was going to have to sort out the senior officer. There were two who alternated on that shift, a doddery old one and a young, fit one. I would much rather have taken a pop at the young one, but on the day we marked down for the escape, the old one was on duty.

For a week or two before the big day I had a few tantrums as we came back in from exercise. I'd go into one, and the officers would stand well back, giving me a wide berth. I'd slam the weights down with a lot of noise:

'Fucking shit, shit, shit,' I'd growl, as I pushed my way angrily through the other lads. They all knew what I was doing.

I wanted the screws to be frightened of me, so that when the moment came they wouldn't fight or struggle. I created the atmosphere; made them very wary of tangling with me.

It was an exciting time, but we all behaved perfectly normally. We knew that everything had to happen swiftly and according to plan. But if it worked . . . The whole of one of Britain's top-security units, apart from one prisoner, would be outside on their toes. There would have been a huge stink – and a huge celebration in prisons up and down the land.

The day we decided to go, Leicester football club was playing at home at their Filbert Street ground, and we could hear the fans cheering every time the ball got anywhere near the net. It suited us: the whole area would be flooded with cars and people, come to watch the match. We could fade away easily enough once we were out.

There was an argument about who would go first, but in the end it was accepted that I would. I spoke my mind and worked my way to the front: I wanted to be first over. Second would be Joey, followed by Brownie, who had been in on the plan from the beginning, then Tommy Wisbey, Bobby Welch and George Elliot.

We went out on exercise as normal, and I was relieved to see that the old officer had got our physical training instructor, a white collar man, to bring us in. I regarded him as fair game. If it had been the old doddery one I'd still have done it, but I was happier taking on someone young and fit. The instructor was the last one to come in from the yard, and as he was going to close the door I put my arm round his neck from behind and threw him on to the floor hard. I got on top of him, laid one of the iron bars from a set of dumb bells across his nose, and gave him some fierce verbals:

'If you move, you c***, I'll smash yer fucking head in.'

He didn't move an inch. Ronnie Brown was supposed to cop for the other screw, but he didn't, so Tommy Wisbey jumped in and got him under control, with the others helping out. It cost us a few valuable seconds and the element of surprise had gone, so he was defending himself and it was a struggle to tame him. We tied them up with their arms behind their backs, plastered their mouths, and stuck them in the corner, trussed up like two turkeys at Christmas. They didn't know what was going on, and they couldn't make a noise, but their eyes opened wide when we dismantled the laundry store, chucking clothes down on to the floor.

We had the keys from the screws, so we opened the door into the yard. The passageway was long enough to assemble the ladders. We bolted the two sections together into one long one and ran out with them. We'd never seen that ladder joined up before, but it was a beautiful piece of work, it fitted together perfectly. But there was no time to admire it. Bobby Welch ran out into the yard first, and the camera that was trained on the area picked him up and tracked him. There was another gate into the yard, and he ran to it with three metal coat hangers which had been straightened, and bent them through the wire mesh so it wouldn't unlock.

I got up that ladder as fast as I could, shouldering a thick, foam gym mat which I put on top of the barbed wire, squashing it down so that I could sit in the V of the concrete post. It gave me a good vantage point, and I saw the security camera swivel away from Bobby and on to me at the top of the wire. Now the screws knew something big was going on.

Joey came up next behind me, and then Ronnie Brown who was carrying the runner. He was passing it up and we were helping. It was heavy, and we knew we mustn't let it go over until it got to the very top because we needed all its length to cover the gap between the fence and the wall. When Ronnie got to about six feet from the top he started to heave it over, with me and Joey yelling that he needed to get it higher. Me and Joey struggled to hang on to it but it tipped over, hit the wall at the other side and swung down towards the ground. I took all the skin off my shoulder trying to hold it and heave it back up for another go, but just as we began to hoist it up one of the screws in the yard outside the wire ran up, jumped and just managed to grab hold of the end of it. For a moment he hung in the air, seesawing up and down like in an old Buster Keaton film. It would have been funny if it hadn't been so important.

The balloon was up and there were a lot of screws out there now, with their batons pulled. We were prepared for a tear-up. But we knew that once the runner was gone, we'd had it. The governor came into the outer yard outside our cage and spoke to us:

'Go in quietly, there'll be no violence.'

Reluctantly, we went in through the first door into the corridor, and they closed the door electronically behind us and then let us back into the wing.

We were so bitterly disappointed, everyone was on a real downer. Brownie said later that the runner was too heavy for him, but I think he might have bottled it. He was serving thirteen years and he'd already done a few, I don't think he wanted more adding on. All that work, months of plotting and planning, all gone. You can't imagine how bad it felt. I'd almost been able to smell the fresh air, see the grass and trees, taste decent food. If it's any consolation, I've been told that our cabinet and ladders are now exhibits in Scotland Yard's famous 'Black Museum'.

I heard that after he was moved from Leicester, Joey Martin got involved in the escape at Durham – where McVicar managed to get out, but he and Wally Probyn didn't. I believe that a few years ago Joey finally got out of prison, but he served many years.

We went straight on to lock-up when they got us back inside. We were in strip cells, which meant all we had was a bed, a table and a chair, and we weren't allowed to have any bedding during the day. It was handed back to us at about eight o'clock each evening. We were allowed books, but there weren't many in the library there, and lots of them had pages torn out. We were still given one hour's exercise a day – which they had to give us, by law. If it was raining they made you walk around the wing. But that one hour was the only time out of the cell.

Two weeks later, the doddery PO had a heart attack and died, and they tried to say it was down to the shock of it all. He probably would have died on the day of the escape if I had got him: you can't mess around, you have to slam them down hard. But if that had happened, the consequences would have been greater.

It was a great shame that we didn't get away. We all got six months' loss of remission for the attempted escape, which was the maximum punishment. Nowadays, you'd probably get five years, because it would all be heard in public, in court. But in those days they kept it under wraps, just had an internal hearing: it was bad publicity for the prison service if news of incidents like this leaked out. We got fifteen days' bread and water and a non-association order for fifty-six days, which meant we couldn't mix with anyone. I also got another forty-two days of non-associated labour, which meant I still couldn't mix with the others. I reckon they put me down as the ringleader.

It was about this time that I first met Lord Longford. He came to visit me after I wrote to him about the conditions in there. I heard about him by reading the parliamentary reports in *The Times* – this was long before he was famous, and before he got a name as a bit of a loony by visiting people like Myra Hindley. After we met he would send me the Hansard reports of his speeches in the House of Lords, and he always spoke up for prison reforms. I never relied on him to help me. He was too mild a personality to get anything radical done: I'm sure the Home Office read his letters and then just put them to one side.

He was a religious man, and he believed in the tenets of his religion – that everyone is redeemable. He should not have been condemned for it, he should have been admired. He was no hypocrite: he wouldn't drop Myra Hindley simply because it would have been better for him in terms of public opinion; he stuck to what he believed in. I talked to him about the awful conditions, and I know he did his best, but he was never going to be able to change things. Lord Longford was a very genuine man, and I was in touch with him until he died. I met him outside prison, and he always promised he would take me to lunch at the House of Lords. I would have liked to have gone to his funeral, but I was in prison again when he died.

One great gee up that I got while I was in chokey was a card from Johnny Cheshire. He was a good amateur boxer, and he'd been selected for the Great Britain team to go to the Mexico Olympics. He got all the British boxers to autograph a team picture for me. I gave Johnny a job at my shop in Deptford when he first came down to London from Scotland and he needed work to fund his boxing. I paid his wages and he got plenty of time off for training. Getting the card from him was a big uplift.

Our wives did their best to highlight the conditions we were being held under. Tommy Wisbey's wife Irene, Bobby Welch's wife Pat, and my wife Maureen – along with some other prisoners' wives – staged a protest outside the gate of the prison, carrying placards protesting about our sentences. Maureen described our treatment as 'inhuman and sadistic'.

Simon Beasley, the chaplain, was so disgusted about our conditions that he complained to the governor many times, and when nothing happened he resigned. It was a great shame, because he was a genuine sort of bloke. I'm not religious, I judge people on how they are, and he was OK. We had a Roman Catholic priest who also used to come round and see us, and I asked him one day:

'Doesn't it prick your conscience that the other chaplain, Simon Beasley, has resigned because of our conditions?'

'No,' he said. 'It has no effect on me, because it's not this world you have to worry about, it's the next.'

We did our own bit to protest. Even though we were locked up, we could still talk to each other through the windows. We thought we might be able to cause enough damage to shut down the submarine. They were giving us plenty of aggravation, so there was a general consensus that we would give them aggravation.

We all got library books and put them in the doorjambs, then slammed the doors on them to buckle the hinges. I'd never seen it done before, because I was still new to the prison system, but some of the others had heard about it. It worked. I made sure my library book was a fat hardback. Some of the others didn't choose big enough books or didn't slam the doors enough, so not all of them got done. I think some of them didn't want any more trouble. Anyway, there were enough spare cells to transfer those of us who did buckle our doors. It cost me another three months' remission.

One of our big grievances was that they'd changed the visits room, and they had installed partitions which we had to sit behind, with our family and friends on the other side. It was another example of treating us like animals: suddenly we weren't allowed to have our children on our laps, or hold hands with our wives. So our next plan when we had finished our punishment was to smash up the visits room, particularly the partitions. I was the first of us to have a visit booked, on 23 December, only a few days after I'd finally come off punishment. I decided I was really going to go off on one, and get rid of that partition.

But at six o'clock that morning I heard the heavy tread of boots coming my way, and I was shanghaied out to Parkhurst. It was the usual deal: no time to pack, no time to say goodbye, handcuffs on and away you go. They didn't let my wife know, so she travelled all the way up to Leicester in the depths of winter, only to find I wasn't there. They don't worry about things like that, it's just an extra way to cause aggravation for you.

For me, it was the usual treatment: a high-security move. But it was a good move.

ELEVEN

HANDCUFFED TO REGGIE KRAY

I arrived in Parkhurst in time for Christmas, and I had a really good celebration with some good mates, including some of the train robbers: Charlie Wilson, Gordon Goody, Jimmy Hussey and Roy James. Also there were Harry Roberts, Billy Gentry, Dennis Stafford – who I knew from Durham – and the spy, Peter Kroger. From their little bungalow in Middlesex, Kroger and his wife Helen had been helping run a sophisticated, electronic spy centre for the Russians. They and their accomplices were known as the Portland Spy Ring, and the Krogers were each sentenced to twenty years in 1961.

Reggie and Ronnie Kray were also there, but Ronnie soon got moved to Parkhurst hospital unit. There was no problem with the Krays, no aggro at all. A few years earlier, walking into a pub and seeing them there, might have been a problem. But inside, you accept things. You all start on the same level in prison, the past is past. It was all new to me anyway, and I soon learnt to take no notice of things that had happened outside. Inside was a different world, with its own rules.

The special unit at Parkhurst was much better than Durham or Leicester. It was bigger, less claustrophobic, the people were good, and I was well pleased to be there. There was a relaxed atmosphere. On Christmas Day we had turkey and all the trimmings, cooked on the prison wing by the lads. There was football, a television room, lots to do. There was a garden with a greenhouse where we grew our own tomatoes and cucumbers. We were eating tomatoes with everything, so every so often we'd do a big parcel for the prison hospital.

There was plenty of hooch, which is easy to make if you can get hold of yeast. In most prisons yeast is smuggled out of the kitchens, but in the high-security units we had to have it smuggled in from outside. Once you've got yeast you can make hooch with anything. Usually it was apples or oranges, chopped up and mixed with sugar and water. You needed to leave it at least ten days, but you had to have a release valve because of the fermentation, which meant there was a smell problem. I never really liked hooch that much but some people spend their whole time in prison working out how to make it, where to hide it: their whole sentence revolves around it. For me, I'd drink it now and again, if there was a party.

We could get newspapers delivered, paid for out of our private funds (you could use your canteen money, the money you earn inside, but I never had to as I always had private funds). I had the *Telegraph* delivered every day. Reggie Kray always had *The Times*, and we'd swap. But when I got it from him there was never any sign that it had been opened and read – sometimes the pages were still stuck together. I suppose he liked the image of having *The Times*, wanted to play Mr Big.

I was with Reggie Kray one day, watching television, and some writer called Norman Lucas came on screen talking about a book he'd written about London's gangland. Every two or three years someone brings out a book about it, and it's all the same old garbage. They were asking Lucas questions about the Kray twins and the Richardsons, and he said they would never be held together in the same prison, that the prison authorities would see to it that we were always kept apart. And there was Reg, sitting on the chair next to me. We just looked at each other, smiled and shrugged our shoulders.

I talked to Reggie once about the death of Frank Mitchell who they sprung from Dartmoor. When he got too hot to handle they got rid of him, although they were never done for his murder.

'That was a fucking liberty, what happened to Mitchell,' I said.

Reggie's eyes filled with tears, whether of remorse or frustration I don't know.

'I didn't want him done,' he said. He didn't say anymore, but I guess it was his brother Ronnie, who was more erratic and dangerous than Reggie, who ordered Frank Mitchell's murder.

Although conditions were so much better in Parkhurst, there were still ways that we were treated which weren't right. The Home Office ordered that all our visitors had to produce passport photos of themselves and fill out long questionnaires. Our wives were in the habit of protesting by now, so they turned up at the gates and refused to give in pictures. They resented it, as all the prison staff knew who they were. They had a showdown with the governor who allowed them to see us, but said that in future they must produce the pictures. These rules still exist today, if you want to visit a Cat A prisoner it can take six to eight weeks to get vetted, and photos are required.

Peter Kroger was an interesting character. He was in his sixties, but he kept himself fit running round the garden every day. He insisted on his toast being burnt, not just blackened but actually alight, because he had this thing about charcoal being good for your stomach. He was a passionate Communist, and we used to have long arguments with him, although there was no chance of him converting any of us.

He spent a lot of time writing to his wife in Holloway. There was a great deal of talk in the press about the pair of them being exchanged for a British businessman, Gerald Brooke, who was being held by the Russians for spying. The press were outraged, saying that as he was an honest businessman, and innocent, why should Britain let these two spies go? First the exchange was on, then it was off. It was a very tense time for Kroger, and his wife was ill, which worried him. We didn't mind the fact that he was a spy: in there he was doing his sentence, just like the rest of us, and he was going through a bad time so we were sorry for him.

The head of the Portland Spy Ring was known as Gordon Lonsdale, although he was really a Russian called Konon Molodiy. He had been sentenced to twenty-five years at the same trial as the Krogers and two others but, after serving less than four years, Lonsdale had been exchanged for another British businessman, Greville Wynne. I had some tee shirts with 'Lonsdale London' written on them, from the Lonsdale sports equipment firm. Peter Kroger was amused by this, so I gave him one which he wrapped up and said he would give to Gordon Lonsdale when they met up with him again on the other side of the Iron Curtain.

Finally, in October 1969, Kroger got the word that his exchange was on, so we laid on a farewell party for him. Everybody pitched in a fiver for him, and we laid out all the tables in the refectory into one long table: there was a real feast, with hooch, biscuits, lots of little extras. I had a record player, so we had music, and when we played

Zorba the Greek he got up and danced to it. Tears were running down his face, and he was very emotional. He made a speech and we all clapped, everyone was very touched.

The next morning he was off early, and on the television news we watched him getting on the plane with his wife and flying off for the exchange with the businessman, Gerald Brooke, in Warsaw. The British press were trying to talk to him but he just swiped them away. People might have thought he was ignorant, but we knew how much stick he had had from them, and how the whole exchange had been delayed by them. Peter Kroger sent us all cards afterwards, from East Germany. Mine said, amongst other things: 'Here's muck in yer eye!' Brooke wrote a book a few years later about how he had been spying after all.

I never judge any man by what he is supposed to have done, except nonce cases, and they were always kept separate from us. I got to know a lot of IRA guys in prison, and I found them very likeable. Each person inside is a human being. They seemed decent lads to me, and they admitted many bad things, including bombs which killed innocent people. They didn't have to own up, but they always did, which makes them honourable in my eyes. They always gave warnings of their bombs, because they never intended to kill civilians, and they were genuinely sorry when it happened. They simply wanted to make their case.

While I was in Parkhurst there was a riot, but it wasn't in the high-security unit, and none of us were involved. We were a prison within a prison, and we had no way of talking to anyone outside the unit. Frank Fraser was involved in the riot, and one of those with him was Andy Anderson, the lad we helped when he was on his toes after escaping with Ronnie Biggs. When the riot was put down the prisoners had to run the gauntlet of a phalanx of screws pummelling them with batons. Fraser was taken into a cell and badly beaten up, and then he got five years added on to his sentence.

The governor at Parkhurst was a bloke called Alistair Miller, and to those of us in the special unit he seemed a decent sort. He didn't believe that just because we were in the secure unit we should be treated like animals. The Home Office let us have record players, radios and all sorts of concessions, because there had been so much trouble in the special units. The train guys got a fair amount of sympathy wherever they went, because their sentences were so heavy. Even the fair-minded screws didn't think they deserved it. Miller was good to them. Roy James was a goldsmith, and a real craftsman, and he was allowed to have gold sent in to make jewellery. He made a beautiful gold-band ring for me to give to my wife.

Years and years later I saw Alistair Miller in a club in Borough, with Jimmy Hussey. He was retired from the prison service by then. A lot of the faces in the club were unhappy that he was there, they still saw him as the enemy. Others didn't mind. I didn't take sides, I just ignored him: although he had been fair with us, I had heard what had happened during the riot in the main prison.

I was very disappointed when I got shanghaied out of Parkhurst, with Reggie Kray. I knew that wherever they were taking us would be worse. Reggie and me went out in the same wagon together. We were both double cuffed – to each other, and with a screw on one side. Double cuffing makes life very difficult. Even if you want to have a piss, the screw has to go with you and stand there.

At least we had a proper van with windows, so we could see where we were going. There were about ten screws with us, and there were police outriders, all the usual stuff again. The screws were delighted, they have a field day on these occasions. On a long distance transfer they get overnight pay, overtime, and a night out with the screws at the other end. They love it. The ferry from the Isle of Wight was packed with holidaymakers, and they kept trying to look inside the van. There were police with guns on the ferry, so they knew there was someone very bad in there. It's like theatre. All the other vehicles were blocked off while we disembarked, because we had priority. It gave all the holidaymakers something exciting to tell everyone when they got home.

I guessed we were going to Leicester from the route we took. Chelmsford had by now got a high-security unit, but the only others were still Durham and Leicester. As usual, we never asked the screws: they wouldn't tell us, so why give them the opportunity to blank us? I didn't want to go to Leicester, because it was where I had lost a lot of remission, and because my brother had been in there while I was in Parkhurst and he had thrown a bucket of piss and shit over one of the senior prison officers. So now I was going back into the frying pan: a dreadful prison, but also all this extra aggravation caused by Charlie. Charlie was shipped out from there the same day we arrived, and sent to Durham. I was never in the same prison as Charlie again for the whole of my sentence, but we wrote letters to each other occasionally, not very often.

'Judging by the landmarks, we're on our way to Leicester,' I told Reg as we travelled north.

He started giving me a bit about the Lambrianou brothers, who were both in there. Tony and Chrissie Lambrianou went down with the Krays, they were there when Jack 'the Hat' McVitie was murdered by Reggie. Reggie said the Lambrianous were a no-good pair of grasses and he wanted to do them. I saw a possibility of getting moved, if I was involved in real trouble again, so I said I'd help him. He said:

'They're fucking nobodies. They're grasses. They've got it coming.'

'OK, I'll make one, and we'll steam into them first chance we get. Fucking sort the bastards out, no problem.'

So he's well pleased that he's got some help, and I'm pleased that I've got a strategy to get moved somewhere else. If I have a tear-up, they'll shift me, I was thinking. I'd never met the Lambrianous but that didn't matter.

When we arrived we were taken into the submarine through the visits room, and the first thing I clocked was that the glass partitions I'd been going to smash the day I got shanghaied out were still there. Nobody else had had a go at them, which made me mad and I heaved one over on my way in. When I got on the wing I asked straight away why it hadn't been done, and Freddie Foreman, who was doing a ten for being an accessory in the murder of Jack 'the Hat' McVitie with the Krays, said to me:

'If you get a good screw he lets your kids come round to you.'

'Wait for a fucking good screw? No way. I don't wait for no fucking screw. We should have it by right,' I said.

I told the others we shouldn't stand for it.

'It's not right. Other high-secure units don't have it. I've just come from Parkhurst and they haven't got it there,' I told them.

What's more, the Lambrianous had been moved, so that plan was down the pan. (Later on in my sentence I met both Tony and Chrissie, and they were alright. I also knew Tony when I was out. He organised a lot of benefits for Reggie, and visited him regularly, so I guess Reg mellowed towards him.)

I still didn't want to be in Leicester but I didn't have much choice. The people in there this second time were not my kind of people and I was miserable and frustrated.

John Duddy was in there, and he made a few comments about Reggie's brother Ron being a poof. Some of the other inmates delighted in relaying these remarks to Reg, and naturally Reg had to do something about it. You can't let things go unchallenged: you have to stamp on them, especially if they have been passed on by a third party. It means everyone is watching to see what you do. The twins were very loyal to one another.

Reg cornered Duddy in the television room and really set about him. I was standing in the doorway, keeping an eye out for any screws. Duddy was a much older bloke, in his mid-fifties, and he didn't work out and keep fit. Reggie worked out regularly, so in no time Reg was on top and he was really pounding Duddy. After a few seconds, I could see Duddy couldn't take it, and I knew that if he was seriously injured Reg would be in deep trouble. I physically dragged Reg off.

'That's enough. It's over,' I said.

Reg turned angrily to start on whoever was holding him, but when he saw it was me he calmed down. Reg never fancied taking me on in a fight, and I reckon I was the only person in there who could have stopped it getting out of hand. He cooled down quickly. He'd made his point.

Nothing happened to make the visits better. The converted cell they used as a visits room had three tables, each with its own partition. Usually there were no more than two visits at once, and often only one.

One day in March 1970, when I'd served five years, my wife and six-year-old daughter, Donna, were on a visit and Donna came round the partition and sat on my knee. There were about six or eight screws around the room and another three sitting at a table. One of them came across and said: 'The visit is terminated.' This was because Donna was on my knee. They were angry because she was round my side of the table. She was only a little kid, she didn't understand their rules. So that was it. It kicked off. I smashed the partition, heaving it up in the air, and they were all on me, thumping me with their batons. I couldn't take them all on, there were too many, about twelve I reckon. I was scrapping as much as I could, I wasn't going quietly, but after three or four minutes they had me spread-eagled, three or four hanging on to each arm. Then one of them started punching me up the bollocks, which gave me a little bit more inspiration, a little bit more strength. I managed to rip the epaulettes off the shoulders of a couple of them. I still had a bit of life in me. They were shouting, 'Hold on! Hold on!'

Two plain-clothes policewomen had swept Maureen and my daughter out, picking Donna up and twisting Maureen's arm up behind her back, like she was dangerous. They got them out of the room, but not before they'd seen what was happening to me. It must have been terrifying for a small child, when all she wanted was to sit with her daddy.

I was marched off to the chokey block, where I got fifty-six days and lost six months' remission. I didn't mind being in chokey, as I didn't want to mix with the other prisoners. After that incident, I refused on principle to have visits. I wouldn't see people under those conditions. For six months I saw nobody from outside, except Lord Longford. I kept in touch with my family through letters. Maureen took up the fight again: she complained to the Home Office about being manhandled by the policewomen, and about my treatment. She also contacted the National Council for Civil Liberties, and our local MP.

The fuss she made did do some good, because the rules for visits were changed. The big square table and the partition were taken out, and a small table installed. Maureen was allowed to sit about a foot away from me and the children could sit on my lap. I resumed visits as soon as it was all changed. Experience has taught me that nothing gets changed in prison without violence, it's the only thing that they take any notice of.

Maureen was feeling the strain of having a husband in prison. She was very supportive, but it was tough for her on the outside. She never complained, but she expressed her feelings to a journalist who interviewed her about a suggestion in the House of Lords that prisoners should be allowed out for short times to prevent marriages breaking up.

'A long sentence destroys a marriage,' she said. 'You just forget you have a husband. You can't see yourself as a married woman. You just go and visit him. You sit there, talk to him for two hours, and he is just a stranger in a way. I can't touch him, I can't give him anything. All the time there are prison officers sitting so close they hear everything you say, even if you whisper. We don't talk about the years ahead, you just try to put it out of your mind. You talk about things that are happening at home, just general information. If you talk about prison, the visit is terminated. Visits are in the afternoon, so I have to take the children out of school.'

Melanie, who was eight when I went down, always understood that I was in prison, but Donna, who was only two when I was sentenced, thought that she was visiting me in hospital.

The whole of my second time in Leicester was awful. I've blocked it all out in my memory. I can't even remember how long I was in there. I got into more trouble for giving this really annoying screw a right rollicking when he was winding me up. I said:

'You're a Welsh c*** and you should fuck off back to the mountains and fuck the sheep, like everyone else in Wales does.'

He nicked me and I had to go in front of the governor. He told the governor what I said in his singsong Welsh accent, and the governor couldn't help it, he started laughing. I got a fine for that, or maybe a bit behind the door. I don't remember. But the screw got the humiliation.

Harry Roberts, who was jailed for life with a tariff of thirty years for killing three cops with John Witney and John Duddy in 1966, was in there with me. He's good with his hands, very good at making models. My wife sent me a big model of a galleon – cost about £70, even then. It was sheets of wood, you had to cut it all out, make all the rigging. It had little cannons, all coming out of little trapdoors. Harry was helping me to make it, although he was doing all the clever stuff and I was just labouring for him. He'd nearly finished it when I got shipped out, and it got sent on to me. But someone had deliberately put their foot through it when I got it. Harry's mother used to visit with Maureen, so I asked if I could send it back to Harry, which I did. He finished it, and I've still got it to this day. It's beautiful.

I always send Harry postcards when I go on holiday. The authorities do everything they can to stop him getting out. Every time he gets near to parole, they claim he's been dealing in drugs or something. They're determined to keep him in there, which is a nonsense because he's more than done his time. Harry was a sergeant in the British army when we were fighting the Mao Mao terrorists in Kenya. He was offered the chance to be a commissioned officer in the Rhodesian army, and I bet he wishes he'd done that. His life would have been very different.

Eventually everything passes, and my time in Leicester did come to an end. I was shanghaied again, this time to Cheltenham, the fourth of the special secure units. It was a relief after Leicester. The atmosphere was relaxed and the staff were friendly: we used to play six-a-side football matches against them. Again, the screws shopped for food for us, so we had decent meals. Bruce Reynolds from the train robbery was there, and we went running together, round the exercise yard. My physical fitness level had dropped in Leicester, but I began to build it up again. Billy Gentry was there, and Charlie Kray, the brother of the twins, was there briefly.

After nine months I was on the move again, and I was finally leaving the high-security units behind. My next prison was Hull, which was about as difficult to get to as any prison in England for my family, on a par with Durham. It was diabolical moving London prisoners so far up north, but it was deliberate, to make life unpleasant. Being in Hull for me was easy enough, especially after all the years in high security. For the first couple of days it was strange being in among a large population of prisoners of all shapes and sizes. It was an eye opener: I'd been so used to being in a small group.

By now, it was impossible for me to move anywhere and not know people. As well as Bruce Reynolds, a few of the other train robbers were there: Charlie Wilson, Jimmy Hussey and Roy James. Roy Hall was there, on the same wing as me, so we set up a little betting syndicate, mainly on horse racing off the telly, but also things like wing football matches. We had community football teams: the Londoners had a team, the lads from Liverpool, Manchester, Scotland, Yorkshire – they all had teams. Again, the first thing you asked a new inmate, if he was a Londoner, was whether he could play football. The Scots lads didn't need to be asked; all the Scottish prisoners played.

The Londoners stuck together. We might have lost a few football matches but we never lost any fights, because we stuck together. No one picked on us because we were a solid group.

There was plenty of money for the betting, although the currency was always tobacco. Prisoners earned about £5 a week. Some people didn't smoke and saved all their canteen money. If they were getting bonuses for their machine work, they might save up as much as £50. I'd 'buy' it off them – I'd arrange for someone outside to send £75 to their family, in return for their £50. They felt good because they were helping out at home, and for me it meant there was plenty of money to buy luxuries. I could buy tinned salmon and chocolate biscuits, and lots of tobacco for trading.

The prison staff knew the betting was going on. It would have been hard to miss all the betting slips on the floor of the television room. But they let us get on with it because it kept everyone happy and quiet.

Roy and me needed a good stash of tobacco to cover the bets. Roy used to breed birds in his cell, budgies. He was devoted to them: he'd have magazines sent in about breeding them. The cells in Hull were relatively large, so he had huge cages, and underneath was a space where we kept the tobacco supplies. Although I didn't smoke, winning lots of tobacco meant we could exchange it for food from the canteen. Not that I was ever short of money in my whole time in prison – if ever my funds were running low I could get a message to a friend, and £100 would be paid in for me.

I got on very well with everybody in Hull. I made sure I never had to work in the workshop: I got myself a job as a cleaner which meant I could stay on the wing, and then as gym orderly, which really suited me. We had a film club, with everyone contributing a small amount of money – a couple of pence a week stopped out of our wages – and then a committee would decide which film we would see that week. John Daly, my childhood neighbour who had been with me when I was arrested as a kid for nicking a torch, was now running a successful film company and he offered to get us *The French Connection*, which was newly released and receiving lots of publicity. Unfortunately, when it arrived, it was 32mm film, and our projector was 16mm.

John, as I said before, was involved in promoting the famous Rumble in the Jungle boxing match between Muhammad Ali and George Foreman, in Africa. He sent me all the pamphlets, posters and promotional material. Billy Williams, a boxer from the East End who was known as Bill the Bomb and who was being helped out by my mate Leslie McCarthy, also used to write to me from the States, and he sent me signed photos, including one from Ali, on which he had written 'To Eddie, All the best'.

Billy had got into a bit of trouble and Les had arranged for him to go to America, where Les had boxing contacts, Chris and Angelo Dundee, who looked after Billy in Miami. He fought twelve heavy-weight contests in America and won them all, and gave exhibitions with Ali and Jimmy Ellis, another world champion. It gave me a gee, it was another window on the world for me. I didn't actually meet Bill until I came home but, later, I met him in prison during my second sentence. He was a hard man, a man you would want in your corner if you were in trouble.

There were interesting things going on in Hull. The prison ran a social studies group, and invited people to come and talk to us on Monday evenings. There would usually be five or six people, and one of them would give a talk, then we would split into small discussion groups afterwards. After such a long time in the high-security units, it was refreshing to meet so many people from outside in such an informal way. John Prescott, who is an MP for Hull, came in once. He was as good as gold, very down to earth, no problem. And a local horse trainer came in once, which was very interesting. Regulars were people like Alec Horsley, who ran Northern Dairies, and the Steigers, a Swiss couple who were also large shareholders in Northern Dairies. They were mostly Quakers, and they ran a Sunday morning meeting, as well as the Monday evening group.

Constance Saville, a lovely lady whose husband was a professor of economics at Hull University, was a regular at the Monday group, and she found interesting speakers for us. We have kept in touch ever since: Constance and her husband came to London after my release and went out to dinner with me and Maureen, and she visited me during my second spell in prison. The Steigers' daughter, Marion, met an inmate called Dougie Pidgeley, a real Cockney, and they are still together. Marion and Dougie came to my art exhibition, thirty years after I first met her and her parents in Hull. I became good

191

friends with her family, and after I was released Maureen and I spent a weekend in Hull visiting them and the Savilles. The Steigers lived in a beautiful house exquisitely furnished with antiques, in a restrained and understated way.

On one occasion we had a geezer came into the Monday group who talked about witchcraft. He was a religious bloke, and he was trying to make out that witches still existed, and were influencing life with their beliefs and their worship. I had to lay into him, verbally, because he was talking a right load of nonsense. Some of the others would just take it, they weren't that bright.

There was a good gym, and I used to weight train. Roy 'Pretty Boy' Shaw came into Hull while I was there, and I showed him round, him being a Londoner. He was a strong boy, and he was OK, not just in the gym. Mickey Williams – a big black guy – Roy and me used to work out together, lifting big weights and doing a bit of sparring. Alex Steene, the boxing promoter, used to visit Hull, and once he brought the brother of Floyd Patterson, the world champion heavyweight, up to see our gym. Patterson's brother boxed an exhibition for us against a prisoner called Paul Sykes, a big lump of a bloke who boxed professionally when he got out. Later, I got to know Alex Steene well, but this was the first time I met him. There was quite a little boxing community in Hull.

There was also a homosexual community. There was a whole network of them, which took me a while to cotton on to. I'd never experienced it in the closed units, and I've never seen it to any great degree since, in normal prisons. There are always some, and you pick up on who is involved with who: but in Hull I had to have it pointed out to me. Then I realised it was rife up there.

All the homosexuals would go and see the wing governor on our wing. They gave him info about what was going down. He never liked Londoners, always gave us a hard time. He was a real little rat.

He gave me as much aggro as he could, but then I was hardly going around pandering to authority. I certainly never found my way into his office to tell him my problems. I could settle my own affairs, without running to the staff for help, like some of them did.

The deputy governor was a Welshman called Thomson, and he was as good as gold, I got on fairly well with him. He was a man's man, into rugby: I always find men like that easier to deal with than skinny wimps.

Eventually, I managed to come off Cat A and I applied to be moved nearer to London. One of the important things about not being on Cat A is that they can't shanghai you: you have to be told where you are going, and be allowed to pack your things and prepare. So when four screws came in at six o'clock in the morning to shanghai me I said:

'I'm not a fucking Cat A man and I have things to sort out here, so fuck off.'

They hadn't come prepared for trouble, so they went away to have a talk about what they were going to do. This gave me the time I needed to pack my stuff. When the unlock came two hours later, at eight o'clock, I was let out with everyone else, which gave me the chance to rush round, see a few people, say my goodbyes and collect anything that was owed to me. I even had a collection of stuffed toys which I'd bought for my daughters: some of the prisoners used to make soft toys to keep themselves busy. I wasn't going to leave all this behind.

They didn't come back for me until lunchtime, by which time I'd sorted everything. I was hauled off to the chokey block, even though I was right about not being shanghaied. They kept me in chokey for a couple of days. The number three governor, a man called Withers, came to see me and explained that the attempt to shanghai me was nothing to do with him, but that I was going to Parkhurst, where I would get on well because Governor Thomson, the Welshman, had moved there. He talked to me properly, which is how it should have been handled in the first place.

After I left Hull the prison became more closed up and the visitors from outside were stopped. If you are inviting outsiders into a prison, it is proof that you are running it well and have nothing to hide. When the regime became more oppressive there was, inevitably, a real bad riot there, and the prison was badly damaged. But that was after I had been shipped out.

This time it wasn't such a high-profile move to Parkhurst – just a van, no police outriders. I had lost quite a lot of remission by then, after all my various problems with the prison authorities. I'd lost 450 days – a year and three months. But a new rule had been introduced allowing prisoners to reclaim lost remission. Governor Thomson was the sort of top officer who wasn't afraid to walk around the prison, talking to the inmates and staff alike. I asked him about my lost remission and he said:

'If you behave yourself, I will personally see you get a result reclaiming remission.'

I said OK. After about eight weeks I filled in a form applying for a cut and went in front of a board to answer some questions. They gave me forty-two days back, which was disappointing. I spoke to Thomson about it, and he said:

'You've only been here a few weeks. Keep your head down and you'll get a result. Just wait.'

So, after the minimum six-month wait between applications, I reapplied and went before the board again. I argued that my record of causing problems had been in my early days in prison, that I had always been held in high-security units which were breeding grounds for trouble, and that this was my very first prison sentence. This time I was given 300 days back. Great! A real result. Near enough a year. It was a relief to me.

As usual, I found myself a good job. I was one of three inmates working in the compound stores, which meant loading up vans with things that were leaving the prison, and unloading stuff, like workshop materials, that came in. Two mates of mine, Billy Grimwood from Liverpool and Kenny Bloom, the long-firm king, were working there and when a vacancy came up they got me in. There were two civilians working there, too, and we all played bridge. So when our little bit of work was done for the day we'd get a bridge four going, with the civilians taking it in turns to join us.

Bill Grimwood was the prisoners' representative, which meant that he went to see the governors or the chief (the highest grade of uniformed officer) when inmates had grievances, and tried to sort them out before they led to trouble.

When he left, I took on the job. Most of the problems I had to deal with were over visits. I'd exaggerate the risk of trouble:

'Look, chief, we can't have this going on. The lads don't like it and there will be trouble if you don't sort it.' It worked a treat.

After I got my remission restored I applied for parole, but I got knocked back. The governor did everything he could, and he told me he would get me transferred to Pentonville to go on the hostel scheme. It wasn't as good as parole, but it was second best.

I was able to leave Parkhurst more or less a free man. I could travel on my own, for the first time in many years. My family, my mum and everyone were making plans to come down to the Isle of Wight to meet me. But I got a few words of advice from some of the others lads inside, and they said the best way was to slip out quietly, get the ferry and the train back to London and meet up with them all at Waterloo. It was good advice, because it gave me a little bit of time to adjust. I had a nice bit of breakfast on the train, watched the world go past the windows, enjoyed some time on my own. There was another fella released at the same time as me, and he went straight into the bar on the train and was paralytic by the time we got to London. Not me. I savoured every minute of that journey.

So for the last six months of my sentence I was at Pentonville, in the hostel. It was a separate building, within the prison. For the first four weeks you had to spend weekends there, but you were allowed out to work every day. I had to have a job to go out to, which the prison were supposed to fix up, but my name and notorious reputation went before me and all the firms they approached refused to have me. I asked John Daly if he could find me something. He couldn't fix me up himself, but he arranged for me to be a van driver for Terry Mills at A. J. Bull, a demolition and rubbish clearance company.

John and Terry were good mates, and I knew Terry from before I was inside. He was as good as gold, he paid me £25 a week to be a van driver. It wasn't a lot of money, even then, but it was reasonable. My wage packet had to be handed in to the hostel, and the rule was that at the end of my six months they would deduct money for my board and lodgings, and I would have the rest.

I didn't actually do any work for Terry, but when the prison officials came round to check up, he always said I was out on the van. In those days there were no mobile phones, so they couldn't keep tabs on me. Then Terry would ring to tip me off that they were checking. I spent my days meeting up with mates, catching up with my family, sorting myself out.

After a few weeks the authorities insisted that I had to earn more, as my wage packet wasn't even covering my accommodation costs: either find another job or get a rise. I explained this to Terry and he gave me a fiver rise. Terry was fantastic: he gave me real help when I needed it. I wasn't supposed to have a car, so I always parked two bus stops away from the hostel, and arrived back by bus. We had to be in the hostel by eight o'clock in the evening, but after the first four

I built up a close friendship with the late prison reform campaigner Lord Longford, who was as pleased as anything with my portrait of him. I was delighted when he came to my niece Susan's wedding *(below)*

I got involved in buying and selling pornographic magazines. Here I am on a business trip to Las Vegas with my brother-in-law Paul *(right)* and Chico

The end of a good dinner: a convivial moment with Frankie Fraser, Charlie *(right)* and other associates. Relations between my brother and me wouldn't always be this friendly...

My dear old mum *(left)* in the box above the Queen at a Royal Variety performance in the eighties. She went along as guest of boxing promoter Alex Steene *(in the shades)*

With my great friends Joan Harris and Jimmy Jeffries

One of the two murals I painted at Long Lartin prison. I think they're both still there

The cover I drew for the *New Law Journal*, illustrating an article they ran about the high rates of prison suicides

Jimmy Jeffries visits me in Parkhurst prison

In October 2003 I had my first private showing of my art. This was the painting I used on the invitations

Lots of my old pals turned up to support me – some even bought paintings! *Left to right:* Tommy Wisbey, Frankie Fraser, Tommy Harris and Rene Wisbey

Actor and genuine East Ender Steven Berkoff has also encouraged me in my art

Some of my work.
These days I don't
get to paint as
often as I'd like

With sister Elaine
and half-brother Chas
in Spain last year

Kenny Bloom –
once king of the long
firms, now retired –
helps me celebrate
my 65th birthday

Hervé Photo

Today, I would not like to meet
the likes of me as I was then

weeks we could spend weekends at home. We cooked our own food – fry-ups, a bit of steak, something like that. We had our own little housewife, too: 'Mary', a gay guy who dressed up as a woman, was on the hostel scheme at the same time as me. I saw Mary again, years later, in prison.

Finally, in August 1976, I was released. I had been inside for ten years and a few months.

TWELVE

'THIS MAN HAS A GOOD WORK ETHIC'

The first and most important thing on my mind when I got out was to get a business cracking away again. I wanted to work, I was hungry to get on with it. I was forty-one years old, and I needed to earn money, but I also needed to be busy.

I have always worked hard. A woman probation officer, writing a report on me when I was up for parole, said: 'This man has a very good work ethic.' She was bang on right.

I've never been afraid of getting up in the morning and getting on with whatever needs doing. But the question, after such a long time in jail, was what? I had no money, apart from the £10,000 I was given by a group of well-respected friends, who took me out to lunch and gave me a grand each. Atlantic Machines had long since gone by the board, but a friend of mine had an interest in a couple of shops selling pornography. I went in with him, and we opened a shop in Earls Court. After a few months, we needed someone to run it, so my sister's boyfriend Paul (now her husband) agreed to take it on.

In no time at all he was doing well. I've always been good at recruiting the right person for the right role, and Paul was perfect. I can eye people up, test them out psychologically, and I'm not often wrong. It's a skill I had before prison, but ten years cooped up with other people makes you an even more acute observer of human nature. Paul's a good man, always has been.

The shop, which was a good size, was in Hogarth Place, near Earls Court Road. Magazines were very big sellers, especially exclusive ones from Los Angeles or Holland, because the laws were more liberal there. Lots of money changed hands – there was a big mark-up. Some of them cost £15 a piece, which would be £60 today. There was quite a big gay community living near that shop, and they have a lot of spare cash to spend because they don't have to worry about wives and children. They've only got their pricks to keep. So we had a large gay section, with gay bondage and sex aids.

It was vital to keep all the different sections separate: men who were looking for big tits (they were known as bounce magazines) didn't want to associate with blokes with rubber fetishes, or those who wanted magazines with pictures of women with whips and high leather boots. It was unbelievable what some people were into, but you soon get to understand the business. You don't feel repulsed by their strange habits, because it's what's bringing the money in. But it was a good game trying to work out who would go to which section – sometimes it would be a real surprise. We drew the line firmly at child porn and anything involving animals.

We sold all sorts of magazines, but we got to know a guy called Chico, who had a shop in Paddington which catered for people with really bizarre tastes, mainly coprophilia. Chico asked if me and Paul wanted to go on a buying trip to the States with him, which we did, of course. It was a working holiday, with more emphasis on the holiday than the work. We flew to Los Angeles, and Chico's contact, who sold him lots of these really weirdo magazines, took us to his house in Beverly Hills. There's money in strange perversions, because he was living next door to Warren Beatty, and the view from his magnificent garden, with an illuminated fountain, was across the whole of LA.

He was giving us a drink and he said to me: 'Do you want some coke?'

I thought he meant Coca Cola to mix with my scotch, so I said: 'No, American dry ginger, please.'

Paul and Chico fell about laughing. The guy took his hat off and pulled out a slim, pencil-like tube, from which he poured a line of coke. I didn't snort any: drugs have never been my scene. I've tried coke once and it did nothing for me. Same with cannabis.

From LA we hired a big American car and drove across the desert to Las Vegas. Despite everyone warning us to be careful with the speed, we did 100mph the whole way. We looked around for a hotel and pulled into one that looked OK, the Hotel Riviera. We booked in and the guy organising the valet parking asked us what kind of car we had.

'It's a big red American one,' said Paul.

'They're all big, they're all American, and quite a lot of them are red, sir,' said the parking guy.

Chico's pal in LA had arranged for us to meet a photographer who was going to find us a few girls. He showed us a load of pictures he'd taken, and we each chose one. He said they weren't brasses (prostitutes) but that they were good fun, and out for a good time.

When we met them, Paul's and Chico's were fine. But mine, who had looked perfectly well proportioned in the picture, turned out to be tiny and very young looking. We were in the famous Dunes hotel, and the Top of the Dunes nightclub was the place to go. This little girl kept grabbing my hand and pulling me on to the dance floor, but I felt embarrassed. I thought it made me look kinky, like some of our customers, as if I was into schoolgirls or something.

Another evening in Las Vegas was spent at the Desert Inn, where I left Chico and Paul while I played pontoon for a while on the gaming tables. When I returned they had a girl sitting with them. As soon as I joined them she started giving me some:

'You, you'd better not think you're leaving here tonight without me.'

She was giving me all this, very bossy, trying to tell me what I should be doing. I'd never met the girl before so I started out being polite, but she was being so heavy with me, on and on, that in the end I had to tell her to fuck off.

Then I noticed the other two were trying their best not to laugh. Seems that while I was away they told this girl that what I liked was women who dominated me, and that she was to take no notice of what I said, but to keep bossing me about because secretly I loved it.

When she realised she'd been set up she turned her sharp tongue on them, and gave them a right going over.

From Las Vegas we went on to San Francisco, to meet more magazine publishers. San Francisco is the gay capital of the US, so we ordered gay mags there. Back home, when we realised what a good market there was for magazines, we started printing our own copies of them: I found a printer who could reproduce them. At first, when I realised I had to order 1000 copies to make it worthwhile, I worried about shifting them, but it was no problem. We could swap them with other shops – we might give them a hundred heterosexual bondage magazines in return for a hundred gay ones, for example.

But then we hit on an even bigger money spinner. We had booths built out at the back of our shop, all kitted out properly, with up-to-date screens, and for fifty pence in a slot the punter could choose a film to watch for a minute. He could feed another fifty pence in and get another minute, and so on. There were gay ones and heterosexual ones, and they were very popular. We kept a big stock of fifty pence pieces, and they'd cash up fivers and tenners and feed the lot into the slot.

Again, it occurred to me that we'd make more money if we made our own films. We would hire a hotel room for the night, and get all the cameras, lights and performers in there. Then we'd get the films printed and we sold them off. There were always people willing to star in the films, we never had to employ actors. We just bunged them a few quid and they were off, at it, in front of the cameras. I went along once to watch them doing it, but it wasn't my kind of thing.

There was one embarrassing situation where a fella asked me to put the money up for a gay film he was making. When it was finished he laid on a venue for a private showing, a cinema in Soho. We got there to find the place was full of gays, loads of them. Me and Paul were the only straight blokes there.

The key to financial success was, like with the magazines, swapping, so that you had a changing selection of films for regular customers. There were no videos back then, it was all film reels. You'd swap ten of yours for ten of theirs. You might even sell five on. But the main aim was to keep the booths at the back well supplied, as they were very good money makers.

Most of the original magazines and films came in from Amsterdam. The wholesalers in Amsterdam arranged for lorry drivers to bring them into Britain, hidden under their seats or wherever. We would pay them at this end. The lorry drivers liked it: it was much better than smuggling drugs, because if they did get caught the sentences would be much lighter.

While he was running the shop Paul was arrested for selling pornography. We thought he would get off, because at the time the law was very muddled about what constituted pornography, and what was OK. I went along to see his court case, expecting to walk out with him as a free man. I went with a girlfriend, and while the case was on we found an empty solicitor's room and, one way and another, we missed the case. We walked out to see Paul being led away in handcuffs. The judge had sentenced him to a month in prison, a bit sheepishly, because he obviously didn't think Paul should be put away, but apparently there had been a statement from Mr Justice Lawton (the same one who had presided over the torture trial) saying that all pornographers should be sent to jail.

Paul served eighteen days of his sentence. While he was inside I sent him a telegram, because if you get a telegram the screws have to read it out to you. So I said:

'You've been offered three quarters of a million for your shares in Bradshaws, do you want to sell?' I did it to wind the screws up. Paul was sharing his cell with a gypsy lad who couldn't read, and was very impressed because Paul took a newspaper every day. 'I knew you were a millionaire,' he said.

We made lots of jokes about Paul's eighteen days. When we went on a visit to Charlie in Parkhurst, Reggie Kray came over to say hello and we said:

'This one's just done eighteen,' so Reggie and the other prisoners on visits were all shaking his hand and congratulating him. They thought he'd done eighteen years.

Once we got the hang of making films, we decided to make a straight one. John Daly encouraged us.

'If you can make a film, Ed, I'll put it out with one of my major productions.'

Looking back, I think he was just being friendly – I don't think he ever expected us to do it. We decided to make a thirty-five-minute documentary about torture through the ages. It was going to be set in the London Dungeon, and we had an actor lined up to do the voiceover. The woman who ran the London Dungeon agreed, so we hired all the technical crew, lighting people, cameramen and everything, and we turned up early in the morning to get cracking while there were no visitors to the Dungeon. But when we arrived, the same woman who had agreed to it refused to let us in. She said she believed we were going to make a porn movie. The film production company offices were above a sex shop in Paddington and she'd checked out the address and decided not to give us access.

We were lumbered. It was costing a lot of money, all paid for by the hour. So, instead, my friend Leslie McCarthy came up with the idea of making a film about Soho. In Soho, there's a whole industry beneath the surface, and we filmed everyone from chocolate makers to gunsmiths, finishing with the familiar bright lights of the clubs and restaurants at night. We filmed the cabaret at the Latin Quarter, where the owner, Peter Tolaini, was delighted to let us in. We even interviewed a wino, living on the streets. It turned out to be a good, lively little film, thirty-five minutes long, which we called *Chameleon Soho*. We had a good soundtrack, and the actor's voiceover: it really worked.

John Daly put it out with a film called *The Passage*, in which Anthony Quinn starred as a resistance worker smuggling people through the mountains under the nose of the Gestapo. It was quite a violent film, and not a big box office success. We were supposed to be on six per cent of what it took, and we wanted to get the money back for what we'd laid out. Leslie had put up most of it. Leslie badgered John and his secretary about the money, which was the wrong tactic. I was not long out of prison and my business skills were a bit rusty, but I think Leslie misjudged it and put too much pressure on John. Eventually, John gave us a promissory note for £15,000, which we would get in a year's time. It was disappointing because it meant that our careers as film makers were over, but we did make a tidy little profit. It soured my relationship with John a bit, although we have remained friends.

We decided after this that the film business was not going to be our future. Although I was making money from the Earls Court shop, I always wanted to get back into the metal trade. It was what I knew, what I was good at, and it was a straight business. I didn't like having to bung the police, which we had to do in the porn trade. The money that flowed through West End Central police station would have run a small country: many were crooked, and everyone in the porn business was paying them. The police weren't paid a fortune, so some of them looked for extras. I always found it painful dealing with them. Over the years I've spent a lot of money with the police, getting relatives out of trouble. I had to do it, but I didn't enjoy it.

Many criminals join the Masons, and end up playing golf with the police: they do it to earn themselves a few favours, to get in with the right people. I never joined the Masons, although I was asked to on many occasions. But I was always happy to go along to social events, ladies' nights. As far as I was concerned, the time, money and effort put into getting on could be better spent elsewhere.

My partner in the shop wasn't too pleased about me going back into the metal business, because I didn't need a partner. So I told nobody about it until it was set up. Soon after I came out of prison Stan Woods, who was very well known in the metal trade and had dealings with me before I went down, asked to see me. He said:

'Ed, if you can find premises you want to buy, I will help you with the money.' He said he knew I was genuine.

So I started looking, and I saw an opportunity advertised in

Reclamation Weekly – a business in Greenwich for sale for £27,000, with a lease of £1000 per annum. I went to see Stan, and he agreed to back me when I got a £15,000 overdraft from the bank. I got the rest of the money from Stan, who kept the deeds. Within three years I had paid off both him and the bank and had the deeds back in my possession. As soon as I took over I increased the door trade.

The most important contract that the previous owner, Ken Shirley, had was to handle all the scrap from the building of the Thames Barrier. It really took off. At one stage I had thirty-two skips on both sides of the river, and I would hire barges and flatback lorries because some of the metal was too big for skips. We could get ninety-five tons on a barge, and we'd send them down the river to unload them. I was paying a lot less than the metal bulletin price: if, for example, the list price was £40 a ton, I'd be paying £35. It fluctuated, but there was always a very good profit in it.

The Thames Barrier, which they started building in 1974, lined a lot of pockets before it was finished in 1982. The crane drivers were making a fortune, and they were always striking for more. Everyone seemed to have a piece of it.

This was at the time when the whole of London's docklands area was ripe for development, and there was money to be made from buying up warehouses along the river. I had a good mate called Paddy Onions, who I met at North Kent Squash Club, where we were both members. (Paddy's real name was O'Nione, but everyone called him Onions.) He was a wheeler dealer, he knew everyone and he could sell anything. He dealt in damaged stock. Paddy could shift dented tins of tomatoes, all sorts of things. You name it, Paddy could find a market for it. He was a lovely man, with a great sense of fun, always playing practical jokes.

Paddy was renting a warehouse to store the goods he picked up. He came to see me one day and told me about a warehouse in New

Caledonia Wharf, with a big river frontage. It was owned by Corry and Co, a company that was well known along the river. Paddy's small warehouse was next door, and he knew the man who managed the property, David Patterson, who had worked for the National Dock Labour Board for over twenty years. Corry's had offered the warehouse to Patterson at the knockdown price of £275,000. He approached Paddy, and in turn Paddy spoke to me.

I could see it was a golden opportunity to make some money, so I bought a shell company called Stalkdean Ltd, making sure that in its articles of association it included wide references to renting, buying, letting and selling property, as well as building. I installed Paddy, Patterson and myself as directors, and then set about trying to get the money to buy the warehouse.

I wasn't financially strong enough to raise this kind of money, so I went to see my old mate Terry Mills, who had helped me out with my hostel job. Terry sent his bankers round to value it, and they reckoned it was worth £400,000. So we were in business. Terry came on to the board as a director, with a twenty-five per cent share: equal to mine, Paddy's and Patterson's. We didn't have to put any money upfront because the bank loaned it to us, and we had to repay at about £60,000 a year.

We had tenants lined up even before we finalised the deal, and as soon as we owned the warehouse we started renting out parts of it, so that straightaway we were bringing in £75,000 a year in rent. We had to make the repayments of £60,000, but we were well covered. Patterson continued running it for us (the whole of the river and docks were unionised, and Patterson was in the union), and we paid him a decent wage of £10,000 a year and provided him with a car. It was a great investment.

The company was registered at Terry's offices in Mitcham, and we bought some more premises in Verney Road, Rotherhithe.

Then Paddy decided he wanted to sell his share, and under our agreement he had to offer it first to his fellow directors. Terry Mills bought it for one of his directors for £60,000. It was all going well, until a terrible tragedy happened: Paddy Onions was murdered. That brought the police crawling all over us, and the other directors panicked.

Paddy's death was part of a chain of events which started at a boxing night at an amateur club in Bermondsey. I wasn't there, but from what I've heard there was a big fight. Peter Hennessy, the one who fought me in the Mr Smith's affair, was involved. (He was never charged with the Mr Smith's case, because we never gave his name to anyone.) Hennessy was drunk, and he was going round collecting money for a boys' club. He went off on one about someone not giving him enough. Anyway, it ended with him being stabbed to death, and the police were after Paddy for it. Paddy didn't do it, but he was on the table that had the argument with Hennessy, and was involved in some verbal with him.

After Paddy was arrested the case was thrown out. But someone thought he'd killed Hennessy, because a gun was fired through his living-room window. I said I would get it straightened out, which I could have done, but Paddy didn't want to do that. He was too much of a gentleman. But a month or two later a contract killer turned up as he was walking out of the wine bar, near Tower Bridge, which he bought with the money from the warehouse. Wallop, wallop, Paddy's dead. The gunman, a lowlife called Jimmy Davey, was nicked, but he died in police custody at a police station in Coventry. The police claimed he attacked a cop as he was being taken from his cell for interview.

Paddy's death was a great shame, because he was a lovely guy. I sold loads of tickets at £50 a time for a benefit for his widow. Anyone who knew him was happy to buy a stack of them, because they knew it was a good cause.

The whole affair caused a lot of aggravation. The police were looking into Paddy's affairs, and the questions being asked were enough to unnerve my wealthy partners. They were straight people, with lots of money, and they were shitting themselves at all this attention from the boys in blue. The police frightened them, and they wanted to sell the property, probably because of me, although they were too polite to say so.

I didn't want to sell. Patterson had made himself busy and had planning permission to turn the top two floors into residential property: when you look at the way Docklands has subsequently been developed, and how prestigious the addresses there have become, we could have made a fortune. Even then, I reckoned the premises were worth well over a million. But we were under pressure so I agreed to sell when they found a buyer, Selective Estates from Jersey, who were willing to put up £750,000. It was still a great profit. The deal was done and was just about to go through when the main man at Selective Estates spotted my name on the letterhead and asked Patterson:

'Is that Eddie Richardson from Greenwich?'

When Patterson said 'yes', he was amazed. We'd just come back from a skiing holiday in Mirabel together, with some other mates: it was Johnnie Parry. We'd never talked business while we were away on holiday having a lot of fun, so neither of us had any idea that we were in the middle of a business deal together. Johnnie was sound, a good man. It was too late to do a deal under the table, which was a shame. Johnnie turned up to our meeting in his new red Bentley: he had lots of money, most of it from laundering the money from Brinks Mat, the bullion robbery where £26 million in gold was taken from a warehouse at Heathrow, which had happened two or three years earlier.

Johnnie was later on the trot for a while from the money-laundering charge – I remember him coming to see me with a beard. But it wasn't until 1992 that he was done for laundering over four million of the Brinks Mat money, and he got ten years. The only two who went down for the actual robbery were Brian Robertson and Micky McAvoy. I served time with both of them, later. They could have done a deal on the sentence, by returning some of the gold, but the others weren't having it, and while they were inside they were both ripped off. The two who should have been looked after, who were doing the time for the rest of them, got cut out of the money.

I knew another one of the Brinks Mat mob. I was out with him one night, just before the Brinks Mat job went down, and at the end of the evening my brother-in-law Paul agreed to give him and a couple of girls a lift home. One of them was a barmaid for Micky Connolly, a publican I knew. Paul didn't know the girls, but he was taking this bloke to Lordship Lane and they needed to be dropped off on the way, so he crammed them into the back of his Mercedes sports car. The bloke, who was out of his head drunk, started being rude to them and they were giving him some back. They were in the back of the car, and when Paul stopped to drop one of them out, the bloke had to get out because it was a two-door motor. As she got out he pulled a tool out and stabbed her. It was outrageous. He stabbed a girl. You don't do that kind of thing.

Then the whole thing went off. Her lung was punctured and her mother was going off alarming. I had a few people coming round to me to see if I could straighten it. They were very anxious to get the bloke in the clear. I realise now, they were about to do Brinks Mat, and he'd nearly fucked the whole thing up. They put up the money and I negotiated with her family and Micky Connolly. It was a very delicate situation, but in the end she didn't nick him. She did recover eventually.

I was happy to sort it out. I know lots of people, and if anyone can gct things done, I will manage it, even though, at the time, I didn't realise the importance of keeping the bloke out of nick. He may have escaped being done for Brinks Mat but he's inside now, doing twenty-two years for cocaine smuggling.

At the time we sold the first warehouse to Johnnie Parry, our company also owned one in Rotherhithe. It had been owned by a mate of Terry Mills's, Freddie Simmons, who was in the waste paper business. He wanted to release some cash, so we bought it and rented some of it back to him, and the rest to others. It wasn't costing us anything: we were covering all our mortgage and expenses with the rent. The company wanted out after the Paddy Onions affair, so this one had to be sold as well. This time, Johnnie Parry and me were able to do a deal under the table.

It was at these Rotherhithe premises that another of the Brinks Mat men, Brian Perry, was later shot dead. I'm not making any accusations about that, I don't know anything about it. He had a lot of enemies, so it was a problem for the police to know who was responsible for his murder.

When we heard about a nightclub coming up for sale, my brother-in-law Paul and me were up for it. I heard about it from a neighbour who lived in the same close as me in Chislehurst, and I knew him because my daughter was friendly with his daughter. He was a friend of John French, who owned the successful J. Arthur's club in Chelsea. He'd opened another club with the same name in Catford, but it hadn't taken off and he'd closed it down. Paul and I had a look, we spoke to the old licensee who was willing to carry on, and we reckoned we could make it work. We met to do the deal at Brown's Hotel, where all drinks served are doubles. We were there all afternoon, and then went on to Tokyo Joe's, where my neighbour, not used to this level of drinking, fell down three flights of stairs.

After we bought the lease we spent money doing the club up. It was on the first and second floor of the building, in Catford Broadway. We set up a disco on the top floor and a piano bar below it. I bought a beautiful white piano, and Ian Gomes was our resident pianist. He's a class act. He now plays at the Palm Court in the Ritz. He has an incredible vocabulary of music and can play any request. I saw him at the Ritz recently, and he remembers me. I got him to play a couple of tunes.

A mate of mine, Johnny Parker, installed the disco, and we had a series of different DJs. The kids paid £3 to come in for the disco nights, and there would be a long queue of them on Fridays and Saturdays, waiting to get in. We also made a nice profit from the drinks and from the food, which was made in our own kitchens by an Italian woman. Once a month we put on big shows, with famous names like Lonnie Donegan, Jimmy Jones, Joe Longthorne, Georgie Fame and many others. The price of the ticket included a buffet. It was a thriving business, well run, and we made a few quid over the years that we had it. The manager at my metal yard, Alan Martin, took the money at the door.

Then one Thursday night, it all went wrong. Roy Hall managed it on Thursday nights – he was out of prison before I was. Thursday was not a big night, we didn't even charge the kids to get in. I'd be there every Friday and Saturday, but it would have been too exhausting to do it every night, so Roy used to cover for me.

On this night two brothers had an argument with another fella upstairs, and a fight broke out. One of them ran downstairs to the kitchen and got a knife, and stabbed and killed one of the brothers. The police were soon swarming all over the club, and that was the kiss of death. The cops were angry that our staff – the barmaids and doormen – were, naturally, saying that they had seen nothing. The parents of the victim were going off alarming. I wasn't even there when it happened, but my name was put right in it. These two brothers were bad news, but there was nothing I could do about it afterwards.

(A few years ago I bumped into the boy who used the knife. I was in a pub in Greenwich and he came across to introduce himself. I didn't know him from Adam, but he knew who I was, and he told me he was the one who got nicked. He said how sorry he was. I said he should be sorry for ruining my business. He got three years for manslaughter, and after he came out he was working for a construction company. He wasn't a bad kid, and he seemed to be making sense of his life. If he'd got a longer sentence he might not have found it so easy to get work, and it might have ruined him for life.)

For two years J. Arthur's had been a very well-run business, and we had a good relationship with one of the local police inspectors. We'd buy him a drink now and again, but we weren't bunging him anything. But after the stabbing a new inspector took over, a real bastard who hated my guts. Our licence was taken away and we had to shut down.

The only thing to do was sell it. There was no way the police were going to allow me to run it, and my name was on the lease. But selling it was impossible: every time anyone else applied for a licence, the police opposed it by saying: 'He's working for Richardson.' The whole thing nearly ruined me, because I had paid £80,000 (more than £300,000 in today's money), all straight money, for a 120-year lease, but it was a diabolical lease. You could hardly move up there without permission from the landlord. The guy downstairs in the chip shop was the landlord, but he'd only been able to buy the freehold with my help. I managed to get planning permission for a change of use so that it could be used as offices, which would be even more lucrative than the nightclub, and I was about to start the conversion work when I was arrested.

After I was inside, some Turks bought the freehold, and planned to use the chip shop part as a venue for Turkish weddings. They tried to claim I hadn't done repairs I was supposed to do, and they claimed this gave them the right to seize the property as I had reneged on the lease. In fact, the only repair needed was the installation of a new fire escape, because they had taken the old one away when they converted the chip shop downstairs. It went to court, and we won.

After that, they decided to negotiate. One of a well-known Turkish family became their intermediary, and went to see Paul, my brother-in-law, and I decided to settle for £10,000 in cash. I couldn't sell it to them because it was listed among my assets for the court case I was embroiled in. So I told them the way to do it was to take me to court and claim the lease, and this time I wouldn't fight it. We went through the motions and they were given the right to confiscate the property, and I was to get my ten grand under the table. I had a lot on my plate at the time, so it was handy. Except that they took money off for the solicitor, and I ended up getting only seven, which was a right liberty. The building upstairs has been empty ever since, which is a shame as it is a lovely property.

Throughout these years I was working exceptionally hard. I was at the scrapyard at eight o'clock in the morning to open up, and while J. Arthur's was in business I was there until late several nights of the week. If I wasn't at the club, I was usually out socialising. I was getting four or five hours' sleep a night but I was able to handle it, so I thought. Maybe, in the end, it would have been better if I hadn't tried to do so much.

While I was getting on with life and establishing myself as a businessman with all these overlapping ventures, Charlie was still in prison. I visited him regularly. By 1980 he had served fourteen years, and had been turned down for parole seven times. He'd worked his way through the system and was in a Cat C prison, Springhill, near Aylesbury. He'd been studying sociology with the Open University for a few years, and he'd got five of the six credits he needed for a degree. It was obvious he was going to get out in the not-too-distant future, but Charlie had had enough. In May 1980 he decided to go on the run.

It isn't too difficult to escape from an open prison, but Charlie messed up the first attempt. Paul went to pick him up, as arranged, and waited for about three hours, but Charlie never showed. Turned out he'd had a farewell party and had stayed longer than he should, so by the time he got out it was just in time to see the car pulling away from the rendezvous. So then he had to get back in. When he rang the next day it was typical Charlie, trying to put the blame on us for not waiting longer. We went down again the next day, and this time he came out at the right time. So now I had Charlie on my plate.

He stayed the first night at my dad's, then I found him a flat. He wanted to go to Paris, so I fixed up a phoney passport for him, and then after some weeks he moved on to Spain. I never stopped heaving money at him. Charlie even persuaded me to give my time and help to a journalist called Robert Parker who wanted to write a book about him – other members of the family were interviewed as well. Charlie believed the book would help him get parole but, in the end, the book was not on Charlie's side at all and he was furious about it. I tried, unsuccessfully, to get it stopped. Parker did, however, reveal that witnesses at our torture trial had lied: one of them gave a signed statement to the *Observer* newspaper (where Parker worked) saying that evidence about Jimmy Taggart being beaten up was grossly exaggerated, and Norman Bickers signed an affidavit stating that his injuries had also been made to sound much worse than they were, and did not involve any torture.

The National Council for Civil Liberties followed this up, and a lawyer working for them called for my case to be reconsidered by the Home Office. The *Sunday Times* took the case up, and even published a long piece headlined 'The "other" Richardson – was he wrongly jailed?', which made out a case for me by going into details of the corrupt evidence given at the trial, and the fact that my appeal had been turned down, wrongly.

I feel now as I did then. In August 1980 I told the *Sunday Times*:
'I can't get the years back now whatever happens.'

I wasn't the only one giving interviews to journalists. Charlie was holding court, talking to reporters from all the national papers about how he was compiling a dossier for his next parole attempt. He was photographed in Paris, and the picture was used across the front pages of newspapers at home. Questions were asked in the House of Commons as to how the press seemed able to find him, but the police couldn't. Charlie loved it all.

He wrote a letter defending his right to parole, and it was described in *The Times* as having 'considerable eloquence' and in the *Guardian* as 'articulate'. Bernard Levin decided to pull it to pieces in *The Times*, repeating all the old myths about torture, so I wrote to the paper. They published my letter, which demolished the stories that Levin was perpetuating, and concluded with a defence of Charlie's university studies in prison: Levin described filling his head with sociology as 'the crime fated to go forever unpunished'.

'What would Mr Levin have wanted him to fill his head with in the confines of the prison, surrounded by thieves, robbers, rapists and murderers?' I wrote.

After a couple of months of courting so much publicity, Charlie quietened down, and found that he could move back to London and live quite openly without the police collaring him. It was quite remarkable: he was supposed to be the most wanted man in Britain, yet nobody seemed too bothered about catching him. He was living just up the road from our old man, with a girl he'd hooked up with.

It was while he was on the trot that a mate of mine, Kenny Bloom, offered to sell me a boat which he had down at Southampton. It was a thirty-two-foot Norwegian motor boat called *Oceana*, with five berths and a top speed of more than thirty knots. I had a good look, and decided to buy it for £9500. I thought it would be useful to get Charlie away if I needed to, so I decided to motor it round to Dover. My brother-in-law Paul was game to come, and my mate Harry Rawlings: Harry was the only one of us who actually knew a bit about sailing and navigation as he'd sailed a boat over to Spain once.

We picked the boat up, and after a four-hour delay over a fault, we set off. It was cold and windy, and we only had two life jackets – we were going to buy a third one but it was so expensive we decided to take a chance. My coat was wet, so I was wearing one life jacket to keep warm, and Harry had the other one. We set off and got quite a long way along the coast. We'd filled up to the top with fuel before we started, but we didn't realise there was a blowback in the fuel pipe, so every time we checked the gauge it still read full.

We were starting to enjoy ourselves – we had some nice music playing from the sound system in the galley, and we could take it in turns to have a rest. We were eleven miles out to sea when one of the engines packed up, followed within minutes by the other one.

'Fucking hell, we're in the middle of a fucking shipping lane,' Harry said.

We got on to the radio and put out a mayday signal, and eventually the coastguard answered. We had to give them our location, so Harry told them we were about half a mile from a buoy that was fourteen feet high – it turned out we were actually two miles from it and it was forty feet high. Those buoys all emit different signals, so it was possible to pinpoint which one we were near.

We had to wait two or three hours before anyone came out to us.

Oceana was a light, fibreglass boat, and we were bobbing about in the waves with big tankers and other vessels passing nearby.

'I wish we'd bought that other fucking lifejacket,' Paul said.

Eventually an RAF launch arrived, but they wouldn't tow us in. They stayed with us until the lifeboat arrived, with a coastguard on board. One of the lifeboat men came on board, and that's when we discovered the fuel tanks were empty: he explained to us about blowback. The lifeboat crew are all volunteers, and they were good lads. I was chatting to one who came originally from Denmark Hill.

'. . . then I found a new model, and moved down here,' he said.

He suggested we meet up later for a drink at a nice little pub in Chichester. We had a whip round for the crew and gave them £80 to have a drink on us. The fella from Denmark Hill warned us about the coastguard:

'That bastard would shop his own mother,' he said.

I told them how we came to buy the boat, and I had the bill of sale on me, all legal.

'So we ain't got no worries,' I said. 'It's not like we're using false names or doing anything we shouldn't be doing.'

The lifeboat towed us as far as the mouth of Chichester harbour then transferred the line to a fishing boat which towed us into the harbour. Just as the harbour wall came into view we could see that the Old Bill was there – police cars, dogs, the lot. They were very excited, all buzzing. We were moored up against two police launches. They put us in the cells underneath the harbour master's offices, then they turned over the boat with the dogs. We had done nothing wrong, and we had nothing to hide, so we weren't worried until they came back saying they had found a substance on board that would have to be analysed.

Harry went crazy:

'You dirty fucking bastards. You've fitted us up!' he shouted.

I was worried in case the previous owner of the boat had left something behind which shouldn't have been there.

They took us to Chichester police station and slung us in a cell, all three of us together. Harry was still going off on one, yelling at them about fitting us up. We didn't sleep, and all through the night the peephole in the door kept opening and someone would stare in at us. At about four o'clock in the morning we were taken out of the cells. They told us that the substance they found was silica gel, which is used a lot on board ships to absorb damp: I think they only took it as a moody to keep us in custody. They let us go, and we had to hang around on the station until the trains to London started running, and when we got back we had breakfast on Waterloo station. I think the police thought at first they had caught Charlie, and that was why they kept peering at us. It must have been a disappointment for them that it was only me.

A couple of weeks later I found myself another captain, a friend of a friend who worked for an oil company, and this time I bought the petrol myself, from a mate of mine, and put in enough to get us to the marina pumps. Every time I went out on that boat something went wrong. We got to Dungeness, which is noted for its rough seas, but this was a big one even by normal standards. We were bobbing about like a cork, going uphill and downhill with the waves. I wanted to get nearer the shore, because I was calculating how far I could swim, but the captain said it would be worse closer to land.

'I'll feel safer, even if it is worse,' I told him.

Luckily, the sea grew calmer and we were able to carry on to Dover. I couldn't wait to get on to dry land, but the captain told me we had to wait because the signals were against us. If I'd been on my own I'd have carried on and we'd have hit the huge ferry which came out of the harbour minutes later – we wouldn't have stood a chance.

Ultimately, we never used the boat to move Charlie. After all, it was hardly a secret possession: the police knew I had it. I did take it out a few more times, but there were always problems. Me and two mates drove down to move it to Ramsgate, but I could see that the sea was a bit rough. They said:

'Don't worry. Where did Nelson come from?'

They were giving me all this verbal. But when we got out there, and it was blowing a gale, and they were turning green, I said:

'Where's Nelson come from?'

When we finally got to Ramsgate the marina was deserted. But as we struggled in, crashing against other boats, there were suddenly loads of people there, trying to help us do the least possible damage.

After three really hairy trips, I was no longer very enthusiastic about being a boat owner. It was expensive, too, as I had to pay mooring fees. We did use the boat a few more times, but what put the lid on it was when I went to Brighton, where it was berthed, to go fishing with Roy Hall. One minute it was a beautiful day and the next, when I came up from the berths below, we were shrouded in sea mist. We eventually got back into harbour, by following the sound of the harbour hooter and then tagging on behind a fishing boat. That was enough for me: I put the *Oceana* up for sale. I actually made a small profit on what I paid for it – but not if you take into account what it had cost me to run and berth it.

There's an old saying that the two happiest people in the world are someone who has just bought a boat, and someone who has just sold one. From experience, I can vouch for that.

We still had the club, J. Arthur's, at this time, and Charlie would forever be sending people in, mates of his, and I'd have to buy them a drink. I had a million things going on with my businesses, and I could have done without all this. I was working hard: I was at the scrapyard by eight in the morning, I had the shop in Earls Court, and the nightclub. I worked at the scrapyard, freezing my bollocks off in winter humping scrap about.

A good chunk of what I earned was going to keep Charlie. Then he did something so fucking arrogant, I still can't believe it. After keeping a low profile for about six months, he must have been missing being on the front pages, because he decided to have pictures taken, of him dressed as Father Christmas, above my shop in Earls Court. Then he gave an interview to the *Daily Star*, in which he said he was in London. The police, who'd been leaving him alone, were provoked. They had to get him because he was openly taking the piss out of them, and the whole operation to catch him went up a gear.

The next day the police raided the shop in Earls Court, and they arrested him as he came out. That it was my shop wasn't a coincidence, was it? And Charlie knew what he was doing. After that the Old Bill were all over us, and that got the shop closed down. It had been a really good business, and it was ruined. We had to close it down. If you listen to Charlie, or read the book or the film about him, you'd think he kept me: he never did a thing for me, but I was keeping him the whole time he was on his toes. He cost me a lot of money with the shop shutting up.

His *Daily Star* interview was just to say the same things he'd said before, except that by the time he gave it he'd been on his toes for eight months. He was arrested on his forty-seventh birthday, and his life on the run was over. Although life was easier for me when he was inside, I didn't feel any relief. I was still very loyal to Charlie, and I visited him regularly, both before and after his time on the run.

Eight months after his capture, Charlie was turned down for parole an eighth time. Despite all the problems he caused, I continued to support his cause: six months later I was one of a group of ex-prisoners – which also included Bobby Welch, one of the train robbers – who petitioned the prime minister, Mrs Thatcher, about the length of sentences.

'You have had long sentences for some time now, and they haven't done any good at all,' I told the journalists. 'They have probably increased the violence. Whereas it used to be "fair cop, guv", now people are prepared to use all sorts of violence to avoid being caught.' I also said that the deterrent was being caught, not the length of the sentence.

I even went to see the copper in charge of the original case against us to find out if there was any reason why my brother was being held so long. Charlie had told me in a letter about his involvement in South Africa, and I wanted to know if that was why. But the police were not forthcoming, they wouldn't confirm or deny that Special Branch were involved because of Charlie's political connections.

Back inside, he was still a continual expense. All he wanted was to smoke cannabis all the time, and that costs money in the nick. It was all he ever asked about: the money for his next load of fucking puff. He even used to send a mate of his, Bobby Bill, round to get money to buy the puff to take into him.

I wasn't the only one working for Charlie's release, of course. His daughter Michelle and our half-brother Chas scaled the scaffolding that was up round the House of Commons. They got right up to the top, near Big Ben, and they hung huge banners that read:

'Public Inquiry for C. Richardson' and 'Free Charles Richardson. 17 years is enough.'

It was another year before Charlie got his first taste of freedom when, in October 1983, he was given a weekend at home. I drove, in a lime-green Rolls-Royce Silver Shadow, to collect him from Coldingley Open Prison, near Woking. Typical Charlie, he stayed out a day too long and lost fourteen days' remission. He got another week out in June the following year, because our mum had been unwell.

Two months later, in August 1984, he finally came out for good, after serving eighteen of his twenty-five years.

When Frank Fraser came out after serving twenty years – Frank kept getting into trouble and had another five years added on to his fifteen – I had a load of tickets printed for a benefit which I organised for him in a West End wine bar. I sold them at £50 each, everything was covered, and the benefit raised £18,700. I rounded it up to £20,000, which was a nice welcome home for him. Charlie kept on at me to do the same for him, but you can't when it's family. In the end I organised a dinner which eight or ten of my friends came to, and they chipped in a grand apiece. That was the most I could do for him.

My dad died in 1988, at the age of seventy-nine. He'd lived until the end of his life with Lizzie, the woman he ran away with to Canada. Mum didn't go to the funeral, but she was sad when he died: she loved him until the end.

After I came out of prison the first time, I soon caught up with the boxing scene. Me and Leslie McCarthy used to put on posh boxing evenings. We'd hire a venue, like the Cat's Whiskers in Streatham, and we'd serve a good meal, there would be three or four boxing bouts, then the floor would be cleared to make way for dancing. There were plenty of companies which specialised in putting up rings, and they could do it in no time. For the gala boxing nights at the Cat's Whiskers, the ring would be dismantled after the fight and tables for dinner put in its place so fast that you hardly noticed it happening. They were very popular events, and earned good money while at the same time giving everyone a great night out.

Later on, I got involved in the promotion of unlicensed fights. I used to put on fights for lots of boxers, including Harry Starbuck – who was a well-known club doorman and an unlicensed boxer. It wasn't bare knuckle stuff, it was with gloves, but they weren't regulated fights. We could sell two or three thousand pounds' worth of tickets for one of Harry's fights, which is good money. By the end of the evening I would have made about £800 after expenses – not bad as I had other people doing all the work for me.

We'd hold the unlicensed fights at Harvey's, a metal company in Charlton Road with a big hall which they hired out, and where we could have a ring set up and dismantled again, quickly, after the fights.

Being unlicensed, we had to be careful, so we would only announce the venue for our fights at the last minute. A guy called Bobby Padgett would find the opposition for me, and if we could put another fight on the same bill – with another fighter with a bit of a name – we could make even more money. We'd have posters printed and put up all around the area.

Harry won his fights, because we made sure he never got beaten. He was a big name draw and the crowd loved him, so we didn't want him to be beaten and we chose his opponents carefully. He was never the real thing – he was too old and too unfit to get a licence – but he was very popular. He worked on the door of a pub with a disco in Eltham High Street, and he'd been a doorman at other venues, too, so everyone in the area knew Harry. And the guys who fought him knew what they had to do: they were being paid, usually about £600, while Harry was getting a grand, and they knew they had to take a dive. One guy fought him twice, under different names, with his hair dyed: that wasn't uncommon in those days, and the fighters made a good living from it. We made a bit from side bets, but that was never the main thing: the ticket money was where the profit lay.

Lots of people really loved seeing Harry fight. The manager of my metal yard, Alan Martin, knew that Harry was being helped to win but still wanted to believe Harry was genuinely knocking them over.

Eventually Harry got an offer from Roy 'Pretty Boy' Shaw, who I'd met in Hull and who was a real fighter. I wasn't involved in promoting that one, but I went to watch – with a sense of foreboding. I knew Shaw wouldn't have been fixed to help Harry, as his career was on the up, and I also knew he was a much harder, fitter boxer. Shaw knocked Harry down twice and gave him a right pasting, and that was more or less the end of Harry's fighting career.

The greatest unlicensed fighter was not Lenny McLean, although he liked to claim he was the guv'nor. The real guv'nor was Cliff Fields, who worked as a doorman at J. Arthur's. When he was a professional boxer years earlier he was managed by Bert McCarthy, who had paid to get him out of the navy. Fields never made it professionally, because he didn't apply himself to fitness and all that, but he was the king of the unlicensed boxing ring: he was a big, hard man, and he knocked Lenny McLean out twice.

Boxing wasn't my only recreation. I had a busy social life with my mates. My friends have always been loyal. One of the first big social events I went to when I came out was Harry Rawlings's wedding, when he married Della: they waited and fixed the wedding date specially so that I was back home and I could be Harry's best man.

It was during this period between sentences that I discovered another great love of mine: skiing. The first time I went skiing, I really wasn't very enthusiastic about it. I was having a drink with some mates in the North Kent Squash Club when Paddy Onions came up to me:

'Eddie, quick, gimme fifty quid,' he said.

I gave him the money without asking what he wanted it for. Five minutes later he came back and said he'd used it to pay the deposit on a skiing holiday. I said:

'Leave off. Out in the cold, falling over, making fools of ourselves. That's not for me.'

But I went, because the crowd who were going were good fun. There were about twenty in all, including Harry Rawlings. And I had the time of my life. I loved it. When I first came out with all my gear and goggles on, the others fell about laughing.

'What's the big joke?' I asked.

'You look like a tank commander,' Harry said.

When I saw the photos afterwards, I could see what they meant.

We went to Seefeld in Austria. There weren't a lot of ski runs, but quite enough for us beginners. On the first day I was heading off for the nursery slopes and someone said:

'Don't be daft, we're not going with all the little kids. Come up with the men.'

So some of us went to the top of the mountain and then, literally, fell down the slopes. It was a right laugh. I fell over lots of times, but it hit the spot for me. Some of the others only went halfway up, so they were all waiting at the restaurant at the bottom when I eventually got down, and I was skiing properly for the last stretch. Everyone clapped.

I love the sensation of going fast, losing control, so this was ideal for me, my kind of holiday, active and exciting: I don't much go for lying down in the sun. We'd spend the day on the slopes, then back to the hotel for a nap, a bath and then out to the clubs for the evening – the après-ski was really good.

Since that holiday, I've never looked back – I've been skiing whenever I can. I've skied at St Moritz a few times, and I've been to Austria, Liechtenstein, France and Switzerland. Each country has its own characteristics. Switzerland is one of the most civilised countries in the world, and the hotel staff all know how to perform – Swiss-trained waiters are the best in the world. In Austria the après-ski was more up beat, with lots of bands playing live. In France it was mainly discos. Once, about ten of us – including Bert McCarthy and Kenny Bloom – went to Badrutt's Palace in St Moritz. It was a beautiful hotel, overlooking a lake, and there was even a bridge room where you could always find a foursome. Maureen and my daughter Melanie were with me on that holiday.

When we first went skiing, the people on the slopes were very different from us – it was like golf, which used to be a minority sport for the upper classes. But we were always made welcome, and over the years skiing has opened up completely. My lot of mates were all racers. There would always be a restaurant or café that we would aim for, and we'd race to it, last one pays. It was quite competitive, but always very funny. Sometimes we would take girls skiing with us, and they'd join in the fun. There were one or two little incidents when we were out at night, in the clubs, arguments and near fights – mainly with Germans, who tend to be as aggressive as us. But we never had any trouble on the slopes.

In January 1984 I also did the Cresta Run, in St Moritz, on a bobsleigh. I'd always wanted to do it, and it lived up to expectations. It only lasted a minute-and-a-half, but it was intoxicating. You are high up in the mountains, the air is clear and pure, and you're hurtling down at an unbelievable speed – I've got a certificate to prove I did it.

I'm a bit rusty at skiing these days, but I can still do it. I went in 2005 for the first time in sixteen or seventeen years: I just haven't been available! I was thrilled to be back on the mountains again, and nothing is as good as that feeling of travelling downhill, fast.

Just as there had been a few celebrities, like Stanley Baker, who liked to mix with us before I went away the first time, there were others when I came out. Richard Harris was one who enjoyed hanging out with faces: I met him with Steven Berkoff, Charlie Kray and my brother Charlie. Me and Richard Harris and Charlie Kray once went out for a meal, and then on to a couple of clubs – Harris was off the booze at the time, and he had a very pretty girl with him.

I was an executive club member at Chelsea Football Club for about six years. I would go over there, along with several friends, for home matches on Saturdays. The club wasn't as big as it is now, and for some of this time it was in the Second Division. We'd get there about noon, to get parking spaces, then we'd have a drink at the bar, sit down at our table for a good lunch and wine, watch the previews on telly, and then it was time to go out and see the match. We'd go back in at half time for coffee and biscuits, then watch the second half. Afterwards, we'd have a drink at the bar and watch the other results on television while we waited until the crowd had cleared, and then into our motors to drive home.

People like Terry Mills, who helped me out on the hostel scheme, used to go to the matches, and John Daly joined us when he could. It was purely social, and we'd have a right laugh. Terry actually tried to buy Chelsea: he had a meeting with the directors but within days it had been sold to Ken Bates.

Another bloke I knew there was a stockbroker, George Miller, who was a good mate of my broker, Vic Andrews, and, later, worked for John Daly. During this time I used to play the commodities market, dealing mainly in lead, copper, coffee and cocoa. I never had a big killing, in fact I think I lost money overall. But every lesson costs you, and it cost me to learn about dealing. I'm still very interested in the stock market, and I have a few stocks and shares. George was doing well, and he knew how to spend a pound note: he'd hire a private plane to take him wherever he wanted to go. He got nicked when the stockbroking company he was working for lost a lot of money, but he was acquitted. I went to the Old Bailey to see the case.

When I look back, I can see a few golden opportunities I missed.

I was offered a box at Ascot for £25,000, for life. I wish I'd taken it: it's now worth a million.

Not that all my interests were sporting. My daughter Donna had wanted to dance from the moment she could walk, and she'd been having dance lessons all her life. She used to get up at six o'clock in the morning to do her ballet stretches against the mantelpiece before she went to school. When she was old enough, she auditioned for lots of different ballet schools and was accepted by them all, but the greatest accolade was to win a place at the Royal Ballet School, and that's what she did.

So many dancers train there, but only a few ever make the grade as professionals as there are only a limited number of openings. Donna danced for the Scottish Ballet, and then for the Royal Ballet. It was everything she had ever dreamed about. She danced for the Royal Ballet for seven years, and I was very proud going to see her.

Unfortunately, her dancing career was cut short by joint problems: she was always needing to have a lot of physio. When I went to see her dance I always booked seats in the royal circle, and then took my guests to the River Room at the Savoy afterwards. I even went to a Christmas party – invited guests only, mostly the dancers' families – which was attended by Princess Margaret, Prince Charles and Diana, Princess of Wales. Again, we were in the royal circle, only about ten feet away from Charles and Diana. The Royals all did a little party piece: Charles came on stage in a cloak and Diana shouted 'One Cornetto please' from the Royal box: he brought a ladder and climbed up into the box. Princess Margaret was at the bar, puffing away on a cigarette, with a bottle of scotch in front of her.

At one time, a famous American artist did a series of paintings of the Royal Ballet dancers, and the one he did of Donna was made into a poster, and later was sold as postcards. I still have the poster up on my wall.

My other daughter, Melanie, has also been a source of great pride to me. Melanie got an honours degree in pharmacology from London University, which was presented at a ceremony at the Royal Albert Hall attended by Princess Anne. It was a tremendously proud moment for the family, and we had a wonderful day.

Another distraction was a new woman in my life. When Maureen gave a newspaper interview, all those years ago when I was only halfway through my time in prison, she spoke prophetically about the problems marriages face when couples have lived apart for so long.

'The readjustment of living together after a long sentence must put an awful strain on a man and his family, ' she had said. 'You are apart for so long, you get used to living on your own, and suddenly you are married again.'

She was seeing the future for our marriage. It was, as she'd predicted, very difficult for both of us. I was still the breadwinner, and proud of my daughters. But Maureen and I had grown apart, and although I had great respect for the way she brought the girls up, and I was grateful for all the support she gave me while I was in prison, we both found it hard.

My life was very costly. I have expensive tastes. Business was not going well. The nightclub and the porn shop had gone. They had both been good earners, and I'd grown accustomed to that level of money coming in.

The scrapyard, too, was suffering, because the Thames Barrier contract was over, and a lot of businesses – factories and the like where I had skips – were closing down and moving out of Greenwich, which was being redeveloped into a posh, residential area and a place for tourists. As property prices shot up, these firms were enticed away with huge offers for their sites and better rates elsewhere. I had a lot of people on my payroll and I still had to find their wages every week, as well as my own. The way it was going, I was looking at having to close the metal business down, and I didn't have the arsehole to do that, knowing that those blokes working for me had wives and kids. What do you say to them?

'Sorry, but I'm not earning enough to keep you on?'

I'm not making excuses. I'd been earning straight money, good money, for years – I've made far more straight money in my lifetime than crooked. But I was vulnerable. And I was tempted.

THIRTEEN

THE DEAL THAT WOULD HAVE
GOT ME OUT OF TROUBLE

I made a mistake. You can moralise on what you should and should not do, and that's all very well, but most people have never had the opportunities I had. Propositions came my way all the time. I've said no to a lot of things down the years, but there were always opportunities. People on the manor knew I was a sound man, so they would come to me with their schemes and plans, asking me to get involved. People say I shouldn't have done it, but wouldn't they, if they'd been given the chance to make two million, and sort out all their problems in one go? There's a lot of bollocks talked about morality.

This one big deal could have got me out of trouble. That's what I thought. I never actually saw so much as a line of cocaine with my own eyes: it was a business transaction. I met the people and thought they were alright, proper people. They were with a big Colombian cartel, they wanted to send gear over here, and they didn't require me to put any money upfront. They wanted me on board because I could lay on the right people to get rid of the stuff. I had the right associations and contacts, and it wasn't difficult for me to find buyers for the drugs: I knew who to go to. It was purely an investment of my time and my contacts, and the drugs were all going to be moved without me, personally, touching them.

I did have to meet a few people I didn't know very well, but I was very careful, and I mainly concentrated on sound people who I knew would not give me any problems. I didn't want to be greedy, especially if it involved dealing with people I didn't know.

Of course, the South Americans were new to me. But I met them, and they came over OK, as if they knew what they were doing. They were from the Cali cartel, named after their base in Cali, a major city in Colombia. (The Cali, along with the Medellin cartel, became known in the nineties as the two biggest and most successful cartels.)

At first, they simply wanted my advice as to who to deal with. A fella I knew from the East End was married to a Colombian girl, and that's how they made contact with me. I put them in touch with some people in Liverpool, and they went up there to talk to them. Unknown to me, the Liverpool lot had been infiltrated by informers, and the police were tracking the Colombians from that moment on.

When they came back to London, I started to get involved. They were going to send the cocaine over, I was going to organise its distribution, and I would get paid when it was sold on. It was all done very carefully, we didn't talk on the phone. Meetings were arranged by word of mouth, and were held in public places, like restaurants, where you can be aware of who's around.

I met two of the South American cartel. I liked one of the men, he was very sensible. He was a chemist, involved with processing the cocaine – he wasn't based here – and I had faith in him. The other was their man in England; Antonio Teixeira was one of the names he used, and I was none too happy about the fact that he brought his family over here.

I thought: 'Fucking hell, why's he doing that?'

In the end I was right: it made him vulnerable. From the very beginning I didn't really trust him, and I should have gone with my instincts. You have to sum people up very quickly, and I am a pretty good judge of character. When it's blokes from London, you've heard about them before you meet them and you can ask a few questions, but with these fellas I had to make my mind up on the basis of a meet and a chat. I felt this Teixeira talked too much. Silence is golden, where criminal matters are concerned. I did say to the other Colombian:

'Is he OK?'

He assured me he was.

To be honest, I was so busy at that time, trying to sort out my straight businesses, and maybe I should have been more vigilant than I was. A couple of things happened, and now and again I was aware I was under observation. But that was normal. The police had never forgiven me for my surname, and they were often outside the metal company site, keeping tabs on me. There was a building society opposite the scrapyard, and someone who worked there used to mark my card when the cops were in the top office watching me. Then a new hotel was built on the corner of the same street, and customs people moved in there. But I didn't know that, and I assumed they had dropped their interest in me for a time. They used to watch me, on and off, for a few years.

A couple of times I was aware of police cars following me, because I drive quite fast and if someone's behind me they have to keep up, and I always use my mirror a lot. I noticed a couple of cars on me when I drove through Docklands one afternoon. So I put my right indicator on, and the car behind did the same. I pulled over and he went past me, and he was obliged to turn the corner because he had been signalling. Then another car came round the bend, so I turned round and followed both of them. They knew I was on them. They weren't supposed to be seen, so they knew they hadn't done their job properly.

After I'd lost the cars, I heard the whirr of a police helicopter overhead. I parked the motor up and hid myself under a tree while he was diving around. He circled for a while and then he found the car – there was probably a tracking device planted on it. Once he'd located it, off he went. There were a few incidents like this, but they didn't worry me, as the police were liable to be on me anyway. If you are known to deal in drugs you get put on 'obso', which means they're observing you. They put people on you, not necessarily customs people, but freelancers, working for customs. But they had no reason to suspect me of being involved with drugs, I thought.

I didn't have any cops in my pocket, but I didn't need them – I was running straight businesses. I never wanted to go near the police, I was never comfortable with them like Charlie was. I wanted to keep a million miles away from them. I think they started watching me because they thought I was involved in something that I wasn't, and they got lucky because they were hanging around when the drugs thing started.

We started with a small shipment – a parcel with twenty-four kilos – which came through the airport successfully, was distributed, and everyone got paid. I made about eighty grand. It was a satisfactory transaction. I didn't see it or touch it, it got collected and then went to the distributors. Everything was done by word of mouth, and nobody was told any more than they needed to know. Customs knew that some gear had come through, but they did not know what happened to it. Don Tredwin, who was working with me, had contacts at the airports and the docks, and they handled it efficiently.

Tredwin introduced me to a Thai girl called Toy, who said she could get Thai grass put on a plane at Bangkok airport, which could then be handled by his people at this end. It was worth looking into, as it was not a problem getting a good price for Thai grass in London at the time. I made several trips to Thailand to meet people who had ways of getting it through the airport there, but nothing ever came through, and both me and Tredwin did quite a lump of money investing in their scams.

The first time I went I had to meet Toy in Pattaya, a few hours' journey from Bangkok. Driving through Pattaya on the way to my hotel, I saw lots of bright neon signs flashing above bars, and the place looked really exciting. So as soon as I booked in and unpacked, I was off out to sample the night life. As I left the hotel I could hear good music coming from a bar that looked upmarket compared to the others, so I went inside and ordered a scotch and water from the waitress. There were a few couples in there, and a few men on their own at the bar. After my second scotch I intended moving on to check out the rest of the local scene, but the waitress told me that if I fancied anyone, there were rooms upstairs which I could use for a small fee. At that moment the music changed, the stage lit up, and I was wondering what was going to happen. Then eight or ten young men came out on stage, gyrating to the music, and with numbers around their necks.

I now realised I was in the wrong kind of club. I left immediately, and when I met up with Toy she told me there were no women in that bar at all, not even the waitress. They were all men.

I went back to Thailand a few more times, staying in the famous Oriental Hotel. I had some excellent seafood in first-class restaurants. On one trip I booked a guide to show me round, and a young Buddhist monk turned up. Everywhere we went he was bowing to statues of Buddha. He took me to see factories where they were making amazing wood carvings, jewellery workshops, and of course lots of temples, where I had to take my shoes off. It was a fascinating experience and Thailand is a fascinating place, even if it proved to be very costly for me.

The next load was coming through by sea, in a container, and Don's contacts at Southampton were going to let us know as soon as it arrived. They would handle it, put it in a certain place and watch to see if there was any interest in it. It was all laid on, but the customs people were on us and they diverted the container to Portsmouth. It was addressed to a regular company here, one that routinely imported legit stuff from Colombia. The company knew nothing about it, we just used their name. The idea was that we would nick it from the docks. They would never miss it, as it wasn't theirs in the first place. But the paperwork has to be bang on, or someone will spot it, and it wasn't. This cartel seemed to know their business, and so you expect them to do the things you tell them to do. They were making good money out of this, so I can't accept that they offered us up. No way. They were buzzing with the deal at the time. There was enough money to go round. So they must have just been incompetent.

The customs men were already on to it. They called the investigation 'Operation Revolution'. They had been watching the South American: he'd been sending money back home in suspiciously large amounts, £500,000 in all, and they had secretly raided his flat in Blackheath. From London he had to relay to South America how we wanted the consignment labelled and packaged – who it was to be addressed to, that kind of thing – and the customs investigators had copies of all these messages. So when the container arrived, it was already in their sights. But I wasn't worried because I thought it was

238

still at sea. As far as I was concerned, my part of the business started when it landed, and that was when I would have to make myself busy.

So it was a shock when I was stopped by the police, just before Christmas 1988. When they pulled me I had £19,000 in cash on me. It was sloppy, it should never have happened like that. The money was owed to me from the first drugs transaction. It was close to Christmas and the next day there was a party for my staff and all the firms near me, which I was involved in paying for. I rang the guy who owed me the money, which I would never normally have done in view of the tight security – nothing was ever done over the phone. But it was so close to Christmas that I figured I wouldn't get it if I couldn't get hold of him. He was in partnership with young Frank Fraser, Frankie Fraser's son. They ran the Tin Pan Alley club together, and it was young Frank who answered the phone. I didn't have to say anything, as soon as he heard my voice he said:

'I can do that for you. We have to have a meet.'

We arranged to meet at a cab rank at the Elephant and Castle in two hours' time – he was coming from the West End, I was coming from Greenwich, so the Elephant, between the two, was a good place to meet. It was also a good place for the cops to get on my tail.

Young Frank handed me a plastic bag full of money and I put it in my motor. But I wasn't pleased: I was never supposed to have to collect money. It should have been paid to me. I set off back towards Greenwich and I got pulled. It was the drugs squad. They searched the car, which was loaded with fruit and other things I had bought for Christmas, then they took me to Eltham police station, and kept me there until four in the morning. I told them the money was stock money from the yard:

'Some days I think nothing of laying out £40,000. This ain't nothing,' I said.

But it was in a plastic bag, which doesn't look good. They had to let me go, but they hung on to the money. It was three months before I got it back, and during that time they were obviously keeping me under close surveillance.

I went to my solicitors, and eventually they rang to say I could have my £19,000 back. The cops made sure they gave it back at about four-thirty on a Friday afternoon, too late to take it to the bank. I counted it all out in front of the police. I hid £10,000 under the stairs in my friend Joan Harris's house, which was in the same street as my yard. The next morning I was spending the rest: I had money to lay out at the yard.

Early on the Monday morning, at about four o'clock, as I was in bed at my home in Chislehurst, I was woken by the sound of the front door being smashed down. There were about thirty cops, some with guns. If they'd knocked, I would have opened up. And, as I was never armed, I don't know why they turned up mob-handed and armed – except they love it, playing the big guys, waking the whole street. They had a metal pole clamped across the door and they were hammering it until the frame split. I ran downstairs in my vest and pants and yelled at them to stop, but by then the door wouldn't open anyway. They were pointing guns at me through the windows. I was worried about Melanie and Maureen, who were upstairs. As they searched the house I was shouting, 'My daughter is in there!' because I thought they were dumb enough to shoot anything that moved. They clamped my hands together behind my back with plastic ties and that was that, I was under arrest.

They searched Joan's house as well, and found the money. Obviously, they had marked the money, and they thought I was going to pass it to the South Americans, which would prove a link between me and them. They were hoping for this, but it would never have happened, because the money was not due to be paid to them. The police had the link anyway: the South American had mentioned me in his contact with Colombia, in the papers they found at his flat. I later learned that the customs people were angry when the police stopped me and took the money, as they were tailing me. But after it happened, they made sure the police gave it back, marked.

I didn't know it until later, but they already had the South American in custody. They'd arrested his wife and kid, and he made a big statement naming me and the others, in exchange for letting his family go. He didn't need to do that, they had no grounds for holding his family and a good lawyer would have had them released immediately, but I suppose he came from the kind of country where family members, including kids, could be held in custody. He tried to retract his statement later but they wouldn't let him, and he'd been taped. He was the weak link, and I suspected it from the very beginning, but I ignored my own feelings. They'd also got the container with the drugs: they picked it up about a week before I was arrested.

I was taken to Southampton police station and charged with importation of drugs. They made out we imported far more than we did: they said it was forty-four kilos which came through the airport in a suitcase, which is a ridiculous amount. One man could not lift a case containing forty-four kilos, plus packaging.

I was in custody for eighteen months before the trial, mainly in the special unit at Brixton. A couple of the others were in there with me. The police never tried to get into me, never asked me to help them. They knew they wouldn't get any change out of me. But the South American had made his big statement, told them everything, all the shit. He regretted it afterwards, because without his statement they didn't have a lot on us. I told him early on that if he ever got arrested he had to repeat: 'On the advice of my solicitors I've got nothing to say,' to every question they asked.

The other South American was never arrested.

I was held as a Double Cat A prisoner from the beginning, which meant I was sealed off from visitors. They had to make an application to see me, and I was being fucked about. Frank Fraser and my brother Charlie were allowed to see me, but I wasn't allowed to see witnesses like Jimmy Jeffries and other people who would have been useful for the case.

There were some good blokes in Brixton and we had some good games of football. There were three black lads, successful robbers, one of them was called Dennis Ellington. He was a diamond of a man, and I would love to see him again.

There was another Irish team who only got nicked because the shotgun they used on robberies was so unusual – it was a great big thing, and there were lots of jokes about it. They were OK, good fun. I was fifty-four, and they were all quite a bit younger, but I got on great with them.

I was taken backwards and forwards from Brixton to Winchester for remand hearings, but when the trial started at Winchester Crown Court I was moved to Winchester prison. I was handcuffed in my cell every morning and transported to court in a sealed unit, inside a little box van. There was the usual fanfare: a convoy of vehicles, bikes, cars, lots of sirens.

In the middle of my trial there was a riot at Winchester prison. One night everyone was banging on their cell doors about something, and then they broke into one another's cells through the walls and the ceilings. There were people up on the roof, and a lot of noise. They were complaining about something, and the screws wouldn't answer, so they decided to have a tear-up. It was sorted out the next day. But I was up in court in the witness box, despite not being able to sleep for most of the night.

I had a lot on my plate at the time the trial started. I was worried that evidence would come out about my relationship with Joan, because the money was found at her house. I would see Maureen in the public gallery some days, and then I would be worried about what would be said about Joan.

The police didn't really have any evidence on me, but I can see they felt it was important to get me because I am a Richardson, and they couldn't afford to see me walk. The case was splashed all over the newspapers and television. I am a big name and they would be left looking stupid if I was acquitted.

Having the trial in Winchester meant an entirely different kind of jury than you get in London, and it was impossible to get into them. The police did their usual business to undermine me before we started. When they said that they were worried about the safety of the jury, it reflected badly on me, because it implied I was up to something. In the same way, all the security surrounding me made me look dangerous.

I was the only one found guilty (some of the others pleaded guilty), and I believe they made a beeline for me because I was the famous name, and that allowed them to let the others off. My co-defendant Terry Sansom, who was cleared of plotting to smuggle cannabis through Gatwick, spat in the customs man's face when he tried to shake hands with him after his case ended. Sansom tried to get off by getting a doctor to say he had a heart condition and could have a heart attack at any minute, but they wouldn't go for it. He was worried about his health: at the time of his arrest he weighed about twenty stone, and couldn't get up a flight of stairs without pausing for breath, but by the time he was in the dock with me he'd lost about nine inches from his waist, and was a shadow of his former self. Getting nicked probably saved his life.

I had to send the South American's wife some money to Argentina to get him to plead guilty, because he would slaughter me if he gave evidence. I had no chance while he was still in the case, because he was dropping me in it completely. The worst evidence against me was that I was seen going round to his house in Blackheath with some plastic bags, which I said contained bottles of wine, because we had also been seen wining and dining in restaurants a couple of times. Carrying plastic bags didn't mean I was involved with drugs money, I argued. I said he had given me some South American wines to try, and I returned his generosity by taking him some Chablis and Sancerre.

Once the South American changed his plea to guilty I thought I had a very good chance. But the prosecution gave a lot of information about the case against me without even calling witness evidence, and I don't believe my legal team challenged it enough.

I wanted to bring up in court my previous convictions, because I didn't have that many, and there was nothing to do with drugs on my record. I thought it would explain to the jury that half the reason I was nicked was because of who I am. But they all knew who I was anyway, because of all the publicity.

I was very dissatisfied with my legal team. My wife came up to the trial one day, and on the train back she saw my barrister and the prosecution barrister sitting together deep in conversation. I know it happens all the time, but they were supposed to be opposing each other in court.

Three-quarters of the way through I asked my brother-in-law Paul if he could get another firm of solicitors to take over the case, but by then it was too late. My co-defendants were shitting them-selves because they didn't want me to defend myself.

I was in the witness box for a day and a half. I had drilled myself up and I did a good job. The judge kept pulling me up, but I didn't do too badly. But it felt as if my own side were not helping me. I was taken to pieces by the prosecution: they even questioned me about a cheque for a skiing holiday that Jimmy Jeffries bounced. My legal team should have challenged the relevance of this, because there was none.

The trial lasted thirteen weeks. The jury was out for a while, which gave me hope. But once they found me guilty of one charge, importation through the airport, I knew I was in trouble. The person who was supposed to have brought the drugs through got found not guilty on the basis that they thought it was pornography. They didn't admit doing the run on the day in question, but admitted doing others with pornography. So if I was guilty, who brought it through?

I was found guilty of smuggling two tonnes of cannabis and 153 kilos of cocaine into Britain, and a charge of money laundering. I was found not guilty of plotting to smuggle cannabis through Gatwick, something which I knew nothing about. They said the drugs were altogether worth £40 million, which was way over the top. It was dubbed by the newspapers 'Britain's biggest drugs plot'.

I was sentenced three months later, after they had held a hearing into my finances. I was so busy with this that it did not register with me fully that I was going to go down for a long stretch. I was numb. It was unreal. It was like a fantasy world. Hope springs eternal: you always think something will happen to make it all change.

John Daly wrote a good letter supporting me, and Lord Longford volunteered to speak on my behalf at my sentencing hearing, which I really appreciated, although I knew it wouldn't make any difference, because they'd already decided what sentence I was going to get. He said:

'I have a great liking for Eddie. There is another side to him. There is much good in him. If he is sentenced to prison, and I hope not, I will visit him, and visit his wife and two daughters, if they want to see me. I plead for mercy.'

I was expecting twenty years, but in the end I was given twenty-five. Teixeira, the Colombian, got twenty and Don Tredwin got fifteen.

When you are in trouble, your real mates support you. But all sorts of pond life crawls out of the water to have a go at you. A bloke who used to work on the door for me at J. Arthur's sold a story to the *Sun* about how I had a £2000-a-day coke habit.

It was complete crap. Apart from the early days when we were running the clubs, when we all took a few pep pills, I've never used drugs, at all. I live on my own adrenalin, I don't need artificial stimulants. That lowlife probably got a few hundred quid for saying what he said. Newspapers don't bother to check things when it's about people like me: they can print any lies.

That toe-rag was the lowest of the low. Once, a girl he was living with came up the club, crying that he'd nicked all her jewellery and her furniture. That's the kind of bastard he is.

Talking about bastards . . .

While I was on remand, I let a young relative run the metal business. He had been working for me for several years, anyway, so it was logical he would take over. He was family, after all, and like an idiot I believed you could trust your own family. I let my brother have the use of the offices upstairs. He was supposed to pay rent to Maureen, which would have helped her out a bit, but he never did. He ran up bills. I had some paintings I had bought, Parisian scenes that I commissioned from Larry Rushton, who I met when we were both in Hull. Since he came out, he's become quite well known and successful as a painter. Charlie took the paintings, along with bits and pieces, and he also took all the depositions from my original trial, which I had carefully stored.

The young lad who was looking after the yard was selling out the metal but didn't pay the VAT, leaving a bill of about four grand. Maureen then took over running it, with the help of Chicken George, a bloke who had worked for me for years. He wasn't the full shilling, but he could do the physical work, and they kept the door trade going.

But there was a spate of break-ins at the yard, and they always happened when Maureen had bought some metal in. She'd get there the next day and the place would be cleaned out. It looked like the thieves were getting in over the back wall. But one day a local shopkeeper came to tell her what was going on. He was disgusted, and he felt she ought to know: my brother had keys and was letting himself in but making it look like a robbery. After everything I had done for Charlie, it was a very poor return. I even paid for his daughter Susan's wedding, because Charlie came to me and asked if I could front up the money. It was a great day and Lord Longford came to the wedding.

Maureen told me about the robberies, and what Charlie was doing, when she came on a visit. There was very little I could do, except to tell her to change the locks.

By now, I was beginning to find out things about my brother. The first clue came while I was on remand and I asked him to see someone for me, someone who could be helpful for my defence. It was at the end of the visit, and he suddenly stood up and shouted out:

'I'm not getting nicked for you.'

I wasn't asking him to do anything that would get him nicked. The visit was over and he was leaving, so I didn't have the chance to say anything. Not that I could think of anything straight off. I was thinking, 'What's he doing that for? If he didn't want to do it, all he had to do was say so. Why's he shouting my business out?'

It really threw me, but it started me thinking about my brother.

Now, after what Maureen told me, I realised the truth. I'd spent a lifetime being a brother, never thinking he was anything other than my friend. Now he was showing his true colours. I believe he has dulled his brains with all that cannabis he has smoked. In the early days, he was a true brother, he was alright. But ever since he came out of prison, he was envious of me, with my successful businesses and with my friends, who have been loyal to me all my life.

When, after my sentence, his autobiography came out, I realised just how envious of me he was. He never visited me or wrote during my second sentence – if he'd tried to, I'd have sent him packing, and he knew it.

The police and customs were claiming that, under the criminal asset recovery scheme, they should get my house, the lease on the night-club in Catford and the metal business, which alone they valued at £100,000. I had owned the house for twenty-eight years, from before my first sentence; there was a small mortgage on it, and it had all been done with straight money. I had ten years of accounts to prove that the metal business was straight. They had no rights to any of this. Anyway, the metal business had fuck-all money in it by this time. The metal business was me, and without me it was only worth the lease on the premises.

They took the money they found at Joan's house, and another few thousand from the safe at the yard, and a couple of thousand from my home. Metal is a cash business, so I always had cash about me. That's all they got. I sold the lease on the nightclub under the table.

Maureen's solicitor suggested we should get a divorce, so that Maureen could get the house in settlement. She started proceedings after my arrest and before the trial. It wasn't acrimonious. We'd fallen out of love, and we were growing further and further apart.

Customs objected to her having the house, but she got it in the end. She didn't get anything she wasn't entitled to, and by making sure she had it, I knew that my daughters would eventually inherit from her.

Meanwhile it was no use to me: I did not have to worry about a roof over my head for the next few years.

FOURTEEN

'YOU'VE SOLD YOUR SOUL FOR A BOWL OF CURRY'

I'd been held in Winchester prison during the trial, and that's where I went back to when my sentence was announced. For three months, between the verdict and the sentence, I'd had the chance to get to know people there a bit, but because I was a Double Cat A, and considered a serious risk, I was mainly banged up for twenty-three hours a day. They were frightened to let me out: I was out of their league.

After I got my sentence, I was soon moved to Full Sutton, near York, which is a Cat A dispersal prison: a holding prison for men who are going to be inside for some time. As a Double Cat A, I had more restrictions than the others. I had to have a screw with me at all times, and they keep a diary of everything you do, writing down your time in the gymnasium, and so on.

251

Full Sutton was alright. If I was rating prisons out of five, I'd give it four stars (with Durham and Leicester on no stars). It was a modern building, which means no draughts, and it was clean and bright, and the staff were OK. It felt like freedom after being banged up all the time at Winchester. I had my own cell (I always had my own cell, in every prison), and I could do my own cooking. There were a few blokes I knew from Brixton, and I also knew two of the Arif brothers, Mehmet and Dennis, who were in for a raid on a Securicor van. All the Londoners stuck together, because we were in a minority. We had our own football team, and we'd play teams of lads from Yorkshire, Lancashire, Scotland or wherever. As usual, if a new Londoner turned up, the first question was:

'Do you play football?' It was always disappointing if they said no.

There were a couple of noticeable differences between my second sentence and my first one. For a start, there were far more prisoners using drugs. At least a third of the prison population in every place I went to were on drugs, a much higher percentage than my first time round.

Another difference was that there were women prison officers. On the whole, they were alright: better than the men because they were less macho; they weren't in a testosterone competition with the inmates. Some were openly lesbian. Most of them were pleasant, but you got the odd exception, and one at Full Sutton would have won prizes for unpleasantness. She was a right nasty piece of work, she used to give women visitors a real rub down, and even go through their hair. Everyone had the needle with her. She used to sit in her little office, enjoying her bit of power. One day a couple of Geordie lads masked up, and shitted her up – they poured a bucket of piss and shit over her. Nobody would say who did it, so nobody could be punished. I saw a few screws shitted up in my time, and I put a few bob into it if I felt the screw had it coming – we'd have a whip round for the lads who did it.

But I also saw a black prisoner badly beaten up because he kept digging out this screwess, who wasn't a bad sort. She was a nice lady. He was a big lump and he kept insulting her, so a couple of Geordie kids came to me and told me they were going to do him. Those Geordie guys are game, they don't fuck about. That black geezer was a real pain: later on, in another prison, he got done for pouring boiling cooking oil over a screw, disfiguring one side of his face. We were all bloody annoyed about the consequence of this, because they stopped all prisoners having cooking oil, so we couldn't cook chips or battered fish.

I met Charlie Bronson at Full Sutton. He's alright. We used to walk around the exercise yard together and he was a real comedian, full of funny stories. Half those kidnaps he does, when he holds a prison officer hostage or whatever, are a big joke. He just wants a cheese sandwich and a blow-up doll! He told me how, when he was in Broadmoor, he got a load of grass cuttings, dried the lot out and sold it to the nutters as weed. They loved it and kept coming back for more.

Charlie's done a lot of chokey and he's used to imprisonment. He keeps fit in his cell: he works out using bedposts for weights, and he does sit-ups – more than 2000 at one go. Roy Shaw did it, too, that's how they got through their bird, they were happy doing it. I could never work out in my cell.

Bronson's time in Full Sutton was going sweet. He was working out in the gym, no problems, good as gold. As a reward, the governor restored a hundred days' remission to him. The next thing, Charlie's running round the wing with a couple of home-made spears. The governor had been trying to help him, but maybe Charlie didn't see it that way. I always send him a Christmas card, keep in touch, because he's a decent bloke. He sends me cards, which he draws himself: he's good at caricatures.

Another prisoner I got on well with was Brian Keenan, head of the army council of the IRA. He was a sensible man, and he kept the peace in there, because whenever the Irish prisoners were having problems, they would bring them to him and he would sort it out. We played badminton and bridge together. He wasn't bogged down by religion: he regarded his cause as just on humanitarian grounds, because the Roman Catholics had been an oppressed minority in Northern Ireland. I have a great deal of respect for him and the cause he was fighting for.

Talking about religion, it was at Full Sutton I decided to become a Muslim. It wasn't a religious conversion: I wanted to have the same food as the Muslim prisoners. They got a special allowance to buy food, and it was all cooked, carefully, by their mates. It was much better than the standard prison scoff: they had curries and fresh fruit. I was friendly with Bob Shamel, in there doing twelve for cannabis smuggling, and he took me along to one of the Muslims' Friday meetings, so I could join. I didn't do the prayers, but it was enough for me to get on to their diet. The chaplain came round to see me:

'What have you done, giving up Christianity?' he said.

'It's nothing personal, just that they have a very much better diet than normal,' I explained.

'You've sold your soul for a bowl of curry,' he said.

I'm not religious in any way. I've seen so many religions, close up, in prison, and they've all got their good points and bad points, and I haven't signed up to any of them. I didn't observe the Muslim Ramadan, or go to any of their prayer meetings. I just went through the motions. After I joined, quite a few others 'converted', to get the better food.

We weren't allowed to have televisions in our cells at this time, but

I had one. There was a clever prisoner who could doctor a tin so that it looked completely untouched, and it could be used for storing things. He would remove the label from a can of beans, very carefully take the bottom off the can, clean it out, and then fix the bottom back on so that it looked perfect – a very thin cardboard tube, with the label on, fitted over it. He did them for a few prisoners, to keep money, watches and things safe. It was his way of earning a few bob. For me he did a powdered milk carton, which was larger, and I kept a small television inside it. There was always a television room, but when we were banged up at eight in the evening it meant that we missed the best programmes.

My second sentence was a much quieter time than my first. I was older and not so explosive, and I preferred to solve problems mentally rather than physically. This time I didn't feel so despairing, because I knew that time in prison goes by. There's always something to hold on to. There was talk about letting prisoners out after half their sentence, instead of two-thirds. You grasp at straws like that, then all of a sudden you've done a few years. You put it out of your mind and just carry on, and you wake up one day and realise the years have moved on more, and you can apply for parole. You start filling in forms, and you begin to see light at the end of the tunnel. Even though I was looking at a lot of years, I knew I'd get there. Some people may have buried me in prison, but I never buried myself.

This time round, I decided to use my time in prison as best I could. The first thing I concentrated on was getting fit again, and I spent as much time as possible in the gym. I was still good enough at football to be picked on merit for the wing team, even though I was twenty or thirty years older than the others on the team. Then I applied to go on education, mainly because I didn't want to go into the workshop with a load of nutters trying to earn a few extra bob by doing piece work. I wanted something more intellectually absorbing, and I started with a business studies class, and woodwork. It was another prisoner, Peter Cameron, one of the more sensible ones, who persuaded me to have a go at the art classes.

I don't think I would have had the patience to paint earlier in my life, but I had mellowed. The first picture I painted was of my nightclub in Catford, and I did it straight from my head. It was very difficult. Even though I had slowed down and become more contemplative, I still liked to get on with things, and I liked to get them right. Peter Cameron, who was in for importation of cannabis, and is a successful artist now, was very helpful, and so was the art teacher who came in once a week. He told me to copy pictures and photographs: he explained that even top artists copy, they don't try to draw straight out of their heads. They either draw from life or they use photos. This put me on the right tracks. My next painting was a copy of a Degas portrait of a woman, and it was easy after what I had been trying to do. I soon found I was enjoying it, and getting good results.

I did my portrait of Lord Longford while I was in Full Sutton. He'd been visiting me for some time, so I asked him for a photograph to work from. He would never have suggested it himself, he was far too self-effacing. He was very pleased with the end result, and so was I – I felt I really caught his likeness. I had only been painting for eight months when I did it, so it wasn't a bad effort. It is much easier to paint someone like Longford, with a lot of lines and character in his face, than someone younger, especially a child.

Lord Longford wouldn't dream of hanging the portrait at his own house – he would have thought that was vanity. So he gave it to a charity which supported prisoners, and they sold it for £300. It was possible to get your work sold outside, but most prisoners wanted to sell their stuff independently, not give it away for peanuts. There was a whole industry inside prison: if you could draw or paint, people would pay you to do things for them. I never did anything on commission, and I never sold my works to prisoners. I was once offered £1000 for a big painting I did of a horse sale, but I refused to part with it. Later, after I was out, it sold for £3000, so I made the right decision.

The woman in charge of the art department was into pottery and sculpture more than painting, so I made a few clay figures. Another woman, a real human dynamo, headed the whole education department, and she helped organise an exhibition of our work at York Minster. I exhibited a painting of my daughter, Donna, with her little girl. It was one of my early efforts, not very good. I gave it to Donna, but I wouldn't blame her if she's thrown it out.

I also started writing poetry at Full Sutton and, fifteen months after I was sentenced, *Inside Times*, the newspaper for prisoners, published one of my verses:

LIFE IN A HURRY

The frustration and worry
Of life in a hurry
Builds walls of suspicions
That affect your decisions
And leave friends and relations
With constrained conversations
Turns love from its beauty
And leaves nothing but duty
And the haste I should mention
Will also cause tension
It's always the same
So beware of the pain
There's nothing to gain
When you join the fast lane

257

I think I would have written more poetry if I hadn't become absorbed by painting. I had the *Oxford Book of English Verse*, and I read a lot of it. I love *The Ballad of Reading Gaol* by Oscar Wilde. It's beautiful, very moving, very powerful and an education in itself.

But painting was my main love, and I started to win awards for my work. Twenty years before his death in 1983, Arthur Koestler, the writer and philosopher, had endowed prizes for creative work in prisons, mainly writing and painting. I won my first award in 1994 and I then won an award every year until my release, with two in 1995 and three in 1997. The actual prizes were not large: I usually received £100 worth of art equipment. But it was very satisfying to know that I'd been chosen, and made me realise that my work must be pretty good. Whether I would have kept going without this incentive, I don't know. But painting certainly helped time to fly by: I worked very intensely, in my cell, for hours at a time. Several of my paintings were made into greetings cards to be sold for the Koestler funds, and lots of my friends would buy them and send them in to me.

After I'd finished a painting, I'd give it to one of my friends or family who came up on a visit. I always had plenty of visitors. As well as my mum and other members of my family, Maureen came, for a time, even though we were divorced. Eventually Maureen and I lost touch: I stopped ringing her. We had a small falling out when she sold the house in Chislehurst: not because I minded her selling it, but because I thought she let it go too cheap.

I'd settled in nicely at Full Sutton, and was preparing for Christmas: I'd ordered a couple of turkeys, nuts, mince pies, a few other things. We had plans to cook ourselves a decent lunch.

Then it happened. At five in the morning, on Christmas Eve, heavy boots along the landing, and a sinking feeling that it was me they were coming for.

'Up you get Richardson, you're on the move.'

Handcuffs on, no time to say goodbye, no time to take any of my stuff, into the van, police outriders – all the same old Double Cat A rigmarole to take me to Whitemoor, an ultra-modern, 'escape-proof' jail – another Cat A dispersal prison – near March, in Cambridgeshire. I was much older now than on my first sentence, and it was all a struggle. I was no threat to anyone.

I was at Whitemoor for about twelve months. It was not a good prison – I'd only give it one star – although I believe it's much better now. It was effectively two prisons run together: one self-contained, one for nonces, who wouldn't have survived if they'd been put in with the rest of us in the main prison.

There were a few people I knew in Whitemoor, and plenty of others would come to introduce themselves to me – they did that wherever I was. As usual, we had a food boat going: that's when everyone puts in a certain amount of money, say £15 a month from their canteen, and food is brought in for us to cook ourselves. I was never short of money: I could always ring friends or send a letter, and they'd send me something in. I wasn't smoking by this stage, and that's where a great deal of money goes.

While I was at Whitemoor, I was transferred for a few days to Belmarsh for my leave to appeal hearing. Belmarsh was a fucking pisshole (no stars) but there were plenty of bent screws who would get you anything you wanted – tobacco, drugs or whatever, most of the gear came in through the screws. And it was in South London, which made it easy for visits as well as meaning there were people I knew in there. But it's very close confinement.

During my appeal hearing three or four people came in and sat in the public gallery. They looked like caricatures of gangsters. I looked at them and thought:

'Who the fucking hell are they?'

I'd never seen them before. But it made me look bad, and I think they were planted for that reason. The first panel of judges to hear my appeal looked very promising, and I thought I might get a result, but the case was put back because of a dispute about whether or not it was right to confiscate property that had not come from drugs money. The second panel, under the Lord Chief Justice Lord Taylor, were not so receptive, and I lost the appeal. By the time the appeal came up I had changed my solicitors and my barrister was Lord Longford's grandson-in-law, Edward Fitzgerald, QC. He's a famous human rights lawyer, and did well for me. But the damage had already been done.

When my next move came it was the same old procedure, but I was glad to leave Whitemoor. I was even more pleased when I arrived at Parkhurst. Now that was a good prison, five stars even. Unfortunately, after an escape attempt in 1995 (three prisoners got out and attempted to fly off the island in a light aircraft) it was taken off the Cat A list, and I was shipped back for another two years in Whitemoor.

But for the eighteen months I was there, Parkhurst was great. It had a good governor, who let us play tennis on a padded tennis court with wooden bats. There was a football pitch, and there were good cooking facilities. Billy Gentry was there, and there was another inmate called Dick Reid who was in for murder. He was a brilliant gardener, and he knew the Latin names of every plant. He grew specialised plants in the greenhouse, which he used to sell to the screws in exchange for food – three pounds of sausages or whatever. The screws used to go shopping for us, and we'd order in steaks and all the trimmings. I always had fish on Fridays – a nice bit of skate.

Most important, there was an excellent art teacher. Even prisoners who couldn't paint at all started to learn with him, and he encouraged them all. He taught me about mixing paint, what to mix with what to achieve just the right shade I wanted. There were eight of us in the class, and we had lessons twice a week. I also did a pottery class, and made five or six bowls, all painted in an original way. One was painted with high-kicking cancan girls, like a Toulouse Lautrec painting: I called it *Legs, Dancing and Knickers*. Another one I called *Della's Dancing Girls*, because I did it for my mate Harry Rawlings's wife, Della. She's still got it, and it's a one-off, personally done by me. I made a teapot, which I decorated with arrows, and wrote on one side 'Parkhurst', and on the other 'Not to be removed'.

I was allowed to carry on painting in my cell, so I'd take whatever I was working on and put in hours on my own. I was allowed to use the art room even when the teacher wasn't there.

We had cookery classes, too. What we made depended on what the cookery teacher brought in. I used to do a lot of curries. I'd cook a big pot of it, ladle it into a Tupperware container and put it in the freezer. It meant I had an instant meal whenever I wanted, all I had to do was cook some rice. Once again, I had a Coke bottle filled with brandy in my cell. The screws brought it in. I'd have it as a nightcap in my coffee.

There was a Filipino prisoner called Victor, who was very game. I first met him in Brixton, on remand. He was a very good chess player, and that's how I got to know him. I didn't mind him, but he didn't know anyone else much. He was such a good player that I would back him in any chess game he played, and I always won a few bob.

But then a new geezer came in, and none of us knew anything about him. We were suspicious of him: sometimes the police slip someone in to try to find things out. Anyway, he was talking about being a shit hot chess player, and he bigged himself up so much that for once I thought Victor might lose. But Victor finished him off in ten or twelve moves, two games out of three, and we were over the moon. Victor jumped right up on my shoulders – he was an agile little bastard – and I carried him around the crowd, who were all cheering.

Another time, I had a bit of a set-to with someone who shouted something out through his cell window after lock-up, and I shouted back. Victor heard it, and the next day he said to me:

'I gotta blade here. Do you want me to go down and see him?' He was offering to cut the geezer. He was like my own personal Rottweiler, really loyal to me.

'Leave it out, Victor,' I said.

I don't know where Victor is now, but if I did I'd put him on my card list.

Victor was in for setting fire to his bosses, who ran pinball machine arcades. They sacked him, so he went back, tied them up and set them alight. He'd been living with a married woman who brought him into Britain, and when she dumped him he went a bit scatty. But he was as game as anything.

When I returned to Whitemoor there was a good art teacher, a young fella, who tragically died of cancer. He encouraged me a lot, and when he stopped coming I corresponded with the education department and they told me he was ill. I was upset: he had a couple of little kids, and he used to work as a roofer to supplement his income.

During this stay in Whitemoor there was a horrible incident. Our food was prepared by the nonces, who worked in the kitchens. That was their job, no one else got a sniff at our food. There was a big hoo-ha about AIDS at this time – the mid-nineties – and there was a lot of fuss about homosexuals needing to use condoms. We never saw the nonces: the food was brought over on trolleys and left for us on a round hotplate in the middle of the landing. Blokes from our wing dished it out.

It was lunchtime and everyone was queuing with trays for their food. The fella serving scooped up some custard, then he yelled:

'It's got a fucking Durex in it!'

It had, and a used one at that. The whole food queue kicked off:

'Fucking nonces, if we could get our hands on them they'd never need a fucking Durex again,' that kind of thing.

Everyone put their meal down, started banging trays, going apeshit. There was a strike, with everyone refusing to go to work. I hardly ever ate off the hotplate, and after that incident I never did again. Everyone tried to avoid eating the prison food, even those with hardly any money were buying tins of beans and trying to survive on them. The authorities said it was a wind-up, and eventually people did start eating the food again.

I did all my own cooking. I'd get some bread in the morning for toast – they couldn't fuck around with bread. Then I'd cook my own bacon, sausage, whatever. I had a kettle in my cell for tea and coffee. The evening meal from the hotplate was served really early, about half-past four in the afternoon, so I would cook my own, at six-thirty, when we were on association time. We had our food sent in from Iceland, the supermarket. You'd compile a list, and it would arrive back with your name and your wing written on the bag. You could get more or less anything you wanted: I had a stock of spices, and I used to buy fish, lamb chops, tiger prawns – anything I fancied. Food is very important in prison: there's not a lot else to think about.

There was one inmate who was in my food boat, Stevie Waterman, an armed robber, and a proper Cockney, who only had about nine months of his twenty-year sentence to do. The probation service came to see him and started making themselves busy.

'If you'd come two years ago, I'd have spoken to you,' Waterman said.

'You'll need help when you are released,' they said.

'No, I won't, I've got money,' he told them.

He'd sold his house when he went inside, given some money to his kids, but he still had a decent lump and he wanted to go to New Zealand when he got out because he had relatives there.

'What happens when the money runs out?' they asked.

'I'll just have to get the guns out again, won't I?' he said.

Waterman fucked them off. He didn't need anyone, and they left him alone after that. As far as I know, he went to New Zealand, and he's still there.

There were a few flare-ups, but I didn't take any notice and I didn't get involved. I got quite a lot of respect in prison this time around. People looked up to me, they would come and ask my advice. I was an elder statesman, although I didn't mix with many people. I've always been careful about who I talk to, I would never talk in depth with anyone other than someone I knew very well. I wasn't unfriendly, I just didn't associate closely with those I didn't know.

There are always fights in prisons, and there are always weapons. Sometimes a knife will have been smuggled in, and it will be passed from prisoner to prisoner, as they move on. One way of making a weapon is to sharpen the plastic handle of a toilet brush. A favourite way of dealing with someone was to pour cooking oil (before it was banned) all over his cell and set fire to it. Boiling water, with sugar dissolved in it, is another favourite; thrown over someone, the sugar makes the burns far worse. I never carried a weapon, didn't need to.

There was a special secure unit in Whitemoor where they mainly kept IRA men and the most dangerous prisoners – the sort of bloke I was on my first sentence. I wasn't in there, and I never saw the blokes from there. In 1994 there was an escape attempt, two IRA men actually got out for about three hours, and then they were recaptured. Three others, and an armed robber, were also in on the plan but they didn't get out. It didn't affect the rest of us, although there's always a little bit of excitement when something like that happens.

One character I talked to was an old Dutch sea captain, who was arrested by British coastguards even though he was 150 miles off the coast, and the cargo of cannabis he had on board was bound for Holland, not here. They boarded his boat from a helicopter while he was moored up waiting for someone to collect the stuff, so fast that he didn't have time to ditch the stuff. He was gutted; if he had been arrested by the Dutch he would have got a quarter of the sentence he got here, and he would have served it in a much cushier prison. He was always very rude to the screws. We made a pact that when we were out we would meet in the South of France for a meal. He was cunning, though: he said he would pay for the food and I would pay for the wine. We've never done it, but if we ever do, I'll be the one with the bigger bill.

Gambling always happens in prisons, and we organised a proper party for Derby Day. We had a great spread of food, and we ran a book. At first, we could place bets by telephone but that tightened up while I was there. They gave us all pin numbers for phone calls and we had to register the numbers we would call, five or six only. By the time you've listed your family, there are none left.

It was while I was in Whitemoor that I was asked to draw a cover for the *New Law Journal*, a magazine for members of the legal profession. The editor of the magazine knew Frank Fraser, and approached me through him: it was a professional commission and I was paid a couple of hundred pounds. The magazine was running an article on the high rates of suicide among prisoners. The Woolfe Report, a wide-ranging investigation into prison conditions which was commissioned after the infamous Strangeways riot and was chaired by Lord Woolfe, would have improved matters throughout prisons, but its findings were sidelined by the government. So my cover showed a young man putting a noose around his own neck and climbing up a 'ladder' made out of the letters in the word Woolfe. There was a great deal of symbolism in the picture: the two Os in

Woolfe were handcuffs; I put bars across the O in report; the letters POA, for Prison Officers' Association, were wrapped in barbed wire; and two shrouded spectres, one symbolising capital punishment and one for suicide, were watching the boy kill himself. I was helped with the design by another prisoner, a lad from Hull.

After it was published I received a letter from the editor saying that Lord Woolfe would like the original artwork, and asking how much I would charge for it. I replied that I didn't want money, but cheekily added that I would like a few weeks knocking off my sentence. He wrote back on House of Lords notepaper, telling me he proposed to frame the original drawing and that although he could not reduce the time of my sentence, he had instead made a donation in my name to NACRO (National Association for the Care and Resettlement of the Offender).

The suicide rate in prison is high, especially among young, first-time prisoners. But they're not the only ones. I recently heard of the suicide of Dessie Cunningham, who I knew well from inside. He was doing sixteen for robbery, and he was doing OK. He was a game fella, a very nice bloke. He was brave in all sorts of ways: he had fights in prison. He could cope with all that, but then he got a 'Dear John' letter off his girl, and he topped himself. It underlined what I'd been trying to say on that cover for the *New Law Journal*: prisons are places which distort real life, and that makes people very vulnerable.

From Whitemoor I was moved to Long Lartin, in the Vale of Evesham, Worcestershire, where I stayed for eighteen months. There were no art classes, because Michael Howard, the Home Secretary, had ordered the prison regime to be made more austere. Howard was hated inside prisons. He was only out to further his political ambitions, and prisons are a sitting target. You don't have to be Einstein to come up with the idea of taking privileges off prisoners.

One of the short-sighted moves was to introduce mandatory drug tests for prisoners. Sounds great in theory and everyone applauds it. The reality is that most of the prisoners who used drugs were smoking cannabis, which stays in the body for about two weeks and therefore is likely to be detected. With mandatory testing, they switched to heroin, which clears the system within forty-eight hours, so their chances of being caught were less. Instead of prisons full of laid-back, doped-up prisoners, you now have all these agitated, violent heroin junkies.

The screws were all for the tougher regime. Music, art and cookery were all stopped. Speakers from outside were stopped. As Long Lartin only took Cat A, I'd been taken off my Double Cat A to go there, so it should have been progress, life should have been getting easier for me. Instead, with all Howard's restrictions, it was harder.

I'll give Long Lartin three stars, because I was happy there and I think it was a good prison: it wasn't the prison's fault that Howard messed everything up. We got television inside our cells for the first time, which was a luxury. Although the prison was geared up to receive Sky Sports, they wouldn't let us have it – their argument was that a lot of the prison officers couldn't afford it in their own homes, so why should we have it?

I campaigned hard against the ban on art. I'd lost all my equipment in the move from Whitemoor: they said I wasn't allowed to have it because turps was inflammable. I argued that I could use non-inflammable stuff, or water-based paints. David Ramsbotham, who was Her Majesty's Chief Inspector of Prisons, came down on a visit, and I pulled him about it while he was being shown around by the governor. I said that art was therapeutic, and did no one any harm. After a lot of campaigning they let me have some acrylic paint, and the PO on our wing asked me to do two murals.

I said: 'Yes, but you'll have to supply the paint.'

I ended up with huge containers, enough to keep me going for the rest of my sentence.

The murals are also huge, ten feet by six feet, and I did them in two days – I don't hang about. One, a Caribbean scene, I painted in a recreation area where a lot of the black guys hung out, playing dominoes. The other, in an upstairs recreation area, was of an autumn scene, with a man fishing. I think they are still there.

I had a couple of close mates in Long Lartin. Mick McAvoy, who was getting on with his bird for Brinks Mat, was there, and we played tennis together. My other mate was Ronnie O'Sullivan, father of the snooker champ. His lad has always visited him, still does. He takes his trophies in to show to his dad. Ronnie is a good man. We'd do a Sunday breakfast together, and he loved his bacon burned to a crisp. He got a life sentence with an eighteen-year tariff for a fight in a bar, nothing premeditated, but it was a black man who was knifed. It wasn't racist, but they like to give a bigger tariff if they think it might be. It should have been a manslaughter charge: it was diabolical that he was done for murder.

There was a lot of heroin dealing going on. Someone I knew was a dealer, and a couple of the prisoners who worked in the kitchens were dependent on him for their fixes. One day they smuggled out a chocolate roll for him. He asked if there were any more, and they told him there was a consignment of a dozen, for the visiting magistrates to have with their tea. He said he wanted them all. They told him there would be a stink if they all disappeared, but he said it was the whole dozen or no more heroin. Junkies are always desperate for their next fix, so of course he got them, and the visiting magistrates didn't. I enjoyed helping him eat them.

I was keen to be taken off Cat A, and the Home Office stipulated that I'd have to do an anger management course before I could be downgraded – I've never heard of anyone else being told this. The course is designed to make you think before you do something. When I first tried to get on it the people running it interviewed and assessed me, and said that I didn't need it. So that's Catch 22, as I needed to do it to get a Cat B. I went back to them and said:

'What are you saying, I don't need it? I need it more than anyone, as I can't come off Cat A without it.'

They reluctantly agreed to fit me in, although they said they felt there were others who would benefit from it far more than me. I was on it then for six months, with classes once or twice a week.

We had discussions and acted out situations. I thought at first that it was like a debating group, so when the person running the class told us to write on a large sheet of paper pinned on the wall what we thought about bird watchers, everyone was writing comments like 'intelligent people', 'into conservation', that sort of thing, so I thought I would stir the discussion by putting down 'wankers'. I wasn't serious, I just wanted to put the other side so that we could have a good debate.

What a mistake. They treated it as though that was my heartfelt reaction to bird watching. That comment followed me right through the course. Even when I finished, and went in front of the board to talk about my results, they were all sitting around saying:

'Well done, you've passed. You've got eighty per cent, that's very good. But you don't like bird watchers, do you?'

Once I realised the score, it was easy to manipulate the course. Most of the others doing it took it seriously – I think they'd all been recommended for it because they were so scatty. But I quickly got the hang of the right answers to give to their stupid questions. One question was: 'You're in a pub and there's a bloke sitting next to your girlfriend. What do you do?'

I said: 'I'd join the company and find out who the gentleman is.'

One bloke said: 'I'd smash him over the head with a bottle.' But he'd got a release date and he was going out, so he was just winding them up.

I'm not sure if anyone got any real benefit from that course. They did fail people sometimes. There was a black fella who wasn't too bright, and when he went before the board they told him he'd failed. He was miserable, so I wrote a letter for him to the board. It was apologetic:

'I tried my hardest but I'm not clever enough to do some of the things they asked me to do. I'm sorry, because I really did my best.'

I wrote it in such a way that it was hard for them not to reconsider, and they passed him. He was well pleased. He came running along the wing to tell me when he heard.

I sometimes wrote letters for some of the other prisoners, for all sorts of reasons, or I would improve their letters. They'd ask for my help, treat me like a sort of agony uncle. Not all of them, of course, but a few. When I first went into prison I didn't know the ropes, and other people told me the score: now I could help, because I could talk about what had happened to other people in the same situation as them. I was older, I'd seen more of life, and I'd seen more of prison.

Once I was off Cat A, I knew I would be moved. There's a ruling that prisoners have to be held near to their homes, but they don't worry about that with Cat As. As soon as I was a B, I knew I would be taken nearer to London. It was 1999 when I was transferred to Swaleside, on the Isle of Sheppey, Kent, and I was there until June 2001. Swaleside was a carzey, a real no-star dump. You suffered in there, but you endured it because you knew it meant you would soon be out.

It was a troubled and troublesome nick. There were lots of stabbings, the atmosphere was always tense. The staff were corrupt: just before I got there a couple of officers were sacked for bringing in drugs.

There were no televisions in the cells – each landing had a four-inch black and white set which you were supposed to get for the night a couple of times a week, but you could buy extra nights off other people. I never bothered, I used to give my nights away. I was working on my art in my cell. I didn't go to the art classes, as they were designed to get people through O and A level GCSEs, and all I wanted to do was paint.

I was continuing my push for release, doing every course I could. I did two computer literacy courses and an industrial cleaning course, just to add them to my CV. I even did the Alpha course, which is a Christian course meant to reintroduce people to 'real' Christianity. It's a bit fundamental and evangelical, and if you were doing it you had to go to church every week. At the class, some weeks we would watch a film, and people would stand up and chant, caught up in the fervour of it all. It didn't do anything for me, but I did everything I needed to do, and by the end of it I was more of an atheist than I was at the beginning. But on my parole forms I had to list all the things I'd done in prison, so it helped. I'm very tolerant of other people's religious beliefs, and it helps some people get through long stretches in prison. But not me.

I became a Cat C prisoner and then I knew it wouldn't be long before I saw the outside world again. I applied to be transferred to Blantyre House, a Cat C/D prison for people coming up for release. They accepted me and I was happy: it was as good as being on home leave. But if you have been serving more than five years, the move has to be sanctioned by the Home Office, and I was blocked.

I'd applied for parole four times and been rejected, but on my fifth application I was given a date. It's a farce, because the parole board are very thorough and if they reckon you are ready, you are ready. But it is not unknown for the Home Secretary to turn it down, and with my experience dealing with the Home Office, I wasn't taking it for granted.

This was all happening at the time of the 2001 election, and the Home Secretary changed from Jack Straw to David Blunkett. My parole date was fast approaching, and I guessed then that I was going to be released straight from Swaleside – although I was still expecting to get a weekend home leave in beforehand.

So I was taken by surprise when the wing governor told me, at eleven-thirty one morning in June, that I was being released at half-past one that same day. I had exactly two hours' notice to get ready to leave, after spending twelve years inside. But I wasn't arguing. I rang Joan and asked her to drive down for me. Swaleside is in a god-forsaken part of the country if you need to use public transport.

Then I spent my last remaining two hours in prison giving away all my belongings. It's normal: when you leave, you know that other people need the stuff more than you do. We were allowed six tee shirts, three pairs of trousers, a couple of sweaters and a couple of pairs of trainers. I gave away everything except what I needed to wear. I also gave my china plates and mugs, my backgammon board, my dictionary and my encyclopaedia. I gave them to the right people: the ones who had been borrowing the dictionary and the encyclopaedia, and a guy who loved to play me at backgammon.

There wasn't time for any celebration, but I shook hands with everyone. When I got down to reception I was surprised to find two or three boxes full of my belongings, like art materials which had followed me from prison to prison, but which I had not been allowed to have.

I walked out, chucked the boxes in the back of Joan's motor and off we went. She wasn't driving fast, but it seemed like it to me, after my laid-back time in prison. We went to her place, where obviously I absolved myself for a few hours. Then in the early evening I headed for my mum's home. I don't know how my family heard the news that I was coming out, because I didn't tell them, but they were all there

– with the exception of Charlie and his sons – and they'd been waiting for me all day. After a little celebration I went out for an Indian meal with Joan, and in the restaurant I heard someone calling me.

'Ed, I didn't know you were home!'

It was Dave Green, a bloke I'd known inside. I told him it was my first night out, and he sent a bottle of wine over to us.

It felt good to be back.

FIFTEEN

I CAN'T COMPLAIN, CAN I?

I t is a cool day at the beginning of October 2003. I am standing outside No 5, a posh wine bar and restaurant in Cavendish Square, London. Inside, the walls are lined with pictures of mine, about eighty of them. There are paintings of friends, of sporting scenes, of horses and hounds, of children playing in the street, a middle-aged couple paddling in the sea. There are a few landscapes, but always with people in them. I find people much more fascinating than places.

Some of the paintings already have red dots on them, to show that they are sold. The most expensive one has gone for £3000. A couple of days ago I was interviewed by a nice young woman from the *Independent*, and in today's paper there is a two-page article about me, complete with a photograph of me and three of my pictures.

I greet lots of my friends, who have arrived to support the exhibition, but there are plenty of strangers going in to look at my work, too. There are celebrities: Martina Cole is there, Steven Berkoff, Judge Stephen Tumin. Both my daughters have come. I sell one of my paintings, a picture of a sad-looking dog, to the bloke who got the chocolate rolls in Long Lartin. It is a very busy day, with hardly a second to draw breath.

I am happy, life is sweet. My only sadness is that my mum is not here: she died six months ago, at the age of eighty-nine. She is buried with my brother Alan, whose death she never really got over. I am so glad that she lived to see me come home. She was suffering from diabetes at the end of her life, and she was not well, so it is important to me that I had some time with her. She was the mainstay of our family, and always visited me in prison, throughout both my long sentences. She ran the family shop for many years, eventually handing it over to my niece Carol, who had to pack it in when her family commitments were too great. It was sold, sometime in the nineties, while I was away. After giving up the shop, Mum moved to Beckenham, to live with Auntie Doll, her sister, and that's where I am living now. When I came home from prison they had a room all ready for me.

I still have plenty of family left. Mum's sisters, my Auntie Gladys and my Auntie Doll, are still going strong, and so are my mother's brothers, all in their nineties. My daughter Donna has given me a lovely granddaughter, Stephanie. After giving up dancing with the Royal Ballet Donna did a course in theatrical makeup and became a dresser at the Royal Ballet. Then she qualified as a ballet mistress, and she runs her own ballet school, with 130 pupils. She and Melanie, who works as a hospital pharmacist, have both done well, and I'm very proud of them. I don't see my ex-wife Maureen, but I hear that she's doing well.

My sister Elaine lives in Brighton, and I'm close to her and her husband Paul. My half-brother Chas lives out in Spain with his family, and I see him whenever I am out there. I'm in touch with my brother Charlie's three daughters, Carol, Susan and Michelle, who are all great girls. They've got kids, and even grandkids by now.

At one time, Charlie was my friend. No more. But he is one of very few friends I have ever had who is not still my mate today. I've had good friends all my life, and I've been a good friend to them. They say you reap what you sow, and if I ever needed anything in prison, they were always there.

We still all see each other. Bert McCarthy lives in Andorra, in the Pyrenees; he's a wealthy man so he's a tax exile. I've been over to see him, and when he comes to London he relies on me to get a group of our old mates together for a lunch. Last time we met in the Beaujolais Club, more than a dozen of us, for a good meal and catch up. I see Harry Rawlings and his wife Della all the time – we've recently been to Venice and Spain together. Ronnie Jeffreys is another true mate. And I see my brother-in-law Paul, and all my other friends, regularly: there are too many to mention, but they know who they are. They were loyal to me, and I am loyal to them.

Because I was a famous name in prison, I find lots of people remember me, and I don't have a clue who they are. I was at a birthday party recently up West for a mate called Georgie Riley, and there must have been a dozen blokes came up and shook my hand. I recognised some of the faces, but I didn't know the names. Most of them were going back thirty, forty years in my life. To be honest, I never took too much notice of other people, unless they were close to me.

When I came out of prison, I knew I never wanted to set foot inside a penal institution ever again. I'd been in for twelve years, and although some of the buildings and street layouts in London were different, it hadn't changed too much. The people looked flashier, more expensively dressed, and even young kids had smart motors. I'd seen mobile phones – there had been a few smuggled in towards the end of my sentence, and I'd made the occasional call on them. Outside, everybody seemed to have one glued to their ear. At first I said I wouldn't get one, but when I gave in I discovered, as everyone said I would, that they are indispensable.

Crime has changed, too. But you have to remember that I never really had a crooked mind. I was always working to get money to put on the table, legit money. Of course, I was asked to go in on things, and sometimes I did, and they turned out to be lucrative, and I got a return. Sometimes I didn't, but if I followed my instincts I was usually OK.

But it's not the same, it's changing all the time. Drugs are not making the big money that they once did. Now it's all huge bank frauds and blue-chip crime. The goal posts have moved: a mate of mine says, unless it's over a million, the police don't want to bother to investigate.

To get me started in life outside, I was set up with a few thousand pounds by my mates. They had a whip round for me, everyone putting in a minimum of £500, so I had a tidy little sum to be going on with.

I also made money from selling my paintings. The idea for the exhibition came from Peter Cameron, the guy who first set me off painting. I went to an exhibition of his, and he introduced me to the man who organised it for him. Peter lives in Liverpool, and makes a living from his painting. I don't paint much anymore, because it is such a time-consuming and intense occupation. But maybe one day I'll feel like shutting myself off from the world for a couple of days at a time, to do more.

I didn't want to go back into business. I was sixty-five when I came out, and that's old for the metal business. And the business has changed completely since I was involved: you need half a million quid's worth of machinery nowadays, because everything is put through grinding machines. I've been offered opportunities to go back into it, and I know I'm capable of it, but do I need it? I don't want to get bogged down going to work every day.

My aim is to enjoy life, play a lot of golf and have as many holidays as I can. My first skiing holiday for many years was great, although I realised I wasn't as fit as I used to be. I skied from Italy into France, and by the end of the trip my legs were doing what I wanted them to do.

I regret some of the things that have happened in my life. I reckon everyone would change some of their actions and decisions if they had the chance. But I don't look back. There's no point in harping on about the past all the time. It's history. I've always been more interested in tomorrow than yesterday. I have the greatest gifts life can give you: good health, great mates, a good family.

I grew up in the back streets of South London, and I left school with hardly any education. Unlike some of Prince Charles's friends, I never had a lot of avenues open to me. Yet I have travelled, I have eaten in some of the best restaurants in the world, I've met people from all walks of life and held my own with all of them.

I have seen a lot of life, from both ends of the spectrum: the good and the bad. I have experienced some of the worst conditions in the world, but I have also experienced the best.

For a South London lad, I can't complain, can I?

INDEX

Bates, Ken 229
Beasley, Simon 162, 173
Beatty, Warren 201
Belmarsh prison 259
Berkoff, Steven 228, 276
Berman, Alf 127, 129–30, 144–5, 148
Berry, Neville 71
betting 19, 189–90, 225, 265
Bickers, Norman 145, 216
Biggs, Ronnie 84, 181
Bill, Bobby 223
Birchmore, Peggy 19
black market 19, 20
'Black Museum', Scotland Yard 171
Blake, George 152, 153
Blantyre House (Cat C/D prison) 271
Blind Beggar pub, Stepney 124
Bloom, Kenny 44, 195, 218, 228
Blore, Jimmy 144
Blunkett, David 271
Bonanza gang 59–60
Bond, Dennis 2
bookies 19, 70–2, 113
BOSS (South African secret police) 99, 101, 127
Bossard, Frank 4
Botton, Henry 119, 122, 131, 140
boxing 13–14, 26, 113–15, 173, 190–1, 192, 209, 224–6
boxing clubs 34, 113–14
Bradbury, Johnnie (alias John West) 125–7
Brady, Ian 3, 6–7, 152

Bridges, Bunny 128–9, 150
Brindle, Eva 65, 77, 149
Brindle, Jimmy 63–4, 65, 77
Brinks Mat bullion robbery 210–12, 268
Brixton prison 122, 133, 241–2
Broederbond (white supremacist association) 99
Bronson, Charlie 253
Brooke, Gerald 180, 181
Brown, Ron 163, 167, 169, 170, 171
Burgess, David 3, 7
Burnett, Al 82–3

Callaghan, Bobby 36
Callaghan, Henry 36
Callaghan, Jim 7
Callaghan, Patsy 69
Cameron, Peter 255–6, 278
card sharps 78–9
Casbar club 52–3, 55, 63
casinos 79, 86–7, 103
Cat's Whiskers, Streatham 224
Cavern club, Lordship Lane 53
Chambers, 'Flash' Gordon 4, 154, 155
Chameleon Soho (documentary) 205
Charles, Prince 230
Charlie Chester's (casino) 86
Charlton Athletic Football Club 24
Chelsea Football Club 229
Cheltenham prison high-security unit 152, 188
Cheshire, Johnny 173